Walney Island

A history

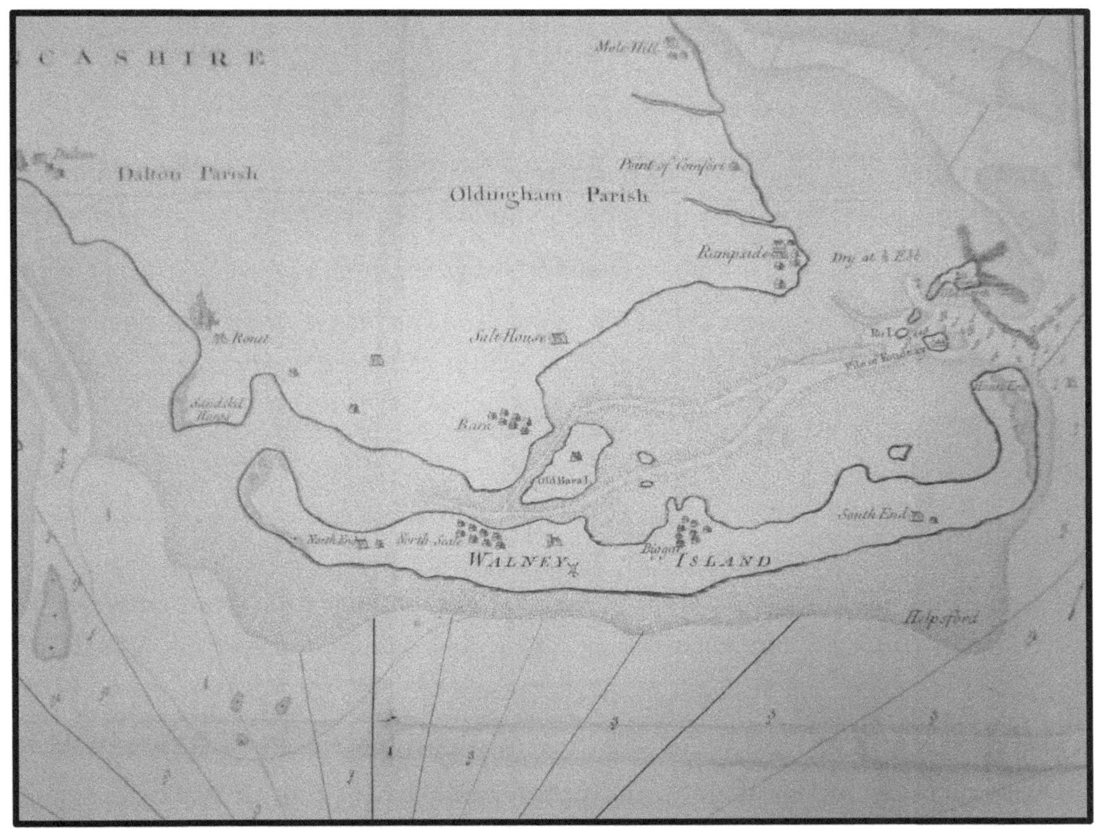

Detail from a coastal map 1775   (Cumbria Archives. BDX/796)

Preface

For centuries, the island of Walney remained an isolated, rural community of tenements reachable only at the mercy of the tides. Little had changed since the times of the monks of Furness Abbey. It was not until significant developments occurred in the nearby town of Barrow that Walney began to evolve into the community we recognise today. With just two main centres of population at Biggar and North Scale there were few roads, only a handful of houses and aside from farming, no notable industry until the 20th century.

The two villages, isolated as they were, contained the few hundred people of the island whose lives depended on a farming way of life, on the protective dykes keeping back the sea, and on the ability to grow their own food and to keep cattle on the wind-swept land.

Walney had few trees, little in the way of building material and no fuel sources other than peat. (The peat was under the sands of Walney channel.) The islanders were a hardy bunch of people.

The aim of this publication is to provide an insight into the development of the island over the past 1000 years.

Acknowledgements

Thanks firstly to Susan Benson, Archivist at Barrow Archive and Local Studies Centre for suggesting relevant documents or maps and for allowing me to use documents and photographs from the collections of the Archives, and to her colleague, Selena Kendall, for her patience in obtaining for me the next document, and the next, and the next.

To my long-suffering wife and family who have had to endure many tales of Walney and local history over the years, thank you. To Sue and to Dennis, thanks for the initial proof reading. For her valuable recommendations, proof reading and advice, many grateful thanks to local historian, Jean Mc Sorley.

I am indebted to the many previous historians of Barrow whose works form the foundation of my current understanding and have guided me towards the relevant information. I am grateful to the late Dr Bill Rollinson whose books and courses first kindled my interest in local history so many years ago.

Thanks also to Barrow Docks Museum for allowing the use of the photographs on Page 10.

Thanks too to Russ at Pixel Tweaks for completing the final bits in the production.

Grateful thanks to the Kirkby Archives Trust for the generous grant towards the publication costs of this book.

Introduction

My interest in local history began over 40 years ago when I attended a number of courses run by Barrow Archives and Liverpool University. Courses on prehistoric man in the Lake District or how to read mediaeval documents were the start of my local history journey.

A specific interest in Walney history began in earnest when I moved to the island in the early 1980s with research into the history of Vickerstown being the first foray into the subject.

In-depth research began during Covid lockdown and continued during the years of involvement as a volunteer on the Sankey project.[A] This led to my participation in the Victoria County History project which aims to update the books written in the early 20th century.[B] The bulk of that research, considerably expanded, and with added maps and photographs, has led to this publication.

I hope you enjoy reading it as much as I have enjoyed writing it. Any errors are mine alone.

All references have been put at the end of the document to make it easier to read.

If you have any comments, suggestions or queries please address them to: -

p.laird@btinternet.com

CONTENTS

[A] The Sankeys were a father and sons team of photographers who documented life in Barrow and Cumbria over a period of around 70 years. Their photographic archive, a result of this project, is held by Cumbria Archives and also hosted on-line at https://www.sankeyphotoarchive.uk

[B] The Victoria County History (VCH), is an English history project which began in 1899 with the aim of creating a history of each English county. It was dedicated to Queen Victoria. It is now in the process of being updated.

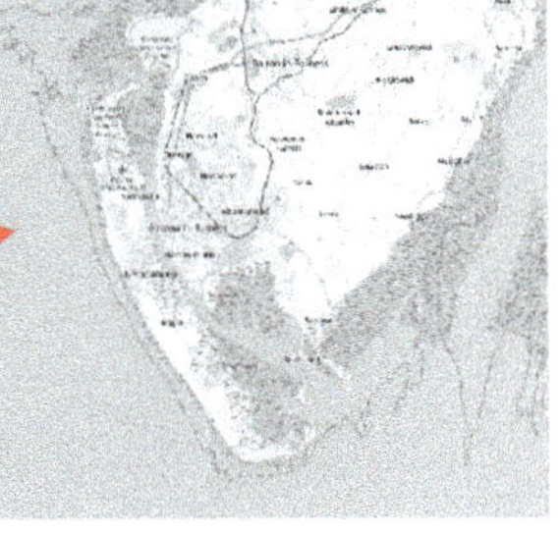

Position of Walney Island, off the coast of the Furness Peninsula, in the Irish Sea.

Maps: OpenStreetMap.org

This page deliberately left blank.

WALNEY ISLAND

Walney Island (hereinafter called Walney), was a subdivision of Hawcoat, itself a brierley[C] of the Parish of Dalton in the south west of the Furness peninsula, within the North Lonsdale hundred[D], Lancashire. It became part of Barrow-in-Furness County Borough on 18 July 1872, following the enactment of the *Barrow-in-Furness Corporation Extension and Amendment Act.*[1]

Walney remained a true island until the opening of the Walney Bridge in 1908. It is approximately 10 miles long, and no more than a mile wide at its broadest point, covering an area of 3065 acres and its highest point is no more than 70ft. above sea level.[2] The island is bordered by the Irish Sea on one side, and the Walney Channel on the other; with a maximum tidal range of up to 34ft. It had a population of 10,651 in the 2011 census, which had slightly decreased to 10,433 by 2021.[3]

The name of the island has changed over time, including: in 1086 Hougenai;[4] Wagneia in the 1127 Charter from the founding of Furness Abbey;[5] Wagenay in 1403.[6] Other names appear in different documents.

Hougen-ai is the island belonging to Hougun – the name given to Furness in the Domesday survey. Both Wagneia and Wagenay are thought to be derived from Old Norse and various explanations have been suggested including 'The Island of the Wagon' and 'The Island of Quick Sands.'

Landscape

Walney was formed at the end of the last ice age when pebbles and boulder clay were left behind by retreating ice sheets. In the succeeding 10,000 years, the sea level has risen significantly and the prevailing south-westerly waves and wind have shaped and reshaped the island into the place we know today. In particular, it has recurved spits at either end and it is now characterised by dune systems at both the north and south ends, low lying salt marshes, grassland and low glacial drumlins. A number of *'erratics'* or stones deposited by ice from elsewhere, can still be seen on the coast. One such erratic, weighing almost four tons, was found in the clay of the brickworks near what is now Dominion Street, and can be seen at the entrance to Vickerstown Park.

Vickerstown Park erratic.

© Peter Laird

[C] A brierley is a quarter sub-division. The other three for Dalton were Dalton itself, Yarlside and Above Town (Ireleth, Lindal and Marton.)

[D] A hundred was a sub-division of a county with its own court and governance.

The boulder clay and pebbles are obvious at Hare Hill (above), on the west side of Walney. The problem is that they erode very easily. Here the hill is around 60 feet high - around 18 metres. One of the highest points on the island, but one of the most exposed.

Occasionally the wind and tides uncover the remains of an ancient submerged forest on the west coast, and more recently discovered human footprints on the west side of the island illustrate how the land has been claimed by the sea. Walney has always been at the mercy of the sea and strong winds, especially from on its west side.

To the north of the island is the Duddon Estuary, to the east Walney Channel, to the south the islands of Roa and Piel before the expanse of Morecambe Bay, and to the west is the Irish Sea.

Dr Close, in his 1813 edition of Thomas West's *Antiquities of Furness,* and Thomas Alcock Beck, in his *Annales Furnesienses* of 1844, both bemoan the fact that the sea is winning the battle. A number of articles appear in Barrow Naturalists Field Club and Photographic Society proceedings describing the diminishing width of the island over time. One of these includes a map (below), showing changes between 1737 and 1951, and the substantial loss of land that had occurred.[7]

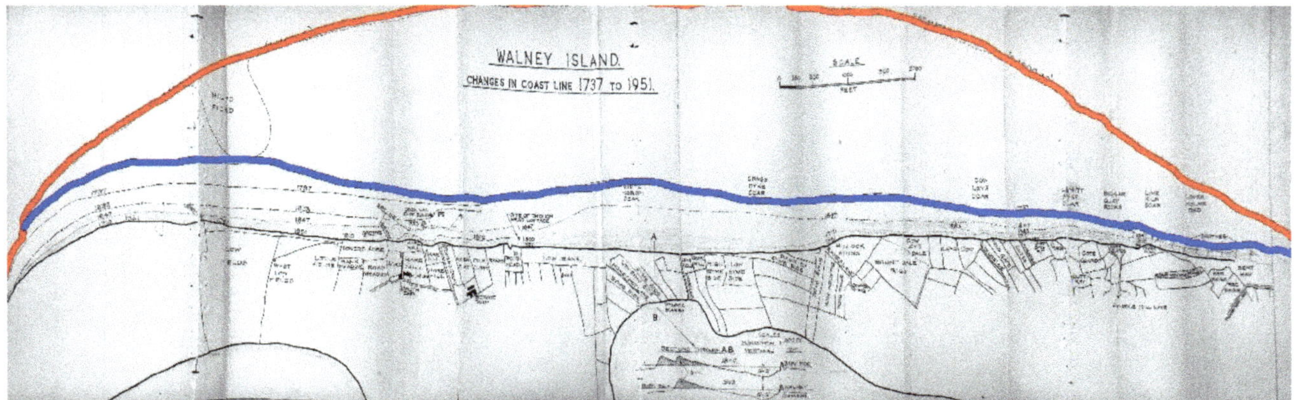

The red line shows the approximate shoreline at the south end of Walney in around the year 1000, and the blue line, the shore line in 1737. The unbroken black line below it was the shore line in 1951. The widest gap between the blue and the black is about 1,000 feet.

Another article notes how a piece of land 20 feet in width near Lamity Sike Pit had been washed away between 1879 and 1882, followed by another 73 feet lost between 1889 and 1906.[8] A map of the changes between 1797 and 1965 shows a depletion of the width of the island coupled with an extension of the length at the south end due to accretion.[9]

The effects of climate change can only hasten this process. Since 2013 the road between Earnse Bay and the North End sandhills has completely been washed away, then in March 2024 part of the wall alongside this beach has been undermined and has fallen over.

The *Cumbria Coastal Strategy* for a substantial part of the west coast of Walney was 'No active intervention'. The current rock armour defences are only temporary and are due to be removed after their 20-year life.[10]
The Westmorland and Furness Council policy for Earnse Bay in 2024 is to stabilise the erosion near West Shore Park, monitor the currents, waves and sand movement and use that data and data collected by a mobile radar station to enable a future plan to be developed.[11]

A glider view of Earnse Bay taken in August 2013. © Peter Laird

A ground level view looking north in March 2024. The road has been completely washed away and the wall has partly gone too. © Peter Laird

Prehistory

The presence of prehistoric artifacts on Walney Island serves as evidence that ancient people inhabited, or at the very least, visited the area. In August 1936, Marjorie Cross was walking in the sand hills of the North End with her sister when they noticed flint pebbles which had obviously been worked by humans. Subsequent research found these to be flint scrapers, arrow heads, stone axes, blades and borers.[12]

Other flint finds have been made at Cow Leys Scar, Cross Dike Scar and Trough Head.[13]

Finds also include stone axe hammers and perforated pebbles from a variety of sites on Walney. A spindle whorl of white sandstone was found by Mr J Thompson-Robinson in 1954 near Biggar.

Although it is obvious that humans have visited Walney for thousands of years, it is less obvious where the flint came from which was being worked. There is no local source of this flint. One answer proposed is that a source exists under the Irish Sea and that during the movement of glaciers that flint was deposited in the boulder clay of Walney.

Further investigations into the North End have found middens of the Later Bronze Age or Iron Age, along with animal bones of wild and domestic animals, and the remains of 'masses of shellfish.'

Two things to remember when considering the changes since the last Ice Age are that sea levels have risen some 15m, (50 feet) or so, and the land itself has risen due to the removal of the weight of the ice. So, it is likely that some prehistoric land surfaces are buried under the sea.

Arrowhead from North End c1300-1399

Polished axe from Tummerhill

Both are held at the Barrow Docks Museum and are part of their extensive collection.

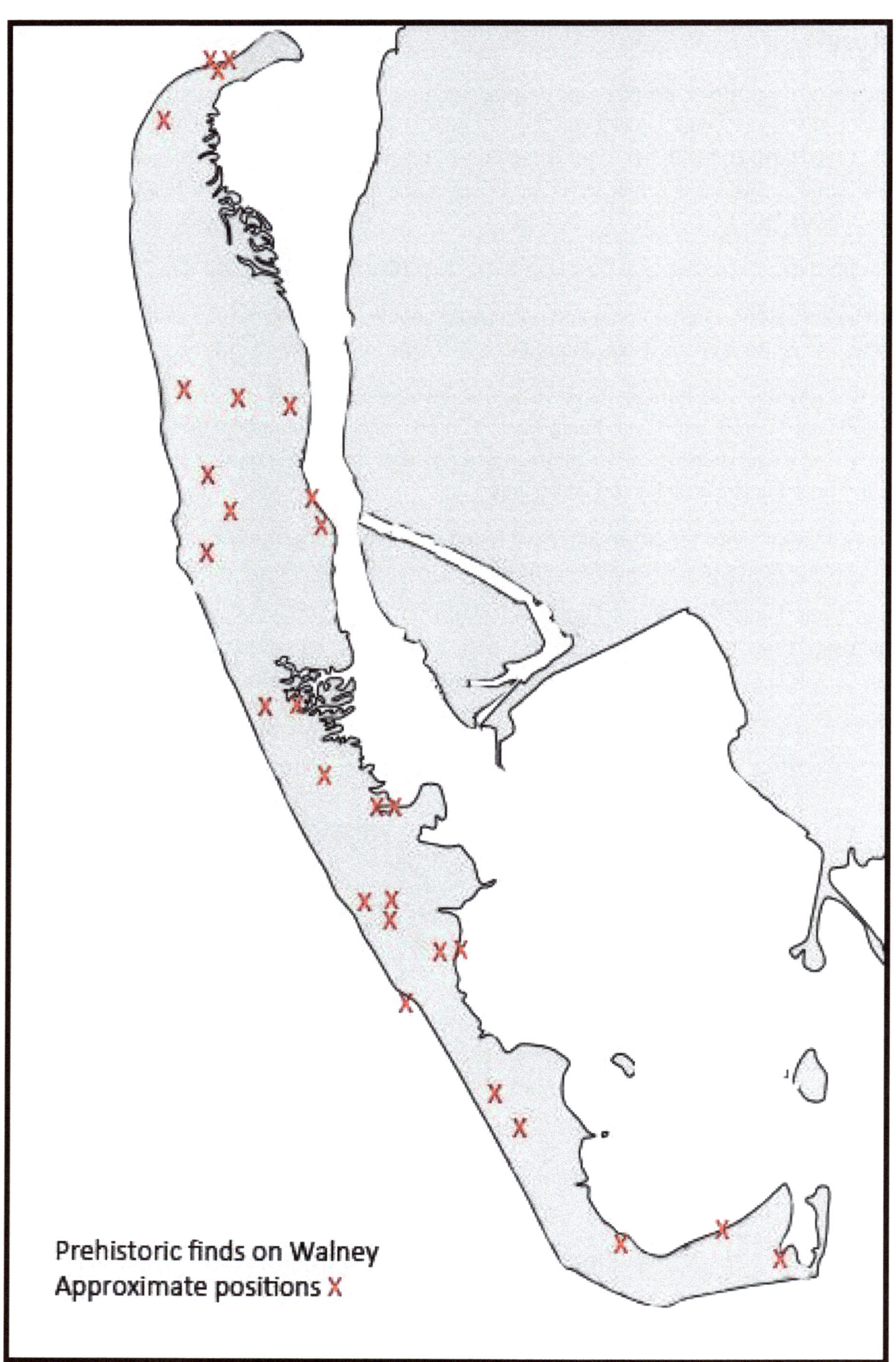

Prehistoric finds on Walney
Approximate positions X

Settlements

The coming of the Vikings

According to Norwegian sagas, at the end of the 9th century, Harald Hårfager (Hairfair), became the first King over all of Norway after ten years of fighting. His conquests and taxation had led many chiefs and their followers to emigrate to the British Isles, Iceland and other lands.

The problem is that there is no contemporary evidence for the story. There probably was a King Harald at that time and there was mass emigration and colonisation by Vikings in and around Iceland, Ireland and the Isle of Man. As for the existence of Hairfair; Historians now view him as part of an 'origin myth' for the settlement of Iceland.

The Vikings, from Denmark and Norway, began raiding Ireland in 795. At that time Ireland was ruled by several Gaelic clans. By 841 the Annals report that the Vikings were already spending winters in Ireland using temporary ship fortresses as bases. One of these bases later developed into Dublin. In 902 however, the Dublin Vikings were driven out by the combined forces of Brega and Leinster, the two kings of the provinces which surrounded Dublin.[14] The fleeing Vikings scattered across the Irish Sea to Wales, Scotland, Iceland and North-West England.

It is thought that it is some of these peoples who first settled, on the east of the island at Biggar, at a time when Walney was up to a mile wider than it is now, and so they were not visible from any potential invaders.

Whoever the first inhabitants were, they probably made the first buildings of boulders from the shore with turf for the roofs, as there was no slate or anything more serviceable. Up until the end of the 19th century it was thought that each house stood almost exactly in the same place as it did from the very first settlement approximately 1,000 years earlier.[15] As can be seen on a plan of the village from the 1842 Tithe Map, no two houses look the same way. Houses and buildings of every description seem to have been set down in no specific order. Similarly, the paddocks and gardens seem to have been enclosed without any order. It looks as if the original settlers built their houses in any convenient unoccupied place, and fenced in what they liked.

+++

Biggar became the first permanent settlement on the island as far as we are aware.
There will be much more about Biggar later, but for now we have a small village, isolated from the outside world, dependent upon the land and the sea for all its needs, and protected from outsiders by its remote position. These settlers were no longer pillaging and marauding, but farming and fishing and keeping their heads down.

> Barrow Dock Museum has a number of Viking artefacts from Furness, including a hoard found in 2011, a Viking sword from Rampside and a lead weight from Dalton.

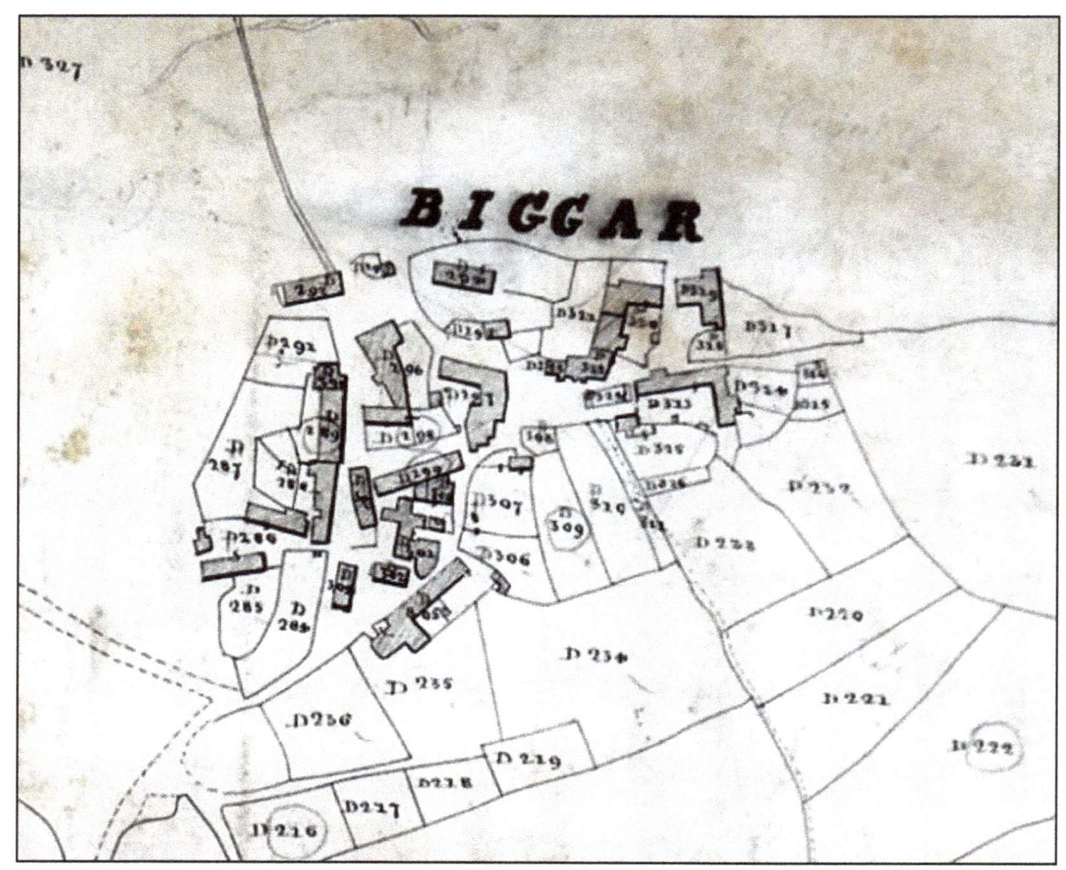

1842
Tithe Map detail

Cumbria
Archives
BPR/I/1/2
Cumbria
Archives

This is the southern entrance to Biggar village showing the cobbled walls, haystacks and a pond. Date estimated to be around 1900. (Cumbria Archives. Z/3384.)

This image shows how Biggar cottages were also built from beach cobbles. c 1900

(Cumbria Archives. Z/3384)

Domesday Book

In 1085, William the Conqueror ordered a survey of all of his lands to be carried out so he could obtain an overall picture of his kingdom to estimate the resources of land, livestock and people and to enable taxes to be assessed. Started in January 1086, the survey covered all of England except the far north. This means only the southern part of Cumbria was included in the survey. The questions within the survey can be summarised as follows: -

1. What is the Manor called?
2. Who held it in the time of King Edward in 1066?
3. Who holds it now in 1086?
4. How many hides or carucates are there? (A hide is approximately 120 acres)
5. How many plough teams on the lords' own land and among the rest of the village?
6. How many freemen, villans, sokemen, slaves and cottars?
7. How much woodland, meadow, pasture, mills, fisheries?
8. How much has been added to or taken from the manor?
9. How much was the whole worth in 1066 and now 1086?
10. How much had or has each freeman or sokeman?
11. Can the Manor raise more taxes?

A freeman was free and might hold land but still owed some service to the lord.

A villan was an unfree peasant who had to give his lord two- or three-days service per week but who also farmed land for himself.

A sokeman was a freeman who still had to attend court.

A cottar, also called a cottager, was an unfree peasant with fewer lands than villans.

There was no Lancashire at that time as it had not yet been established, and so Furness was entered as part of the West Riding of Yorkshire in Amounderness. (Amounderness was a hundred lying north of the river Ribble and South of Morecambe Bay and the river Lune.)

The bulk of Furness was in the Manor of Hougun, (Low Furness), which had been in the possession of the Earls of Northumbria from the time of Canute.[16] Siward the Dane held it from 1038 to 1055 and then Tosti Godwinson, brother of King Harold.[17] Morcar, son of Ælfgār (Earl of Mercia) became Earl of Northumbria after Tosti's expulsion.

The exact location of Hougun is unknown, with Millom, High Haume near Dalton and Urswick all proposed as possible locations. Within the survey comes mention of Hougenai – the island of Hougun - Walney, with six carucates (about 720 acres) under the plough. This is the first documentary evidence of the antiquity of Walney as an entity.

The Domesday Book entry for Hougun. Hougenai circled. (Image from opendomesday.org)[18]

In Hougun Manor Earl Tosti had four carucates rateable to the geld.	
In Chiluestreuic iii c.,	Killerwick
Sourebi iii c.,	Sowerby
Hietun iiii c.,	Hawcoat
Daltune ii c.,	Dalton
Warte ii c.,	Thwaite Flat
Neutun vi c.,	Newton
Walletun vi c.,	Waltoncote
Suntun ii c.,	Sunton
Fordebodele ii c.,	Fordbootle
Rosse vi c.,	Roose
Hert ii c.,	Hart Carrs
Lies vi c.,	Leece
Alia Lies ii c.,	Little Leece
Glassertun ii c.,	Gleaston
Steintun ii c.,	Stainton
Clivertun iiii c.,	Crivelton
Ouregrave iii c.,	Oregrave
Meretun iiii c.,	Marton
Pennigetun ii c.,	Pennington
Gerleuuorde ii c.,	Ireleth
Borch vi c.,	Birkrigg
Beretsiege iiii c.,	Bardsea
Witingham iiii c.,	Whicham
Bodele iiii c.,	Bootle
Santacherche i c.,	Kirksanton
Hougenai vi c.,	**WALNEY**
All these vills belong to Hougun.	

The coming of the Monks

In the year 1124, Gaufrid or Godfrey, second abbot of a monastery in Savigny in France, obtained from Stephen, Count of Boulogne (nephew of Henry I), a grant of land in a district called Tulketh, near Preston, on which to build an abbey of his order. No extensive buildings were erected in the three years the monks were at Tulketh. Why, is not known.

In any event, in 1127 the same Stephen gave to the same monks the whole of the Lordship of Furness with all its appurtenances, its inhabitants, forests, lands and waters, with the sole exception of the lands of Michael Fleming at Aldingham. The Savignac monks came to Beckansgill in Low Furness on 1 July 1127.

Foundation Charter

"In the name of the Blessed Trinity, and in honour of St Mary of Furness, I Stephen, Earl of Boulogne and Moreton, consulting God, and providing for the safety of my own soul, the soul of my wife, the Countess Matilda, the soul of my lord and uncle Henry, King of England and the Duke of Normandy, and for the souls of all the faithful, living as well as dead, in the year of our lord 1127, of the Roman Indication, the 5th and 18th of the epact:

Considering every day, the uncertainty of life, that roses and flowers of kings, emperors and dukes, and the crowns and palms of all the great, wither and decay; and that all things, with an uninterrupted course, tend to dissolution and death:

I therefore return, give and grant, to God and St Mary of Furness, all Furness and Wagnea (Walney), with the privilege of hunting; with Dalton, and all my lordship in Furness with the men and everything thereto belonging, that is, in the woods and in open grounds, in land and in water; and Ulverston, and Roger Brathwait with all that belongs to him; my fish ponds at Lancaster, and Little Guoring, with all the land thereof; with Sac and Soc, Tol and Team, Infangenetheof,[19] and everything within Furness except the lands of Michael le Fleming; with this view, and upon this condition, that in Furness an order of regular monks be by divine permission established: which gift and offering I by supreme authority appoint to be forever observed; and that it may remain firm and inviolate for ever, I subscribe this charter with my hand, and confirm it with the sign of the Holy Cross."

Signed by Henry, King of England and Duke of Normandy; Thurston, Archbishop of York; Audin and Boces, Bishops; Robert, Keeper of the Seal; Robert, Earl of Gloster.[20](sic)

We see from this that Walney has a specific mention and that the incoming monks had power over the inhabitants of the area. For the next 400 years or so that would be the case.

In the past, Furness was regarded as a rugged and unwelcoming wilderness. Undoubtedly, its isolation held a certain allure for the monks. Twenty years after first arriving in Furness the Savignac order merged with the Cistercian order, a process which was resisted by the Furness monks.

The next mention of Walney comes in a Papal Bull of Clement III in 1190 when the granges of the Abbey are listed as Roos (Roose), Newton, Killerwick (Elliscales), Irelyth and Barrai, and all the island of Walney; also, Dalton, Ulverston, Marton and Orgrave.[21]

A grange was an outlying landholding held by the monastery and used for food production or producing livestock. They were usually centred on a farm and outbuildings.

In 1247 a further list of granges changes *'all of the island Walney'* to become Northscale, Northend and Southend and finally a further list in 1292 has Northscale and Biggar but does not mention Northend and Southend. This is likely because of the change to the granting of granges to customary-hold tenants – i.e. a tenant who held land by the custom of the manor, these tenants had certain rights and obligations which could vary according to the local custom. The tenants usually had little security of tenure.

It shows that Walney was originally effectively divided into four settlements or townships.

The influence of the Abbey cannot be over-stated. Although Walney tenants paid some of their rents in kind (as will be explained later), they received substantial benefits in return. These included provisions such as bread, beer, iron, wood and manure - roughly equivalent in value to their own produce.[22] Additionally, each tenant with a plough had the privilege of sending two individuals, for dinner at the abbey, once a week between Martinmas and Whitsuntide.[23]

A monk's diet was fairly frugal, and consisted of grains, bread, fruit and vegetables. At Furness Abbey they refrained from eating meat. That rule changed in 1335 and again in 1485, and from then onwards they could eat meat on Tuesday, Thursday and Sunday.

Harley MS 1526 f. 24v | Source: The British Library

Furthermore, the tenants enjoyed the right to obtain peat from Angerton Moss, near Kirkby.[24] As part of their customary obligations, every tenant took an oath of fealty to the abbot, to be true to him against all, excepting the King. Every tenant of a whole tenement furnished a man and horse of war for coastal defence, for border service, or any joint expedition against the common adversaries of the king and kingdom.[25]

More on tenants' rights and responsibilities later, first back to Walney

North End, as its name suggests was the northernmost part of the island which ran from the sandhills, on the edge of the Duddon estuary to North Scale. Today that would be from the northern tip of the island to part way down the current airfield. There were four tenements. In recent times, and until the building of the airfield in 1940, there was a farm at North End and a windmill. The 1841 census has a John Hobson in the 'Old Windmill' along with his wife Margaret and five children. In 1851 Robert Benson is listed on the census in the 'Old Mill house' with his wife Elizabeth, a niece, a journeyman and a servant. No mention is made of the windmill in census returns after 1851, but that doesn't necessarily mean that the windmill had ceased operating.

In 1835, North End Farm was owned by C.D. Archibald Esq., of Rusland Hall the year William Postlethwaite took the farm.[26]In the 1841 census he is listed in the North End Farmhouse with his wife Sarah, four children, four farm labourers and three farm servants. He is listed there until 1881. In 1891 there are two different families living in North End Farm – one with Henry and Richard Postlethwaite both listed as 'Head of the family' and another with both Thomas and James Thompson both listed as 'Son', nobody listed as head of the family but there was a note saying 'Head temporarily absent'. An older Thomas Thompson (presumably the previously absent head of the family), is 'head' in the 1891 census. Thomas sold his whole holding in the farm by auction on 17th April 1894. This included 31 head of cattle, six horses, 100 sheep and 70 head of poultry. He also sold all of his machinery, dairy utensils and household furniture.[27] Adam Penny is the North End farmer in 1901, and again in 1911 by which time there were a total of nine persons living there. [28]

In 1865, **The Barrow Herald** reports that Mr Postlethwaite has resorted to setting man-traps and spring - guns to deter the theft of his rabbits.

18 Nov 1865

The windmill and North End Farm late 19th century.   Cumbria Archives Z/2915

A 1922 report has C.D. Archibald as still being the owner of the farm with William Mc Lung as the outgoing tenant and Joseph Barnes as the incoming.[29] At that time the farm is growing oats, potatoes, beans and clover.

In the late 1930s sand and gravel extraction were part of a business on the North End estate run by William Mc Lung, now of North Scale. 1,600 tons of sand and 2,600 tons of gravel were removed in 1937. In 1938 almost 4,500 tons of sand was removed and 17,000 tons of gravel.

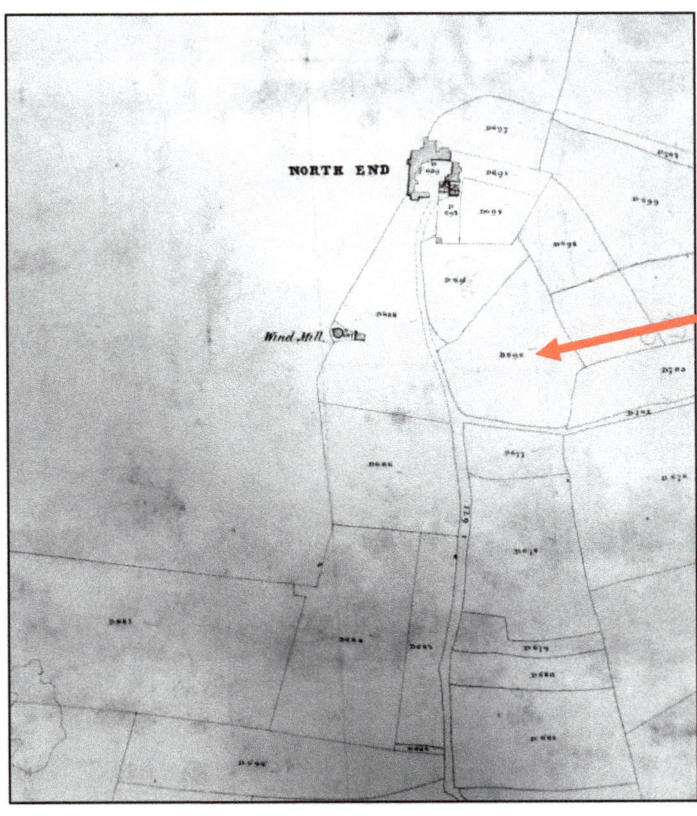

Detail from 1842 Tithe Map

(Cumbria Archives. BPR/I/1/2)

The D numbers are referenced in a schedule which shows who owns and who occupies each section. (D690 arrowed)

Below, is a section of the schedule showing that James Benson occupied the windmill, D687, plus other fields and pasture.

(All were owned by C.D. Archibald of Rusland Hall at the time.)

James Benson	D694	Homestead & Yard	
	D677	Butter field	Arable
	D679	Piper Hole	do (ditto)
	D687	Wind Mill	
	D688	Millfield	Pasture
	D690	Tewit Meadow	Meadow
	D692	Garden	
	D698	Little Marl field	Arable

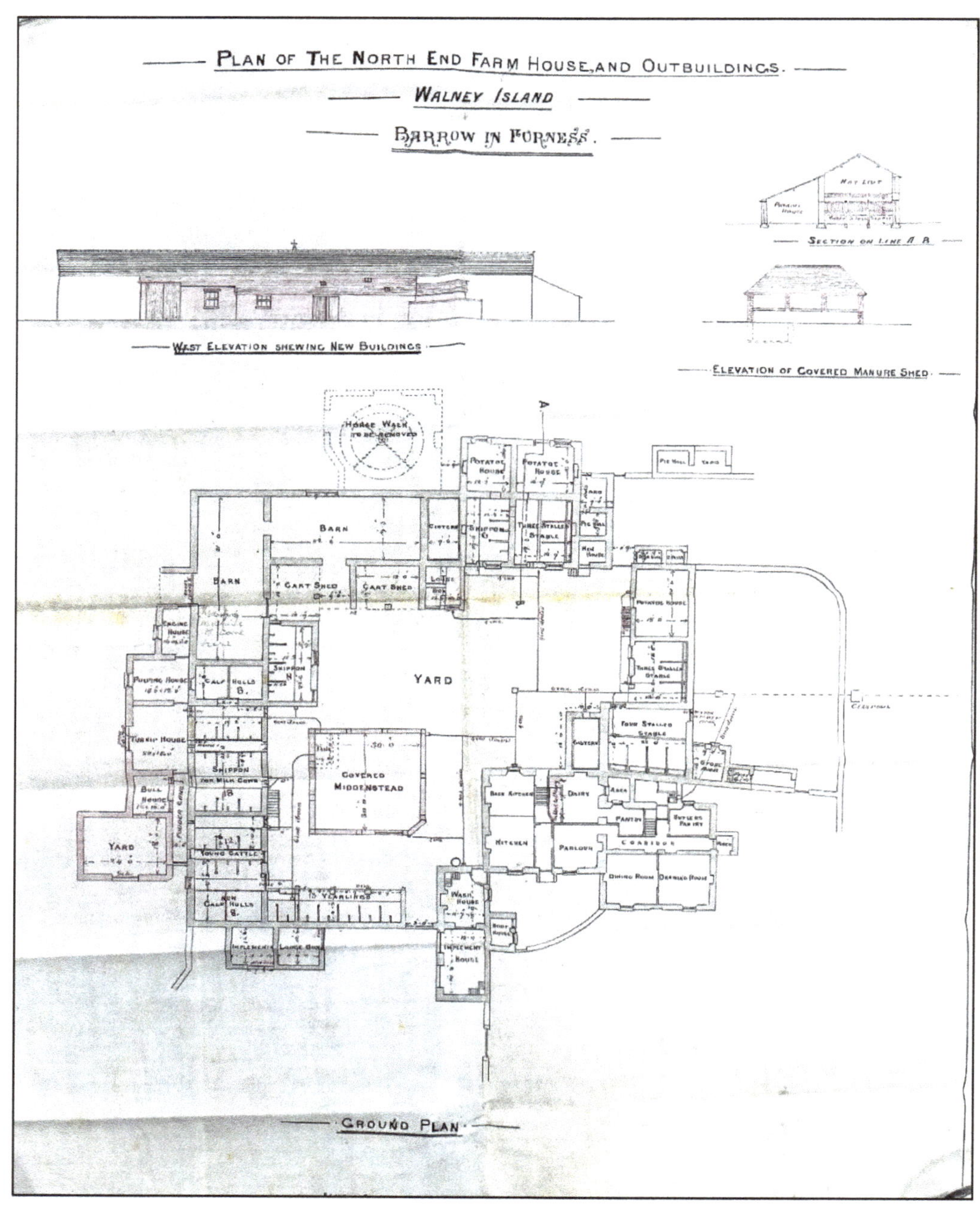

North End Farm plan. (Cumbria Archives. BDBUC/40/1/25)

A compulsory purchase order for the farm was issued by the council in October 1938 in order for an aerodrome to be built. The Second World War was looming. At an enquiry held in February 1939, William Mc Lung's objection was mainly because of the impact of the proposal on his business of sand and gravel extraction. The council had offered £8,030 for the land at the North End. The purchase went ahead and the farm was demolished. It was a substantial range of buildings which disappeared from the landscape.

William Mc Lung originally came to Barrow in 1900 to become manager of the Isle of Walney Estates Company farm at North Scale, a job he kept until 1907. He then started his own business as a farmer and contractor.

Below North End, **North Scale** township ran south to Tummerhill – approximately to Ocean Road today.

It is suggested that the name North Scale comes from the Old Norse 'Skali' meaning hut, shed or lodge.[30] So North Scale was likely a temporary place used by the inhabitants of Biggar in the summer months to take advantage of the north of the island for farming or animal husbandry.

North Scale consisted of 16 tenements and these in turn were divided into 4 'burgages'. [31]Each burgage was *'bound'* to find one man for military service, and the tenants held their lands under a fixity of tenure at a fixed rental according to the custom of the manor. The tenants had to provide services and goods to the Abbey, in common with other tenants on the island. One service they had to perform was to cart (or pay for the carting of) 20 loads of peat to the Abbey. They also had to provide oats, wheat, barley, hens, and geese for the monks. Along with all other tenants of the monks, they also had to provide labour to help in the upkeep of Biggar Dyke.

At North Scale the arable land was laid out in 21 common fields, unenclosed by hedges, with each field split up into 48 narrow strips called 'dales.' Each of the 16 tenants held three dales in each field, or 63 dales altogether. On the west of the island the tenants occupied around 250 acres in common, as pasture for their cattle and horses. Like other tenants of the monks, however, the North Scale tenants held no sheep.[32] (That was a privilege kept for the monks.)

At the end of the 15th century there was a great agricultural depression in England caused by competition from foreign markets, wars and conflicts such as the Wars of the Roses, and other factors. The result was that two of the tenants gave up their holdings, and the dales they had farmed were taken over by six of the other tenants who now farmed one and one-third tenements each. Two of the common fields were left to lie idle, and went out of cultivation altogether. These 'idle' fields were ultimately taken over by the monks and turned into a sheep farm. A cottage (Cote) was erected for the shepherd, and the whole farm came to be known as 'Idlecote.' [33]
At the dissolution of the monasteries in 1537 the Abbey's lands reverted to the King and were controlled by the Duchy of Lancaster. North Scale tenants, in common with all others, now had to pay their rents in cash.

The Civil War between King and Parliament broke out in 1642, and lasted five years. The Royalists were driven out of Furness in 1643, after the battle of Lindal Cote on October 1st, but around the middle of July 1644, a band of the fugitive cavaliers from Marston Moor passed through Cartmel and established themselves at Dalton. They consisted of the shattered fragments of five regiments of Rupert's[E] cavalry, and several foot-soldiers. One of the cavalry regiments was commanded by Sir John Preston of the Manor and Abbey. The local Parliamentary forces had anchored at Piel. Some of the sailors assisted by certain countrymen, marched against the Royalist forces at Dalton, but were waylaid, and defeated on the way. Next day the Royalists prepared an expedition against North Scale, which had been occupied by sailors from the fleet, (aided by a body of Walney men), with the view of holding command of the low-water fords across to the island. The Royalist troops crossed the channel at low-water during the night, and formed on the sands in front of the village, intending to take the place by surprise. The defenders, however, were on the alert, and a sharp volley from them sufficed to disperse the invaders, and drive them in confusion from the island. The victory was

---

[E] Prince Rupert was a younger son of Elizabeth and a nephew of Charles I. He was Commander-in-chief of the Royalist land forces from 1644

short-lived for the North Scale men, as next day the Royalists returned, found the village deserted, and set it on fire. Only two houses belonging to well-known Royalists were spared.[34]

The next event of any note was that of George Fox, from the Quaker movement, in summer 1652. In his own words:

"I went into the island of Walney, and after the priest had done, I spoke to him but he got away. Then I declared the truth to the people, but they were rude. I went to speak with the priest at his house, but he would not be seen. The people said he went to hide himself in the hay mow, and they looked for him there, but could not find him. Then they said he was gone to hide himself in the standing corn, but they could not find him there either. I went to James Lancaster's, who was convinced in the island, and thence I returned to Swarthmore, where the Lord's power came upon Margaret Fell and her daughter Sarah and several others."

He tried again at Walney little later;

"As soon as I came to land, there rushed out about 40 men with staves, clubs, and fishing poles, who fell upon me, beating and punching me, and endeavouring to thrust me backward into the sea. When they had thrust me almost into the sea, and saw they would have knocked me down in it, I went up into the midst of them, but they laid at me again, and knocked me down and stunned me. When I came to myself, I looked up and saw James Lancaster's wife throwing stones at my face, and her husband James Lancaster was lying over me, to keep the blows and stones off me. For the people had persuaded James Lancaster's wife that I had bewitched her husband, and had promised her, that if she would let them know when I came thither, they would be my death, and having got knowledge of my coming, many of the town rose up in this manner with clubs and staves to kill me, but the Lord's power preserved me that they could not take away my life. At length I got up on my feet, but they beat me down again into the boat, which James Lancaster observing, he presently came into it, and set me over the water from them, but while we were on the water within their reach, they struck at us with long poles, and threw stones after us."

In 1778, the majority of the tenants at North Scale agreed to enclose several of the town fields, lay out roads, build fences and dykes and share in 'unequal but proportionable shares' the new lands - as they called them. Their reasoning was that the current system of very small detached parcels of land and large open townfields was a '*Discouragement of good husbandry and a great hindrance to the said townfields.*'[35]

Like Biggar, North Scale was governed by a local 'Grave' up until modern times. The grave or mayor was supported by 'painlookers' and their job was to govern the township. The grave was not elected, but each tenement holder, or their representative, took office and responsibility in turn each year in rotation. The grave and painlookers were referred to as the 'four men'. The workings of the grave were recorded in the Town Book or Grave Book. [36]

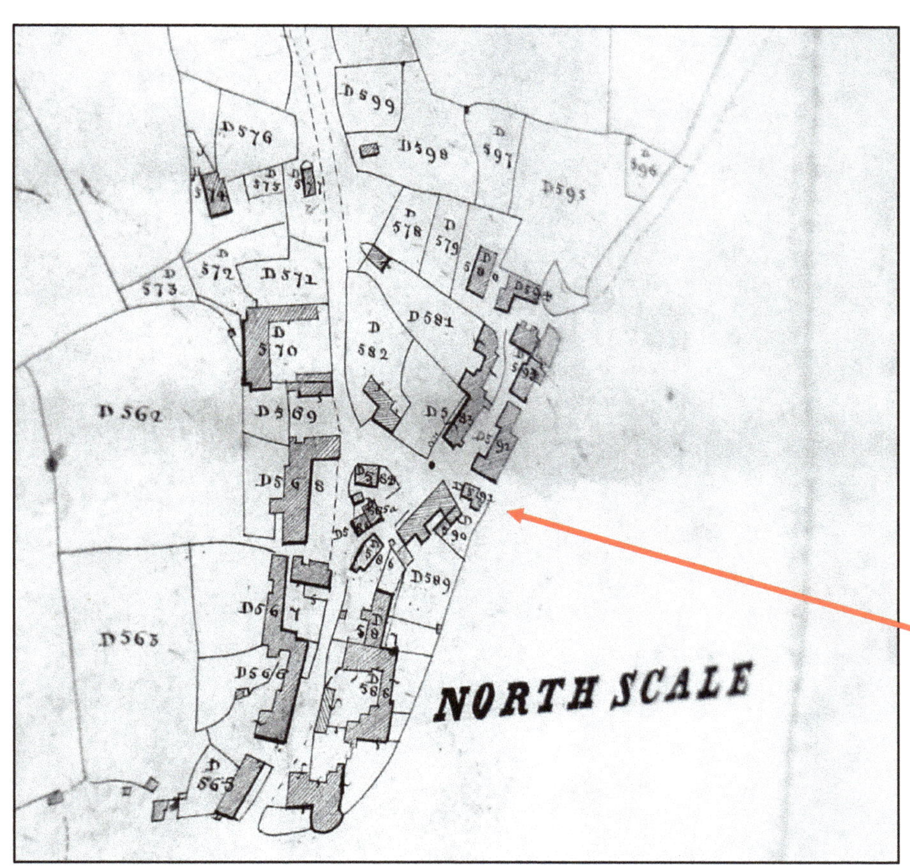

Two maps showing the position of the blacksmith's (Smithy), at North Scale.

The second map shows the field names along with the tithe references. (The D numbers in this case)

The smithy

1842 Tithe map detail. (Cumbria Archives. BPR/I/1/2)

1890 map.   (Cumbria Archives. BDBUC/45/10/2)

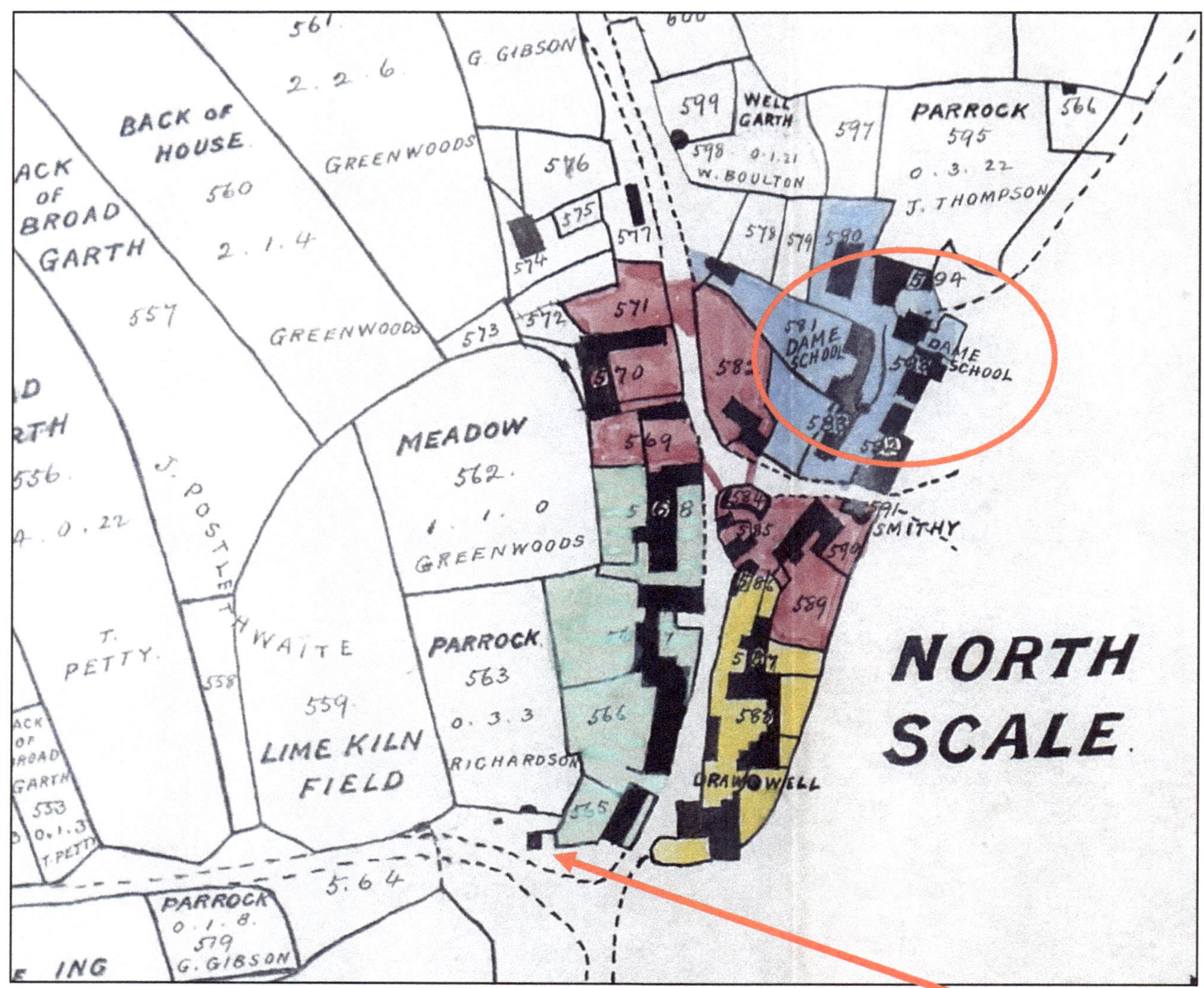

Unfortunately, this map is undated. Possibly c1880 (Cumbria Archives. Z/841/1)

Cobbler's shop

The above shows a Dame School[F], the owners and names of fields, and the position of the smithy. John Kinnish was the blacksmith in 1841, living with his wife Jane, five children, a journeyman, two agricultural labourers and a female servant.[37]

The 1841 census has almost the entire population of North Scale involved with agriculture to some extent, with the exception of people of independent means, the curate and the Blacksmith. By 1871 there are diverse professions listed, reflecting the changing fortunes of Barrow, and the opening of the Iron and Steel-works.

Today there are six listed buildings in the village. All were recently re-photographed, (by the author), as part of an Historic England project, and can be viewed on line. [38]

[F] A Dame School was a small privately run school providing basic education to children. Dames were often widows or unmarried women. I can find no other mention of this particular Dame School anywhere.

In 1841 the house shown, was owned and occupied by James Richardson, a shoemaker (cobbler), his wife Elizabeth, three daughters, a son, and two others.[39]

In 1851 the house was still occupied by James and Elizabeth, along with two daughters, a son, a granddaughter and an apprentice shoemaker.[40]

In 1861 the house was occupied by James, still a shoemaker, now aged 84, his wife Elizabeth now aged 80, along with one son, one daughter, one granddaughter and two grandsons.[41]

In 1871 James Richardson, (the son of the previous James) is living here, he too is a shoemaker. Also living here are two of his nieces, a boarder and an apprentice shoemaker.[42]

We cannot find either a Richardson or a shoemaker in North Scale after 1871, and the census has no house numbers for North Scale until the 1911 census. Presuming the house numbers were the same, in 1911 a Thomas Burney lived at No 1, (the cobbler's house), along with four other males and three females.[43]

There used to be an old stone cobbler's shop attached to the rear of this house, (see photo over). It was demolished sometime after 1974.

Lime Kiln and Old Cobbler's shop North Scale. Early 20th Century.   (Cumbria Archives   Z/3384)

The low-lying land at this north end of Walney Promenade floods regularly at high tides. The photo shows a typical spring tide flood, February 1990.

Biggar Township ran from Tummerhill south to approximately where South End Farm stands today.

The origin of the name? – There's a number of theories - possibly Old Norse – 'bygg'- barley, 'ergh'– hut, or pasture. 'ergh' is Norse-Irish. Second part could be Old Norse 'geiri' or old English 'gara' – 'triangular piece of land.' Another explanation is 'bygg' – barley and 'gar' – garth or field – this is the most often quoted, and the one I favour.

As was stated earlier, the Vikings were driven out of Ireland in 902 A.D. and then settled in Wales, North West England and the Isle of Man. It is thought that it was some of these Vikings who built the first settlement at Biggar.

To be safe from sea-going marauders the village was on the east side of Walney and until modern times all windows faced inwards. The original buildings made of cobbles with turf or peat roofs. Many of the wooden beams used in the buildings over the years have been scavenged from wrecks, as there were many on the west of the island.

There is no main street – as there was nowhere to go other than to the south end – and the layout of the village is still haphazard. The older houses probably stand in exactly the same position as those of the first settlers; that is in any convenient place.

Biggar is first mentioned as a Grange of Furness Abbey in 1292, one of eleven Granges of Furness Abbey at that time. There were 16 tenements, or estates, in the township each originally of around 45 acres.

Every tenement holder enjoyed specific rights and responsibilities related to their land. Each had designated fields: one to the north, another to the south, and additional scattered plots. These parcels were their responsibility. The tenants were allowed to graze one cow at High Bank (now known as Biggar Bank) and another at Low Bank. They had the right to collect tangle (seaweed) for purposes such as manure and burning. Another resource they could gather was whins (gorse), which served as fuel for burning and also for fencing. Unfortunately, there was no available source of wood for them. These rights and limitations shaped their daily lives and interactions with the land and sea. They obtained peat, for fuel, from Angerton Moss near Kirkby – originally by cart but much later by rail.

++++

During the time of Furness Abbey, much money was spent on 'banking' on Walney to try to prevent the ingress of the sea. There may have been a west wall, but only Biggar Dyke, to the east, is left now. It is not known when Biggar Dyke was built but it was certainly there at the time of the monks. Considerable time and much effort was expended in order to keep it in good repair. All tenants of the Abbey, from all of the outlying Granges had to give three days a year 'boon' work with horse and cart to Walney – even those from as far afield as Hawkshead. After the dissolution, The Crown was responsible for repairs. In 1564 Queen Elizabeth 1 issued a decree enforcing the villagers to take upon themselves the responsibility to repair the dykes – for a permanently reduced rent.

The Biggar villagers had to provide 300 days' worth of work between them and the North Scale villagers 20 days' worth, as shown below.

Everyone above the age of 12 would help, and the morning and afternoon each counted as a day. A horse counted as four people, so would complete eight days' worth of work in one day.[44]

++++

The Abbey controlled the lives of the tenants of Walney and all of their Granges until the dissolution in 1537.

In 1631 the plague came to Walney, starting at Biggar. The Dalton Parish registers state:

> 'In this month of July 1631 did the plague begin in Dalton and Bigger (sic). There died in Dalton of this sicknes (sic) three hundred and threescore, and in Waney one hundred and twenty, it ceased about Easter followinge (sic).'

The population of Walney at that time was about 240 people.

Local folklore has it that the dead were buried in Sepulchre field, which is behind the Ferry Hotel. Unfortunately, I can find no evidence to substantiate this claim.

The headman of the village of Biggar was also called the 'Grave' just as at North Scale and they held office for one year in turn – once every 16 years. The position of Grave went with the tenement – two holdings meant two turns in office. In Biggar the Grave had three assistants called 'painlookers' – one of their tasks was to look after the valves which closed the dykes – the name might also refer to pains or fines administered for the Lord of the Manor.

These 'four men' grave and painlookers, also appointed the 'herds' to look after the cattle on the unenclosed land. One herd for High Bank and one for Low Bank.[45] They watched the cattle between 13 May and 10 October. The High Bank was then let for pasturage of fell sheep between October and April.

At Low Bank the herd lived in Trough Head cottage near South End Farm – now long swallowed by the sea. The herd had to bring the cattle to the village twice per day.

The High Bank herd lived in the village, was paid a wage, and had the privilege of going from one house to the other in rotation for his meals.

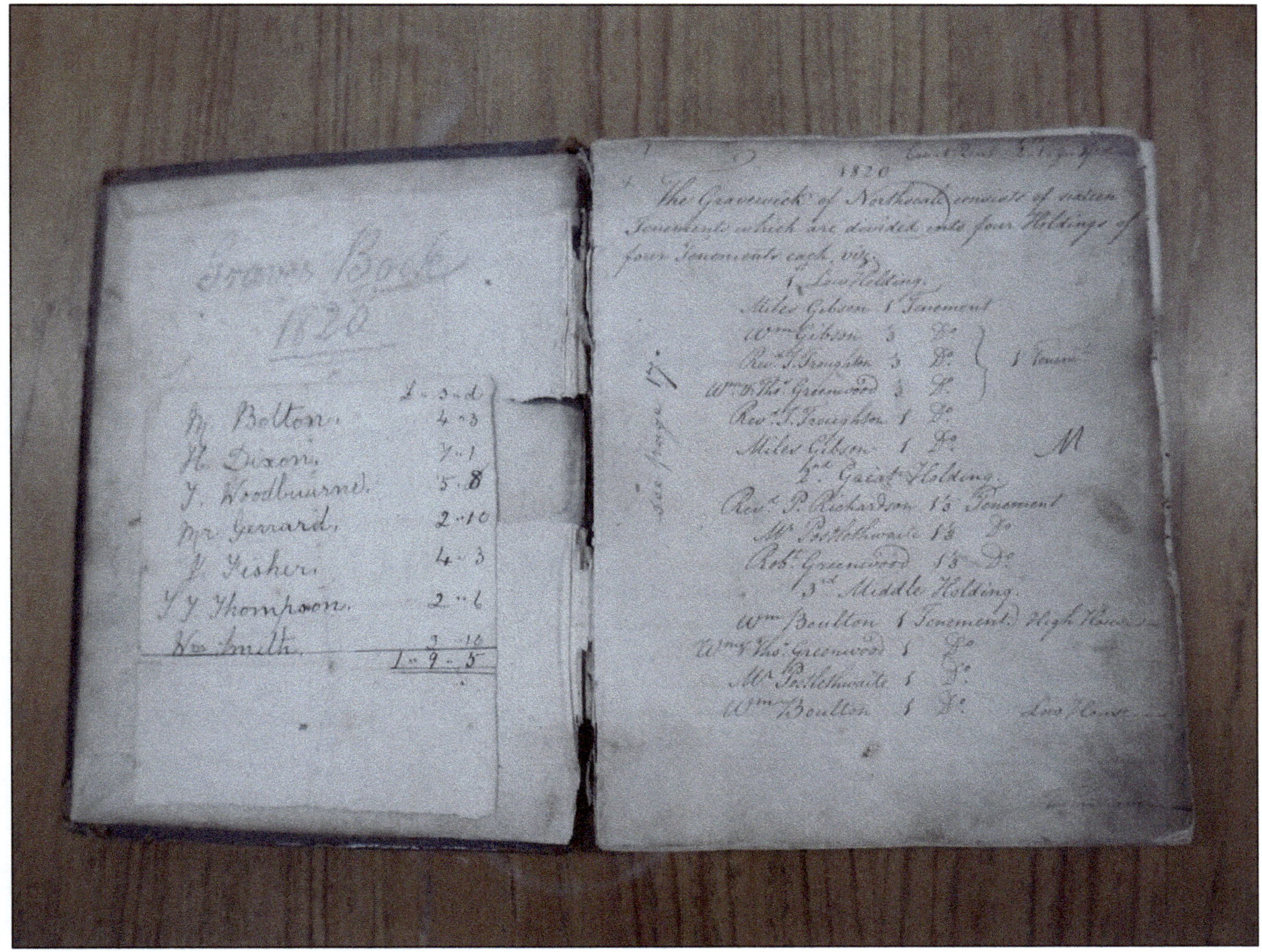

A page from a copy of the Grave Book. 1820   (Cumbria Archives. BDBUC/50/1)

> ## AWARDS.
> To the Labourer in husbandry who has brought up the greatest number of legitimate children without parochial relief, Three pounds ; 2 competitors. John Richardson, Biggar Walney, having had 10 children.

In October 1845, John Richardson of Biggar won £3 at the North Lonsdale Agricultural Association show, for bringing up 10 children without resorting to relief from the parish.

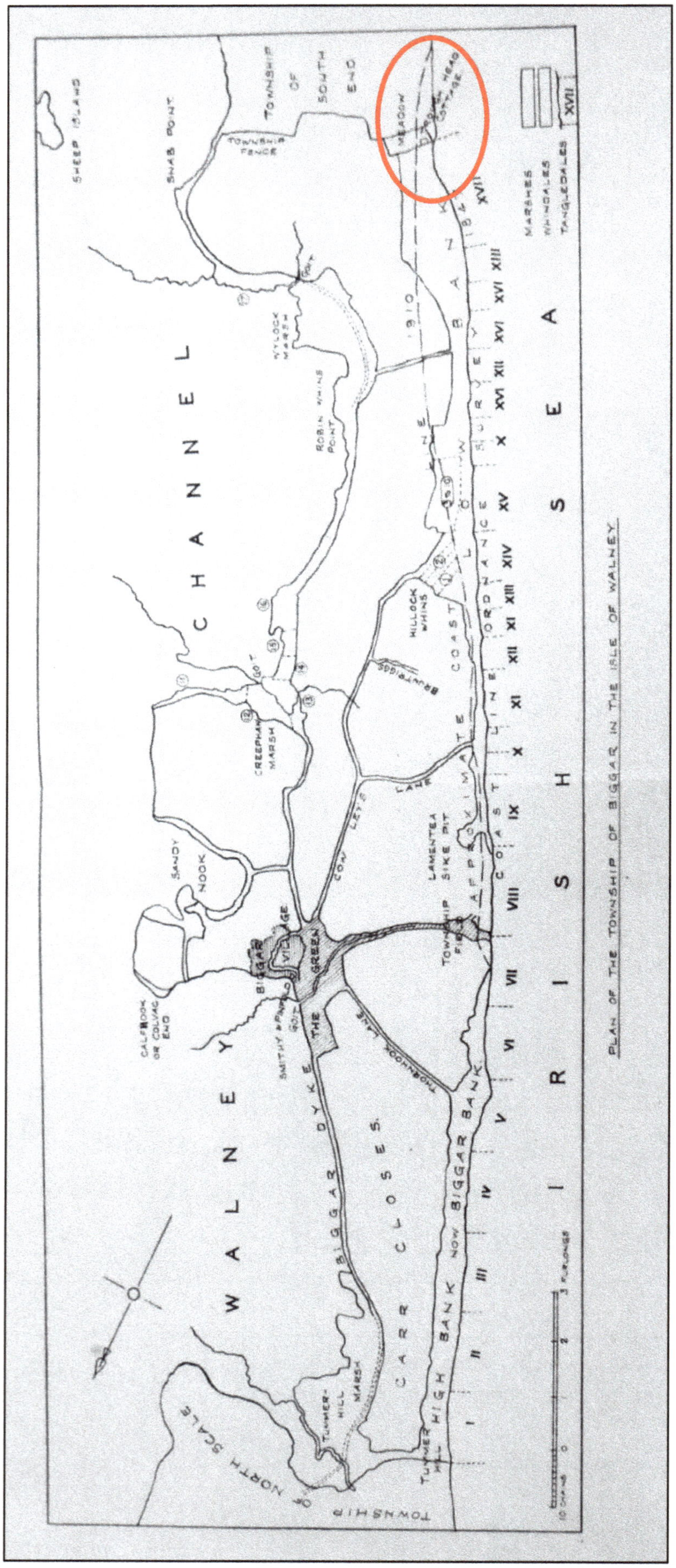

Showing the extent of Biggar township.

The Roman numerals corresponded to which tenants farmed which land.

The position of Trough Head cottage, where one of the 'herds' lived, can be seen circled.

Cumbria Archives BDMH/1/17

A herd's hut at Biggar village.

Cumbria Archives

BDP/169/28

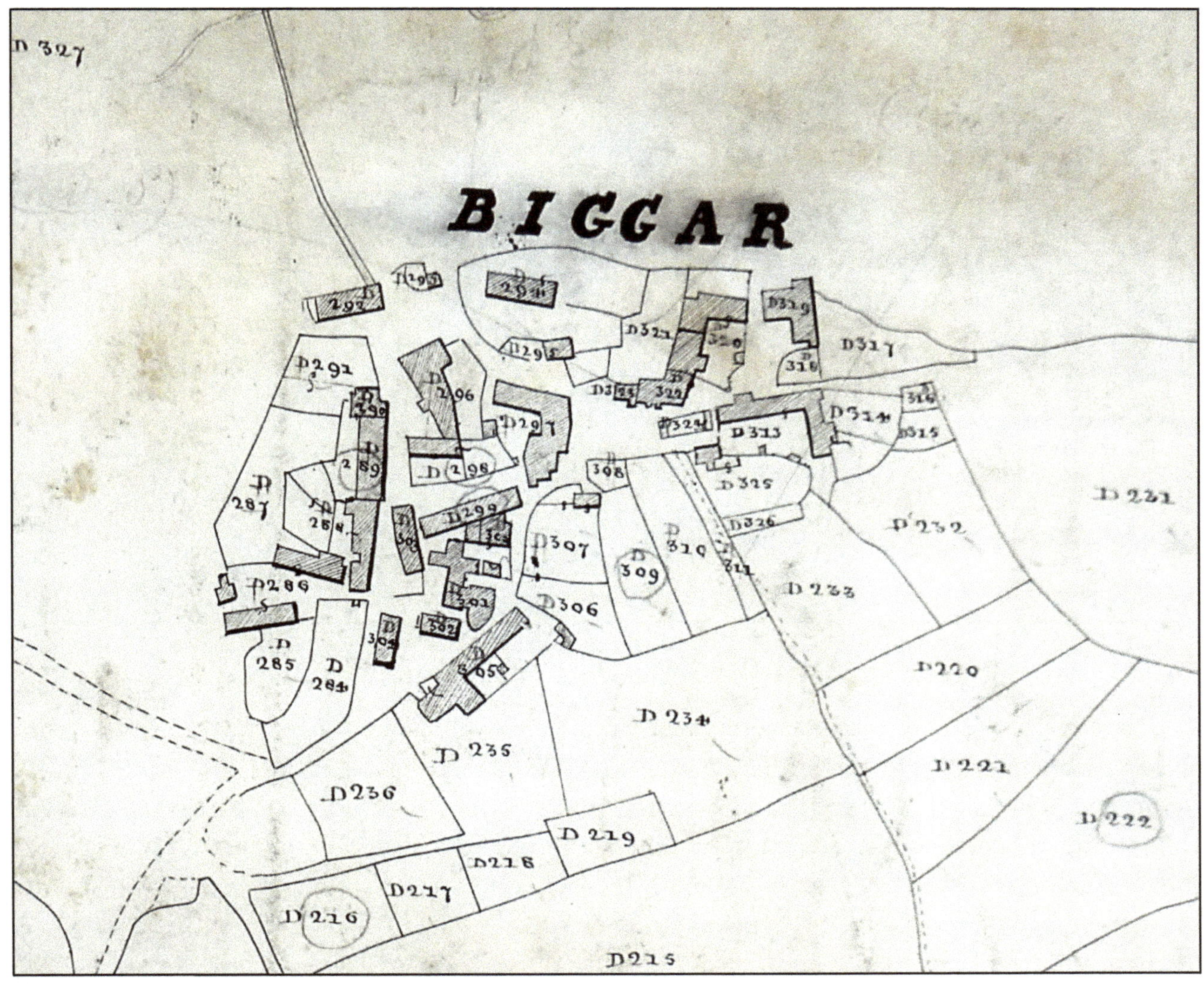

Section of Tithe Map for Walney c 1842.   (Cumbria Archives.   BPR/1/I/3/1/2)

This section of the 1842 Tithe Map shows the layout of the village and the numbered fields. Each field had an entry in the tithe schedule book showing who owned and who was the tenant on each plot of land, plus the acreage and the name of the field. We can subsequently plot who lived in each of the houses shown and then track them through the census returns from 1841 onwards. So, for example The Queens Arms is D286 on this map and the schedule tells us it was owned by John Atkinson and occupied by Richard Spencer in 1840/1.

The Queen's Arms and its associated barn, are currently listed buildings, as are eight other buildings in the village. (More about the Queen's and the New Inn in a later section).

There were 125 people living in Biggar township in 1841. It gradually fell to 85 in 1901 and then rose to 99 in 1911.[46]

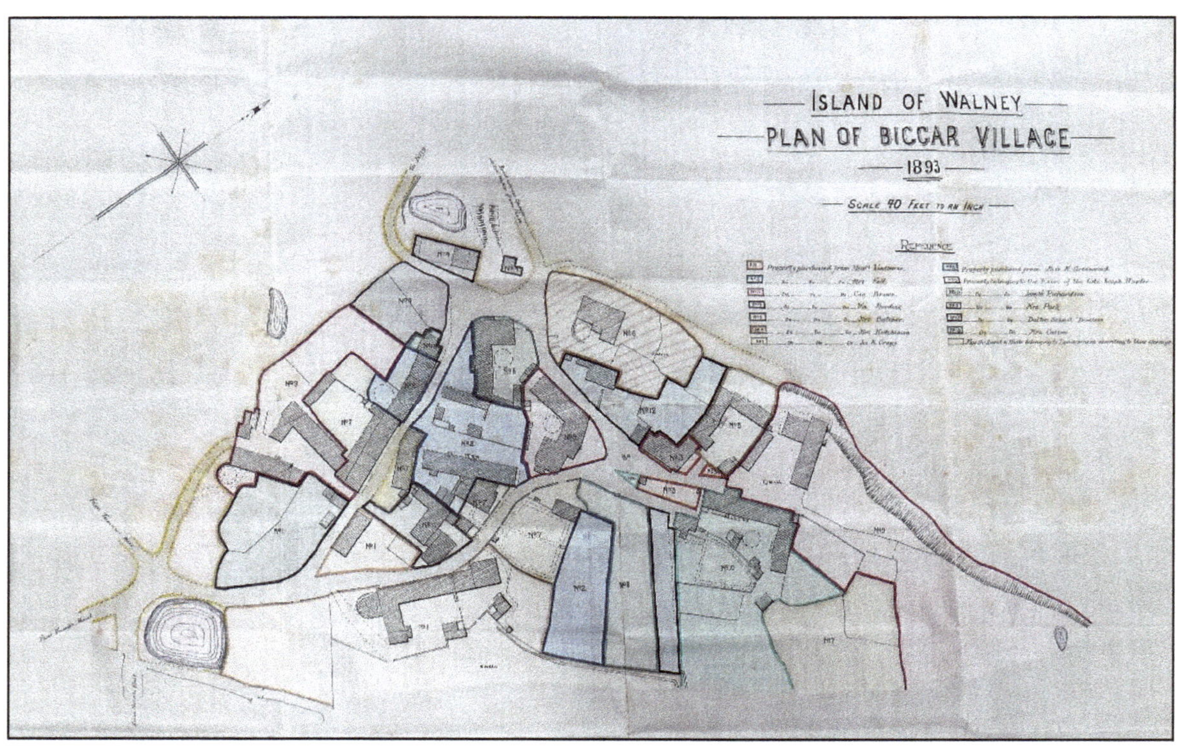

Biggar Village 1893   (Cumbria Archives. BDBUC/43/4/8)

A curious custom used to take place in the village. When a young man from outside came courting a young woman of Biggar, the local men would procure a large sack and waylay the unfortunate suitor, and, if he failed to provide money 'to their satisfaction', they would tie him in the sack and hang it from a beam in a convenient barn until he surrendered. In 1854, Jimmy Wilson, a Cartmel shoemaker was 'sacked' in a barn adjoining the public house. Proceedings were taken before Ulverston magistrates and the custom was stopped.[47]

A peculiarity occurred when the first OS maps were surveyed. The land to the east of Biggar village had always been called 'Calf Hook End' by the locals and it appears as such on pre-OS maps. However, it now appears on OS maps as Cove o' Kend. You can imagine the surveyor asking the locals 'what do you call this bit of land?' and completely mis-hearing the Furness dialect.

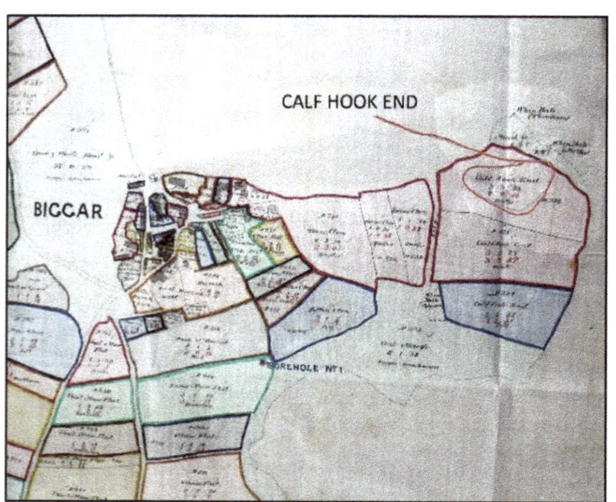

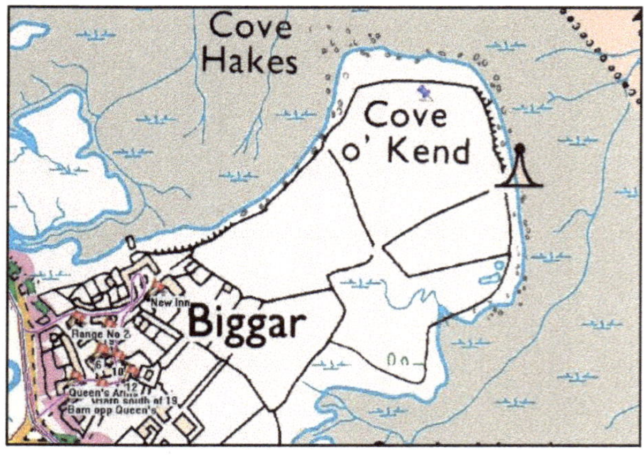

Detail 2021 OS map. Cove o' Kend

Detail 1842 tithe map. (Cumbria Archives. BDBUC/39/60/64)

Tummerhill has an interesting name. One theory is that it comes from Tumbrel Hill. A Tumbrel is a ducking stool. People found guilty of minor crimes might have been brought here for punishment in public.[48]

49

(Image from Chap-books of the 18th century. 1882)

The Fearon and Eyes map of 1737 (below) has the spelling as Tomeril, (bottom left below), and on others it appears as Tumeril, or Tumrel.

A well-known folk song 'The Charcoal Black and The Bonnie Gray' references the cruel sport of cock-fighting, which had been outlawed in this country in 1835.

"Come all ye cockers far and near
I'll tell of a cock-fight, when and where:
At Tummerel Hill I've heard them say,
The North Scale lads had a bonnie grey.
Two dozen lads from Biggar came
To Tummerel Hill to see the game.
They brought along with them that day
A black to match with the bonny grey."

There was a cockpit at Tummerhill and despite the banning of the 'sport' it was reported in 1871 *'The annual cockfighting came off on Walney Island this year as usual. A few birds were killed and a deal of money changed hands.'*[50]

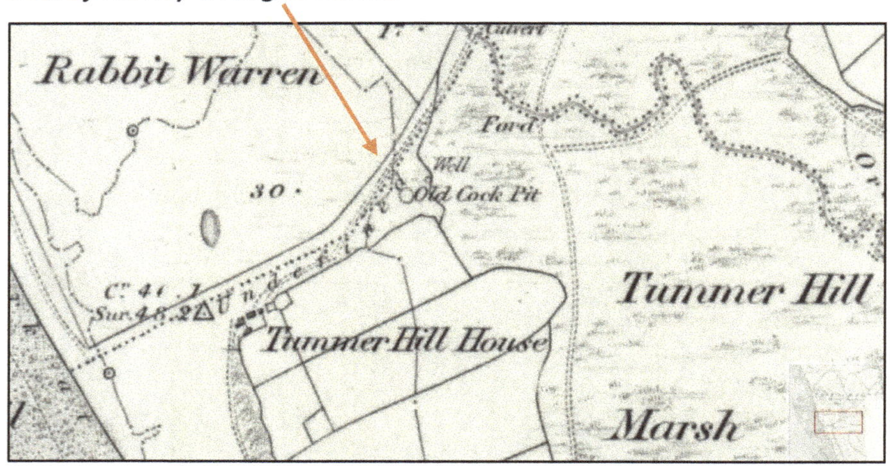

Detail from 1873 OS Map

It is rumoured that the curate from St Mary's – Mr Troughton, officiated at the cock fights - wearing his gown and bands.

Shipwrecks

Shipwrecks were a common occurrence on the west side of Walney throughout the years, and especially during the years of sailing ships.

Walney Island. *During the last few days, many drowned cows and pigs have been cast by the westerly winds upon the shore of this island, some of the pigs weighing 35 scores. These have supplied many of the inhabitants with a large stock of tallow and lard. Several firkins of butter have also been picked up. One person is said to have found three firkins, all good. … Each morning, hours before daybreak, horses, donkeys and carts are heard hastening to the shore in hope of obtaining prizes. Of course, the first maxim of wrecking, the value of the property found is kept a secret profound…..* **Soulby Advertiser. 29 January 1852**

There was the Brig Susan, which was wrecked off Hilpsford on 5th November 1825. The crew all drowned and are buried in the churchyard at St Mary's on Walney. The captain's wife asked for his money belt which he always wore but it could not be found – until it was later discovered stuffed down a rabbit hole.[51] Another disaster saw a sailing vessel flounder off Hillock Whins around 1862. It was carrying red flannel from Lancashire Mills to India. It was said that following this, everyone on the island had red flannel underwear, and red curtains, and bed-clothes.[52]

The Battle of Biggar Bank

What we call Biggar Bank today was originally Biggar High Bank to distinguish it from Biggar Low Bank further south on the island, and it belonged to the farmers of Biggar.

With the huge rise in the population of Barrow from around 150 people in 1841 to well over 47,000 by 1871, the island of Walney became more attractive to the people of the town as a place of recreation. The problem was that the land belonged to the farmers and they began to deter the trespassers, enclosing the land by fences which the trespassers pulled down.

On 13th March 1876 several hundred men, watched over by a police inspector and six constables, began to pull down the new fences and demolish an earth dyke erected by the farmers. According to the *Barrow Herald*, *'A large quantity of free beer was thereafter freely distributed in celebration of the event.'*

BIGGAR BANK.

WHEREAS, certain Persons have been found TRESPASSING on Tummerhill and Biggar High Bank, in the Island of Walney, NOTICE IS HEREBY GIVEN, that any person or persons found trespassing on Biggar Marsh, Tummerhill, or Biggar High Bank, or any other of the marshes or open pastures in or about the hamlet of Biggar, without leave from the Grave for the time being of Biggar, will be proceeded against by the owners thereof, as they may be advised, without further notice.

Dated this 4th day of May, 1876.

W. BUTLER and SON,

Solicitors for the Owners. 8

Despite numerous adverts (such as that above, from the *Barrow Herald* of 13 May 1876), the problem persisted.

It was reported later that *'It is well known that the Bank has been used by the public of Barrow for purposes of pleasure and recreation ever since Barrow had any existence as a place of manufacture.'*[53]

In July 1876 a Biggar Bank Defence Association was set up, not just to promote the rights of the public, but to ascertain 'What are the real rights of the farmers of Biggar, and whether the public have a right in law to the use of the Bank as a place of recreation'. It met in the Hartington Hotel, Duke Street.[54] The groups first action was to set up a fund to collect subscriptions for the purpose of defence for those who were about to be prosecuted.

In August of the same year, one man, Thomas Dawson, who already paid the farmers eight shillings rent for right of way to a new house on Tummerhill, was taken to court for pulling down fences and trespass. He was found guilty and fined 40 shillings.[55]

So here we have a problem. The rights of the farmers to graze their common land versus the rights to recreation on the same land. At the time there were no public green spaces in the town or on Barrow Island.

In June 1877 the Barrow Council decided to lease the land from the farmers at a rent of £70 per year, with a view to opening it as a public recreation ground.[56] That was not the end of the matter however. On 26 July 1877 a mass meeting of about 1000 ratepayers was held on Biggar Bank to hear an address from Mr De Morgan, President of The Commons Preservation Society, in which he held that leasing the land for £70 when it should be free was wrong, and that there were people who would testify that they had had free reign on the land for over sixty years. He also stated that the cost of the lease was too high in any case when compared to the value of the land and the length of the lease.[57] On December 8th, the council, after a long debate decided against the lease by 13 votes to 11.[58]

The first steam ferry began to cross the channel to Walney on 1 July 1878 and this increased the need to resolve the issue. In August, the *Barrow Herald* is again reporting that '*The Reputed owners have again closed Biggar Bank, and the public are once more refused access to it.*'[59] In September the council directed the Town Clerk to write to the solicitor of the 'reputed owners' calling their attention to the fact that the Corporation couldn't permit what is certainly a public highway to be closed.[60]

In October 1878 the Biggar Bank Sub-committee of the council reported back, and it was resolved that '*Biggar High Bank and the adjoining land at the Cock pit, to the extent of 41 acres, be purchased for a sum of £2500.*'

On 16 November 1878, a small notice in the *Barrow Herald* stated that '*Mr Fish moved and Mr Comber seconded that the common seal of agreement be affixed to the following agreements: - Agreement for the purchase of Biggar Bank.*'[61] It took quite a while to conclude the purchase due to the fact that the sellers were 16 in number.

Finally, on 14 May 1883 Biggar Bank was opened officially by John Fell, the mayor of Barrow, and a foundation stone was laid for the new Pavilion that was to be built. The *Preston Herald* reported that upwards of 10,000 people witnessed the event (they all had to cross Walney channel by ferry – a lucrative day for the operators.)[62]

(Cheers) Having proceeded thus far I will now take the formal step of declaring this Bank to be the open, inalienable, and public property of this borough for ever. I hope that for all time it may be a blessing to many generations. (Cheers.)[63]

John Fell's formal opening of Biggar Bank.

<table>
<tr><td>

Borough of Barrow in Furness

Biggar Bank

together with the

Pavilion

was declared free for the use of the public forever
by

John Fell Esquire J.P.

DL Lancashire, Mayor of the Borough by whom
this stone was laid. May 14th 1883

</td></tr>
</table>

A memorial stone from 1883 celebrating the event still stands near to the Roundhouse, though it is difficult to read nowadays, (above).

A number of designs were proposed for the new Pavilion or shelter and it was completed by September 1883, and the road from the Walney Ferry to Biggar Bank was improved at the same time to raise the level above the tide line. [64] The Pavilion finally closed in the 1970s and was demolished sometime after 1975.[65]

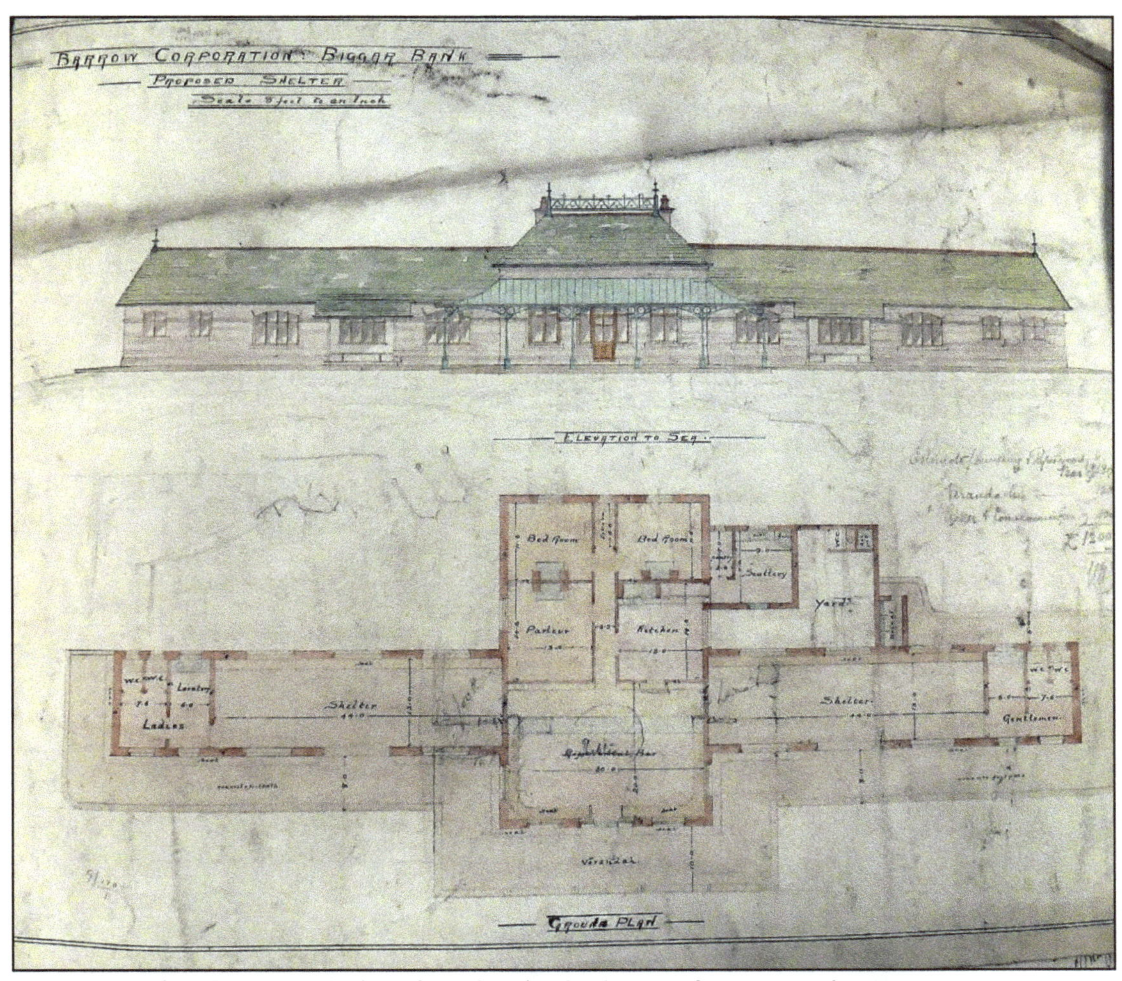

A proposal for the new shelter (Pavilion) which wasn't accepted. c1883

(Cumbria Archives.   BA/S/BC/D3)

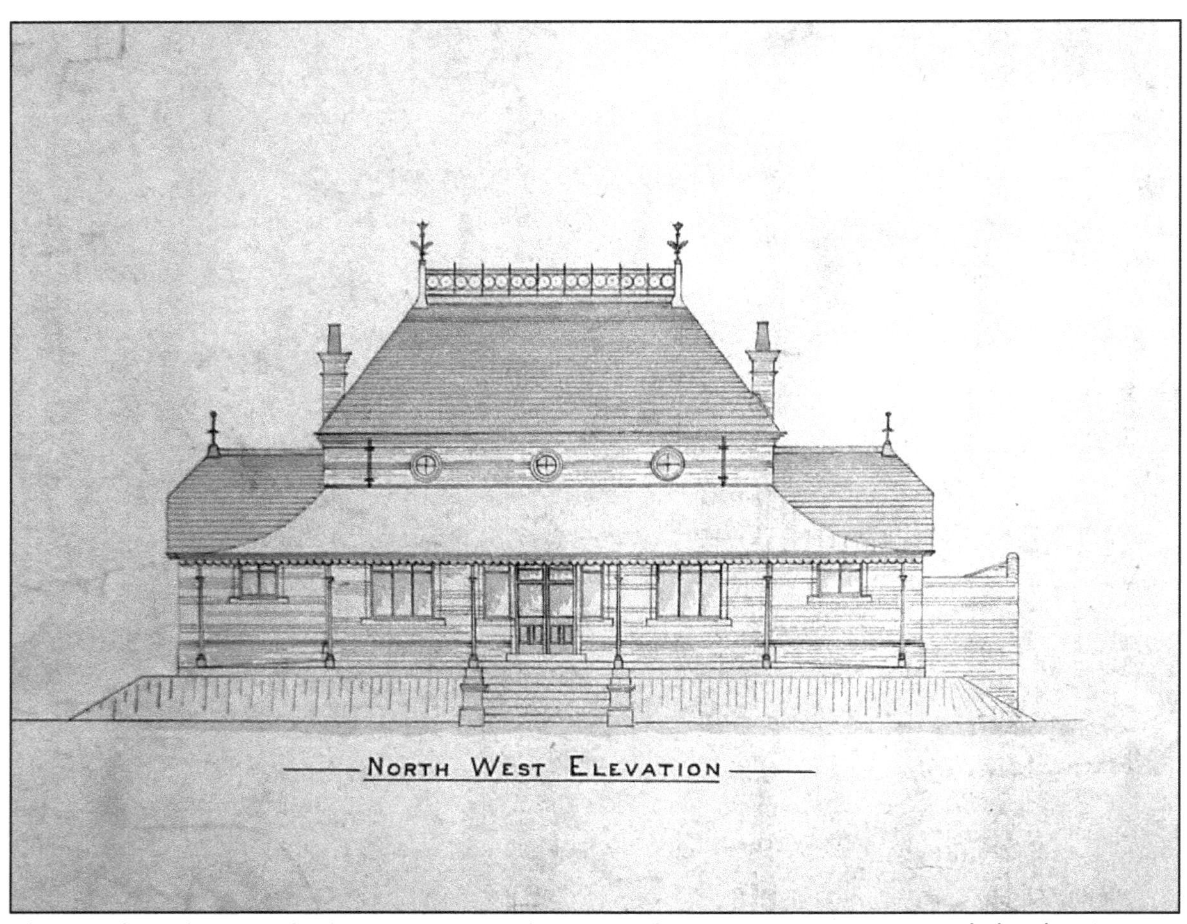

The Pavilion design which was approved. c1883. (Cumbria Archives.   BA/S/BC/D3.)

Sankey Family Photography Collection No 266. c1900 © Cumbria Archives.

The final of the four Granges, **South End,** ran from the Biggar township to the southern tip of the island. It originally consisted of eight tenements. Only one, South-End Farm, remains from earlier times, and this has been rebuilt at least once.[66]

This map shows Trough Head cottage where one of the Biggar Herds lived before it was taken by the sea, and the position of South End Farm.

You can also see the line of the original road from Biggar which ran on the west side of the island before it too was eroded away.

(Cumbria Archives BD/BUC/39/64)

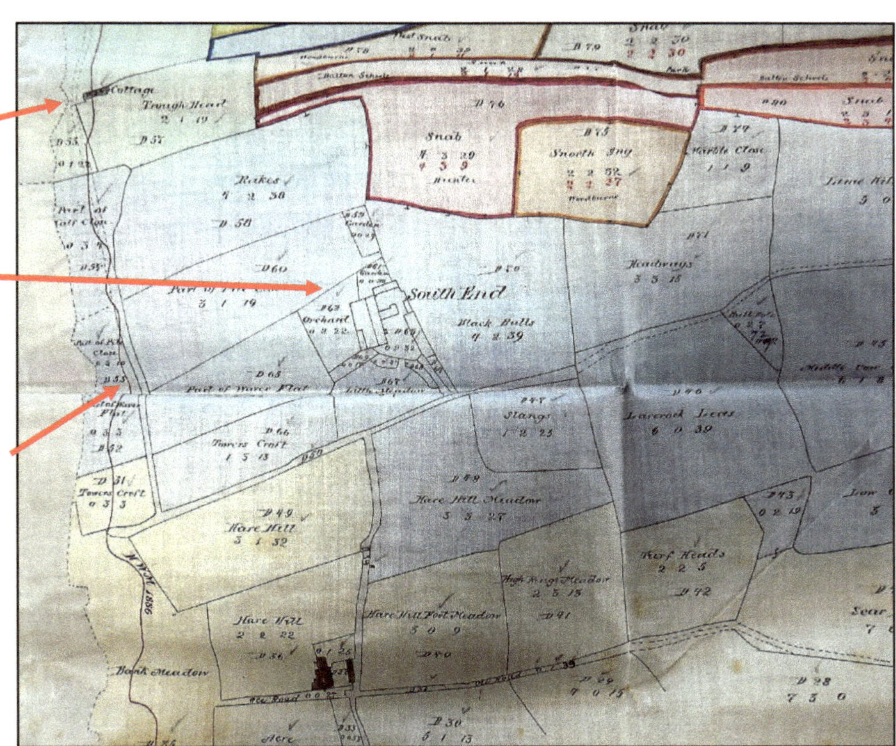

By the early 1800s, the South End had dwindled to just two tenements. This decline may have been attributed to the gradual encroachment of the sea, which had claimed much of the land over the preceding 450 years. Within living memory South End Farm was known as Berry's Farm.

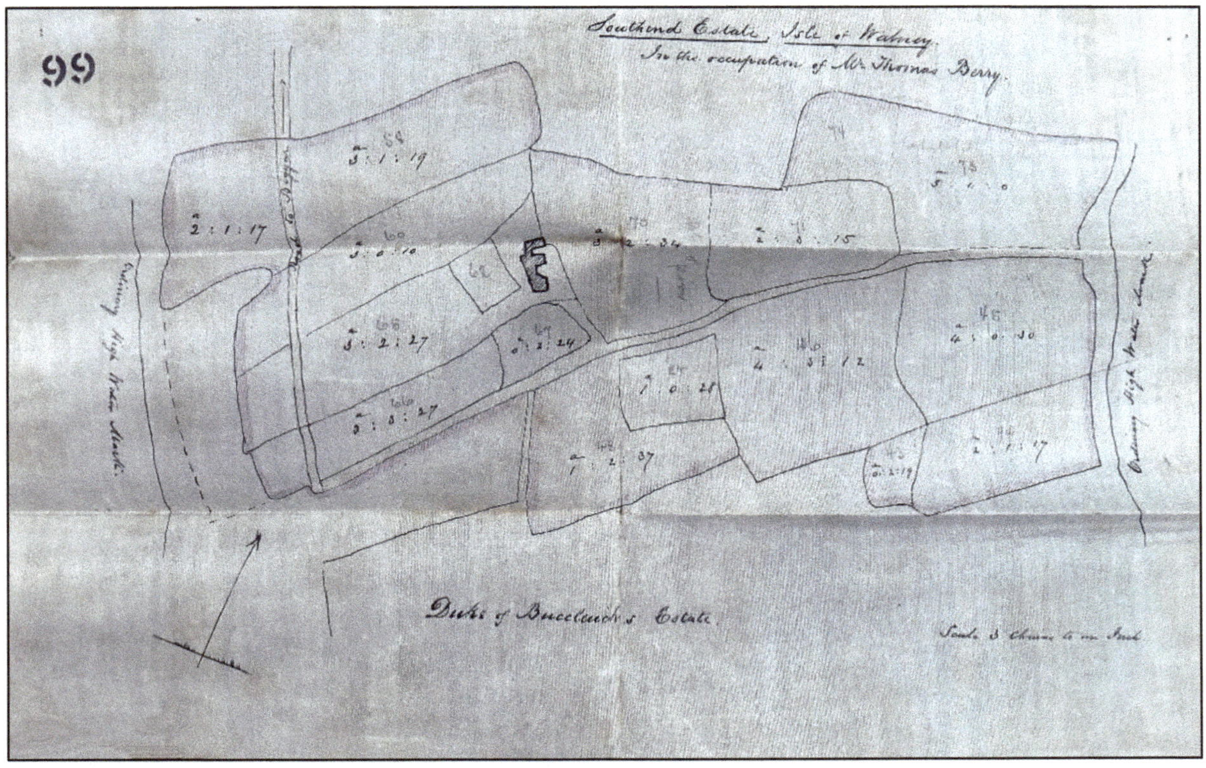

This map shows the Berry estate. (Cumbria Archives. BD/BUC/39/34)

One thing of note on this last map, is that to the right, near to where a later lime kiln stood, was a 'Sod Hut', put up by Margaret Susanna Berry around 1850 as a meeting place for the Baptists who lived on the island.[67] This map also clearly shows the 'road to Biggar' on the left.

The 1841 tithe map and schedule have the owner of South End Farm as William Simpson and the occupier as William and Ann Redhead.[68] The 1841 census has William, his wife Elizabeth, four children, a farm servant, a female farmer surname Redhead along with six children, five agricultural labourers and another farm servant. A total of 20 people.[69]

In 1851 Thomas Berry was head of the household, along with his wife Margaret, three children, Ann Simpson, Thomas's sister-in-law Elizabeth, his mother-in-law and five servants. In 1861 Thomas, Margaret, three children, a governess and three farm servants lived there. Thomas and Margaret are still there in 1871, along with three children, a niece, and four servants. In 1881 Thomas, Margaret, a son-in-law, a grandson, and three servants are listed at the farm.

Again in 1891 Thomas, now 69, Margaret, also 69, one daughter and a son-in-law with their two children, a niece and a servant are living at the farm.

In 1901 Thomas is still at the farm with a daughter and son-in-law, Robert Casson, along with their two daughters and a 70 years old servant. By 1911 Robert Casson is head of the household along with another male and three females.[70]

South End Farm is today a listed building.

South End Farm.

(Cumbria Archives.

Z/3384)

North Scale and Biggar, along with the outlying tenements of North End and South End continued to be the main dwelling places on the island until the end of the 19th century. [71]

Walney Lighthouse.

One of the earliest buildings on the island after the villages of North Scale and Biggar, was the lighthouse at the South end.

Image from Walney church pamphlet 1929. (Cumbria Archives. BLC/PH/280/FJ/WAL 1)

In 1789, The Commissioners of the Port of Lancaster obtained an act of Parliament (29 Geo iii C12) for improving the Navigation of the River Lune, and various other matters – among these were the erection of lighthouses in such parts of Lancaster Bay as they might 'think most proper'. Walney lighthouse was not built to benefit Barrow, as that was only a small village at the time. Its purpose was to improve the navigation of the River Lune and act as a guide for cargo ships from the West Indies bound for Glasson Docks, near Lancaster, which had opened in 1787. The Commissioners thought the South East end of Walney (or Hawse Point) was the best site due to the number of wrecks occurring on the west side of the island.[72] After a survey and negotiations, the land was leased from the owners, James Hunter and John Simpson for ten shillings and sixpence per year for 10,000 years for a plot measuring 20 yards by 20 yards, with a road to the lighthouse. The original lanthorn (lantern) and reflectors were timber, and the light was first used on 1st December 1790. [73] James Hunter and John Simpson were appointed lightkeepers.

Built with sandstone from Overton, near Heysham, the lighthouse had cost £1100 to erect on an octagonal column 70 feet high with a foundation 26 feet 6 inches in diameter diminishing in 57 ft to 14ft. There were 91 steps up to the top of the lighthouse and it had an initial rating of 3,500 candle-power, lit by oil.[74]

At the top of the tower were three, three-foot parabolic reflectors, which from 1791 were driven by a weighted clockwork mechanism to rotate once every 15 minutes. The lanthorn and reflectors were destroyed in a fire on 21st December 1803 and the wooden part of the structure burnt down. In Lancaster Museum is a parabolic reflector made from a concave metal plate, covered in 617 pieces of mirrored glass, thought to have come from Walney lighthouse.

WALNEY LIGHT-HOUSE BURNT.

THE COMMISSIONERS of St. GEORGE'S QUAY, Lancaster, hereby give NOTICE, that the REVOLVING LIGHTS, on the ISLAND of WALNEY, were accidentally DESTROYED BY FIRE on Tuesday last; and should it be found practicable to shew a TEMPORARY LIGHT, until the Light-House is re-built, due notice will be given thereof.

LANCASTER, Dec 23, 1803.

75

76

The light was up and running again by March 1804. In 1820, four silver plated copper reflectors were installed.

Hunter and Simpson remained as keepers until 11 December 1821 when Joseph Geldert was appointed. In 1836 Joseph was paid £40 for his work.

The 1841 census has Joseph Geldard as the lighthouse keeper, living here with his wife Margaret, and five children.[77]

++++

Was it Geldert or Geldard? Similar discrepancies occur whenever we research into the past. The problem is that many people could not read or write and even when they did, they often used their own interpretations of a spelling. When researching family history for example, the spelling of names in census returns demonstrate this often. Census takers would often write down names based on how they sounded when spoken, especially when the respondent was unable to provide the correct spelling.

++++

Back to our story.

In 1846 the light was changed to revolve every four minutes, showing a bright light every minute. Joseph's son, Thomas and Joseph's grandson James, were made assistant keepers the same year and a tidal light was erected at Hawes point in the September and first lit 1 October.

The 1851 census has Joseph, and Margaret and two children. Their surname now written as Geldart.[78]

In 1861 Joseph and Margaret, aged 74 and 71 are still in residence. Next door, in one of the cottages, his son Thomas, also a lightkeeper, is living with his wife Jane and four children.[79] It is reported in 1861 that the lighthouse has been painted three times since erection at a cost of £5 6s 3d each time.[80]

In February 1871, after 50 years at the lighthouse and having brought up a family of 12 children there, Joseph Geldert and his wife Margaret both died.[81] Joseph was 84 and Margaret 80. They had lived at the lighthouse since their marriage in 1807. Thomas was the lightkeeper in 1871, with Jane and an 18-year-old son James, (also a lightkeeper), and two other sons.[82]

Thomas died on 16 June 1879.[83] James then took over the duty of keeper and his brother William was made assistant keeper. [84]

In 1881, Jane a widow, James the lightkeeper along with his brother William, Jane's other son Joseph, and a daughter, Sarah Jane, are living here.[85]

In 1891 James and William were still the lighthouse keepers, living next door to each other. James is living with his mother Jane and a servant girl. William with his wife Bertha a son and a daughter.[86] Jane died on 16 January 1900.[87]

Image from Walney church pamphlet 1929. (Cumbria Archives. BLC/PH/280/FJ/WAL 1)

The lighthouse was connected to the Barrow telephone exchange in 1899. In the lighthouse visitors' book is an entry dated 3 February 1899 – '*Mr Doherty, The Superintendent Engineer of the Post Office Telegraphs, have this day talked to me through the Telephone from the Barrow Post Office to the Lighthouse and find it working most satisfactorily.*'[88] There are regular entries in the visitors' book from a GPO linesman who checked on the line and repaired faults. Other regular visitors were the Port of Lancaster Commissioners who inspected and reported (favourably) on the condition of the lighthouse.

By 1901 James had a younger wife Mary living with him and William and Bertha are living with a daughter.[89]

In 1909 the lighthouse was converted to run on acetylene gas.[90] In 1937 the light was increased from one flash every 60 seconds to one every 15 seconds and the power increased to 12,000 candle-power.

The 1911 census has James living with two females and William with one female.[91]

Fred Swarbrick became Walney Lighthouse assistant keeper in 1920 moving from Piel Island with his wife and two daughters, Ella (born 1915) and Peggy (Margaret Grace born 1919). In 1933 he became Lighthouse Keeper.

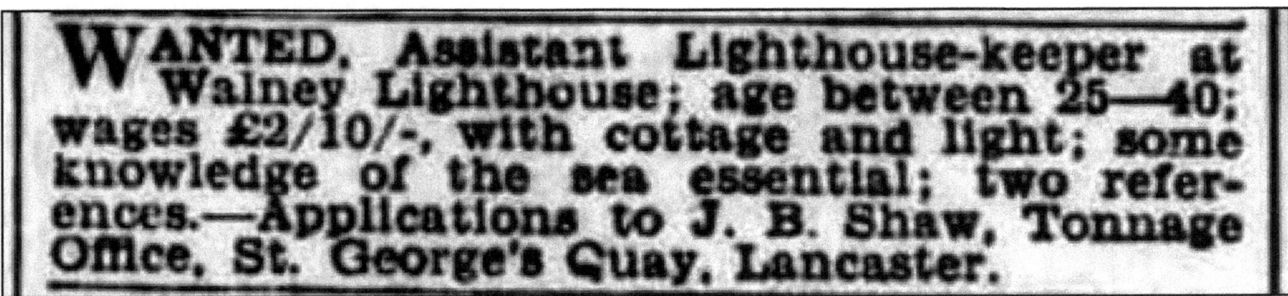

Lancashire Daily Post 23 April 1937

During the Second World War, the lighthouse had a telephone at the top and would receive coded messages telling them when to light and when to douse the light so as to guide convoys down the Irish Sea.[92]

An accident occurred in December 1949 when the plant which generated the acetylene gas exploded and Fred Swarbrick, was burnt on his face and wrists.[93]

Both of Fred Swarbrick's daughters married on the same day in 1952. Ella married Albert Wheeler at Barrow Register Office and Peggy married Ken Braithwaite, an engineer and wartime wing commander, at St Mary's, Walney. Between 1952 and Ella's death in 1967, Albert and Ella were in charge of the lighthouse. In 1953 the lighthouse was converted to electricity supplied by a diesel generator. The light would now flash every 15 seconds and be visible for up to 18 miles and be 450,000 candlepower.[94]

++++

Peggy Braithwaite became assistant keeper when Ella died and on Albert's retirement, in 1975, she took over charge of the lighthouse. Peggy was awarded the British Empire Medal which was presented to her at the Lakeland Rose Show by Princess Margaret on 14 July 1984. She retired in 1994 and died two years later in 1996.[95]

© Peter Laird

In 2003, the lighthouse was the last in the country to be automated. It is a grade II listed building.

Vickerstown.

The spectacular rise of the town of Barrow from the 1840s onwards led to a chronic shortage of housing in the borough and led to a few short-term solutions. The huts on Barrow Island, (some built by the shipyard for its workers), were declared unsanitary and were mainly demolished by the early 1880s[96]. The ex-liner Alaska was used for about 18 months by Vickers, Sons & Maxims Ltd as temporary accommodation for about 250 workmen.[97] The local council was seemingly opposed to municipal housing most likely because of the vested interests of many of the councillors. At least nine of them were connected to the building trade in one way or another.

Benjamin Fish, a local builder who had been a councillor for many years, and who was Mayor in 1898, was one of an original syndicate which proposed a sea side resort to be made at Earnse Point and for workers' housing on the east side of the island. In January 1899 the local press reported on the scheme to develop Walney *we never get any further forrader than rumour.'*[98] In April 1899 Fish announced a new steamship service to the Isle of Man from Barrow in an interview with *The Manxman*. He spoke of the formation of a new company with £100,000 backing from Vickers, Sons & Maxims Ltd. The company was to be headquartered at Walney-on-Sea and a new pier built for the service.[99]

It was with this background that the Isle of Walney Estates Company was formed in 1899, with a plan to develop Walney Island into a seaside resort with up to 1,000 houses.[100]
Fish was however unable to raise the money, Vickers had bought the company and made Fish the Manager by 1900. (He resigned from the council in Oct 1899.)[101]
The original plans drawn up for a village on the east side of the island, north of the Ferry Hotel and to be called Vickersdale, show a collection of small terraces and a large central square. (called Albert Square). The idea of a seaside resort had disappeared.[102]

A NEW SEASIDE RESORT.

A BIG PROJECT AT BARROW.

A new company has been registered, the Isle of Walney Estates Company, Limited, with a capital of £100,000, all of which has been subscribed, to develop Walney Island, Barrow-in-Furness, into a seaside resort. Already practically the whole of the land in the north of the island has been purchased with this object. A part of the land has already been disposed of, on which Messrs. Vickers, Sons, and Maxim are about to build at once from 600 to 1000 houses for the workmen employed by them at the Naval Construction Works. There is a great scarcity of houses at present in the town. The rest of the land purchased will be laid out on a big scale as a watering place, with an extensive frontage and a fine promenade on the west shore, washed by the Irish Sea. Here are located fine bathing sands, and many advantages likely to make Walney-on-the-Sea a very popular seaside resort.

[103]

By September 1899, the Vickersdale idea had been abandoned, and instead the Vickerstown scheme of around 1,000 houses north *and* south of the Ferry Hotel was now the favoured plan.

Detail of Vickersdale plan 1899.   (Cumbria Archives. Z/312.)

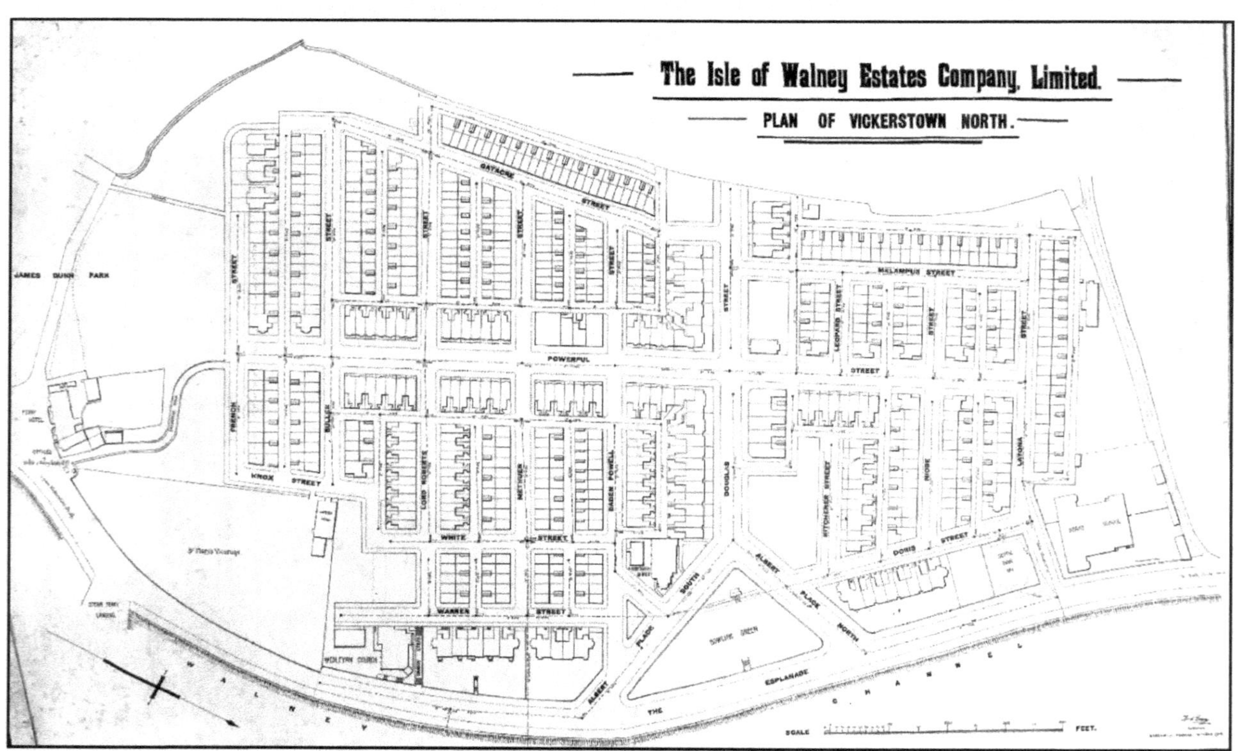

Vickerstown North.   (Cumbria Archives. BA/S/BC/D7/7)

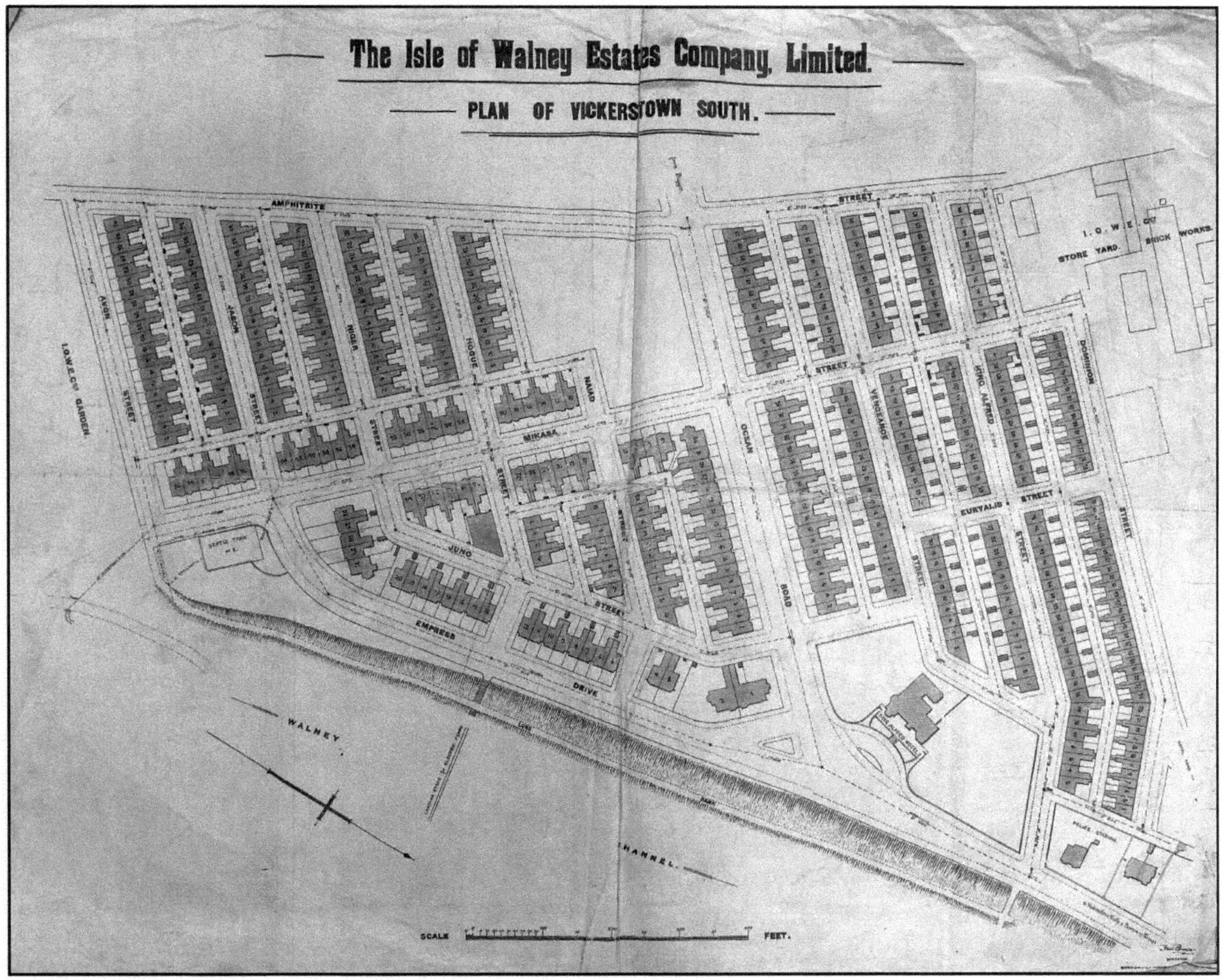

Vickerstown South.   (Cumbria Archives. BA/S/BC/D7/7)

By 1900 the company had purchased 343 acres at a cost of £100 per acre.[104] The whole estate, both north and south, was designed by William Moss Settle, an Ulverston architect.

++++

Work began in earnest in 1900, with the project using eight major contractors. Benjamin Fish was not one of them, was replaced as manager of the Isle of Walney Estates Company by Vickers, and from then on was a staunch critic of both Vickerstown and the later plans to build a bridge to Walney.

++++

Bricks for the estate were produced at clay pits and brickworks at North Scale and at a site close to where Dominion Street is now. To transport those bricks to Vickerstown North a wooden trestle bridge 600 foot long, was built across the valley which now houses Vickerstown park, by one of the contractors, William Gradwell, one of the town's most well connected and prolific builders. Some of the slate for the roofs, curiously, was imported from America. It was claimed that it could be brought over cheaper than slate from the quarries of Kirkby.[105]

The *Lancashire Evening Post* reported that the first houses were occupied on 1 November 1900.[106] The first tenant to move in was a David Mason, a clerk at Vickers who moved into 28 Latona Street.[107] By 1904, about 950 houses had been built, north and south. The houses were sturdy, well-constructed, and equipped with flush toilets, running water, and electricity. However, during that period, there was no gas supply to the island. The estate was run from the offices of the Isle of Walney Estates Company next to The Ferry Hotel.

Trestle bridge for transporting bricks across James Dunn Park 1915.
(Cumbria Archives   BDP 150/4.)   This picture can be dated by the building of the semi-detached houses on French Street occurring in the background.

Part of the layout of Vickerstown included the park, still in the centre of the island today – James Dunn Park, opened in June 1903.[108](James Dunn was a Vickers director.) The park had a swan pond, and a bandstand. Regular Pierrot shows also took place there. In addition, six acres of land to the east of the park were laid as allotments and a nursery and small market garden was built near Avon Street to help supply the plants for the allotments. The Company established a farm near North Scale for the supply of fresh milk and cream.[109]
Lord Dunluce was the first estates manager, appointed in 1901, a post he held until August 1909. He lived initially at 2, Empress Villas, near the King Alfred Hotel, before moving to the Old Vicarage near the Ferry hotel.[110]

++++

Obtaining a tenancy to a Vickerstown house for the average worker was however not straightforward. A man had to be recommended by his foreman and the condition of the house had to be maintained in order to ensure continued occupancy. The houses were all painted in estate colours of chocolate, green and cream.

++++

Originally none of the houses were to be sold. Rents varied from 5s per week to 13s per week depending upon which type of house was rented. The most numerous houses were type 'A' such as Niobe and Vengeance Streets providing basic accommodation for ordinary workers at 5s.

Houses such as Powerful Street, type 'J' were for the likes of foremen and some had bathrooms at 7s. Type 'L' in Avon Street were for Estates Company personnel, with the rent at 9s, rising to 13s for houses on The Promenade - reserved for the elite of the estate.

Pierrots in James Dunn Park, pre-1915. Sankey Family Photography Collection No 279.
© Cumbria Archives

The streets on the North estate were named after generals, and in the southern part were named after famous ships built in Barrow.
There were many clubs to keep people occupied. These were;
- The Football club was formed in September 1901
- The Cricket club was formed from the previous Naval construction cricket club in 1902
- The Bowling green club was originally on Barrow Island, and moved to Walney in 1903. In 1908 it moved to The King Alfred Hotel.
- The Lawn Tennis club had two courts in the grounds of the King Alfred Hotel, and on the Promenade.
- Vickerstown Institute was formed in 1902 in a large house in Baden Powell Street before moving to Central Drive in 1917. (The old Institute was then converted into two houses.)[111]
- A couple of garden or horticultural organisations flourished and there was an Orchestral Society and a Male Voice choir.[112]

The Isle of Walney Estates Company, Limited.

CONDITIONS OF LETTING

OF

Dwelling-houses, Farm Buildings and Lands at Walney.

1—The premises will be let for one year as to the lands from the 14th day of February and as to the dwelling-houses and buildings from the 12th day of May 1900.

2—The Company will in or before the month of July inform the tenants if they can continue their tenancies for another year at the same rental.

3—The tenants shall keep in repair the fences gates and gate posts belonging to their respective lots and shall deliver up the same at the end of their respective tenancies in as good repair and condition as at the time of entry. In case any two fields adjoining each other shall be let to separate Parties the fence dividing the same shall be kept in repair as to one half thereof by each tenant. The tenant paying the higher rent having the right to select which half he will keep in order.

4—The tenants shall keep clean all ditches drains cuts and watercourses belonging to the lands they hold.

5—The tenants shall repair and keep in repair all dwelling-houses and buildings (except main walls main timbers and slate and damage by fire excepted) and shall so deliver up the same at the end of their respective tenancies.

6—The rent shall be paid by equal half-yearly payments on the 12th day of August and 12th day of February as to the lands and on the 11th day of November and the 12th day of May as to the buildings but the Company may by writing require the rent to be paid half-yearly in advance or security to be given for its payment such security to be to the satisfaction of the Auctioneers.

7—The tenants shall pay all rates taxes and outgoings now due or to become due in respect of the premises (Landlords' Property Tax only excepted).

Part of a letting agreement c1902. (Cumbria Archives. Z/597)

Shops were provided on Douglas Street, and Mikasa Street, and also land was provided for churches (more on these later).

The original plan was for there to be a public house on the north estate and one on the south estate. The King Alfred, on the south estate was built. It was opened by Earl Grey, and was operated on the Public House Trust principal, whereby the tenant made more from the sale of non-alcoholic drinks.

The King Alfred Hotel, Vickerstown, was opened on Monday night the 15th inst. The Hotel has been established on the Trust principle whereby the profits accruing, after the payment of 5% on the capital outlay, are handed over to the Trustees for disposal for the public good. Not only so, but in hotels governed by the Trust ideals, the sale of food and temperance beverages is encouraged and the sale of liquors is not pushed. The manager, in point of fact, is given a commission on the sale of food and non-intoxicants, but on alcoholic liquors he receives nothing.

Vickerstown Chronicle. 26 February 1904.

The "KING ALFRED" HOTEL, to be opened by EARL GREY, and a Distinguished Party on Monday next.

A second public house, to be called the King Edward, was to be built on Douglas Street. Unfortunately, due to the increase in costs it never materialised and an off-licence was opened in Methuen Street instead.

In order to correct an erroneous impression conveyed to the public, by the publication in a local paper a few days ago of a picture PURPORTING TO BE the New Trust Public House proposed for Vickerstown, we have pleasure in presenting to our readers, by kind permission of the Walney and Barrow Islands' Trust Public House Co., Ltd., a perspective sketch of the Public House, which the Company aims at erecting in Vickerstown.

The one that got away. The pub that was meant to be built on Douglas Street.

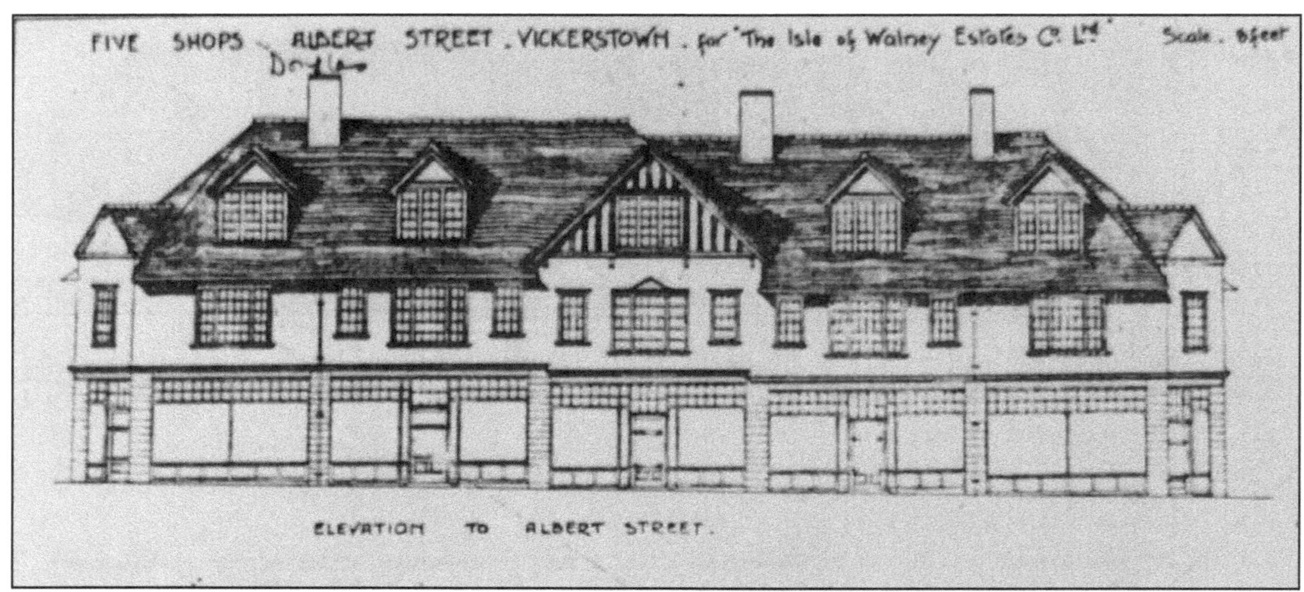

Detail from the original design of Douglas Street shops. (Cumbria Archives. BDY/116)

The above differs from what was eventually built, there are no dormers now and the basements of the design didn't materialise either. Note it says Albert Street, but there was already an Albert Street in Barrow.

Mikasa Street Shops.   Sankey Family Photography Collection No 72.   © Cumbria Archives

A second phase of building in Vickerstown started in 1913, with the addition of some houses in Delhi and Dominion Streets followed by new houses in Douglas Street, Lord Roberts Street and Gatacre Street in 1915. The semi-detached houses of French Street were built in 1915 and 90 extra houses were built on South Vickerstown in 1916 with another 44 in 1920.[115](Plymouth Street, Cardiff Street, Bristol Street)

The sale of houses began in earnest post the First World War when a house in Powerful Street would set you back £515.[116]

Further housing development

In 1934, debates were ongoing in the local council chamber concerning another possible housing scheme at Vickerstown.[117] (As an aside, in January 1934 it was also reported that 75% of houses on Walney didn't have bathrooms.) In January 1935 the council advertised land for sale near Ocean Road.

In March 1935 it was reported that the land had been sold to a Lancaster firm, Parkinson and Sons, for £5,350.[118] [119]

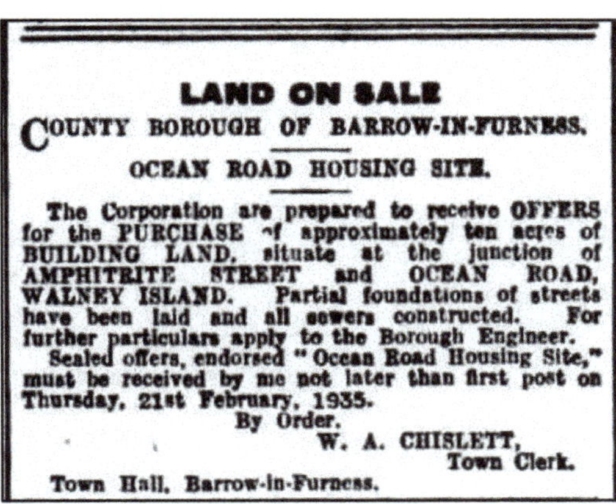

The Ocean Road estate including Strathnaver, Strathaird, Strathmore etc houses were built in 1936-37, closely followed by Southport Drive, Maryport Drive, Black Butts Lane etc. These are typical between-the-wars semis, built by private contractors.

Ocean Road estate plans. (Cumbria Archives.   BA/S/A/6)

Tummerhill Prefabs c1947   (Cumbria Archives. BA/S/10/42)

To help ease the dire housing situation after World War II, prefabs were built at Tummerhill and in other parts of the town.

The local council estates of houses at Rainey Park, and Tummerhill were built in the 1950s.[121] The West Shore council estate was built in the mid-1960s, with Shearwater Crescent and others built at the same time. Carr Lane estate, near Biggar Bank was built in the 1980s [122]

During the 1960s, the Red Ley Estate was also constructed, between North Scale and the airfield. In the early 1970s, additional housing developments, including Lowther Crescent and Muncaster Road, were added to what had previously been a quiet village.[123]

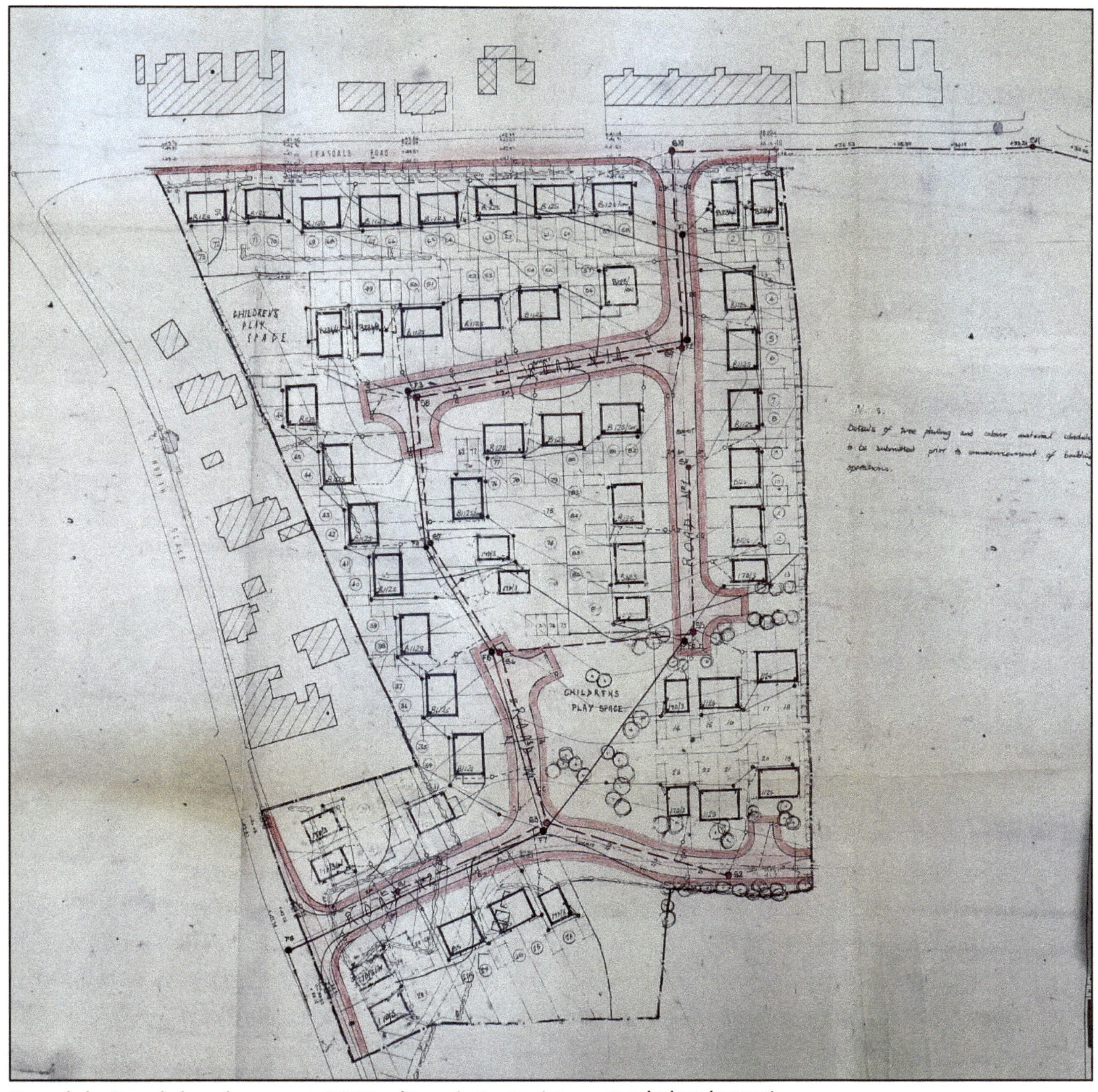

Teasdale Road development 1971. (Cumbria Archives. BA/S/BC/D257)

A residential park complex has been at Earnse Bay since 1957,[124] and in 1963 you could buy a new caravan from £210.[125]

A popular holiday home and caravan complex now also lies at the south of the island today. That started in 1986.[126]

Despite the developments of the 20th Century, the vast majority of housing, or indeed building of any sort, is still in the centre of the island.

Communications

Roads

A writer to Ulverston's Soulby Advertiser, in 1849, going under the name 'A traveller,' lamented the lack of roads on Walney.

> *"Mr Editor, happening to be in Walney, on a Sunday, not many weeks ago, I was led to conclude from observations on the spot, that it retains as many traces of the primitive state of things as any place in Furness. The march of intellect and improvement seems to make slow progress here. I understand from some of the natives, who are originals, that few townships contribute more to the highway rates than the islanders; while their contributions are so sparingly laid out among themselves. In fact, they may be said to be, in a manner, without roads. Many of the tracks, which they call roads, are covered by high tides and rendered impassable for several hours each day. I saw no roads that could be called good ones, except for two from North Scale towards the west, where wreck is found. On the Sunday I alluded to I went to the chapel, and to my surprise, when we should have returned along the beach, the road was covered by the sea! But the people seemed quite to enjoy their usual mode of proceeding under these circumstances. Immediately on leaving the chapel, a regular steeplechase commenced, in which old and young, men, women, and children joined, over hedge and ditch for the distance of about a mile towards North Scale, tearing down all the fences before them. I followed of course, there being no alternative, though not by any means so expert at scaling their dikes as the natives; and this I was told, is what happens nearly every fortnight in winter; the inhabitants never entertaining a thought of change. To me, after breathing awhile on the termination of the chase, it seemed strange that there should be good roads to the west, where as I before observed, wreck is found – but none to the chapel and school. If going to church had been as much prized as going a-wrecking, there would surely have been a better provision made; a footpath at least, for going to the chapel, when the tide covered the way on the beach. But from what I could learn, on my making this suggestion of a foot road, it would seem that things are expected to go on here, just as they are, till the consummation of all things."*[127]

Until the building of Vickerstown (1900-1904), the road system on the island was rudimentary. There were the fords across to the mainland and Barrow Island, and there was a system of lanes between the fields both north and south. There was a lane between Biggar Village and South End which went via the west side of the island until it was eroded away, and there were lanes between Biggar Village and the ferry crossing. Cows Tarn Lane ran from North Scale to Earnse Bay and Mill Lane from North Scale towards Moor Tarn, where it joined Sandy Gap Lane and continued to the west side. Chapel Lane ran from St Mary's to Tummerhlll. Thorny Nook Lane connected Biggar Village to Biggar High Bank and Rakes Lane and Mawflat Lane connected Biggar Village to the south.[128] So, although it was possible to get from north to south and from the east side to the west side of the island, the roads bore little resemblance to what we see today.

In 1893 the council bought land from the various owners on the route of the lane which ran from the old school on the Promenade to Biggar Bank, then called New Lane, in order to widen it.[129]

This eventually became Ocean Road. The road system really emerged as the various estates were built over the 20th Century.

A glance at early maps shows that James Dunn Park stretched from the Ferry Hotel right up to the church grounds, (below). In 1915, the Isle of Walney Estates Company came to a deal with the council and transferred ownership of James Dunn Park to them in return for 50% of the costs towards the new Central Drive.[130] Building Central Drive meant removing 29 of the allotments behind the park, and so extra allotment gardens were provided behind Latona Street, Gatacre Street and Melampus Street.[131]

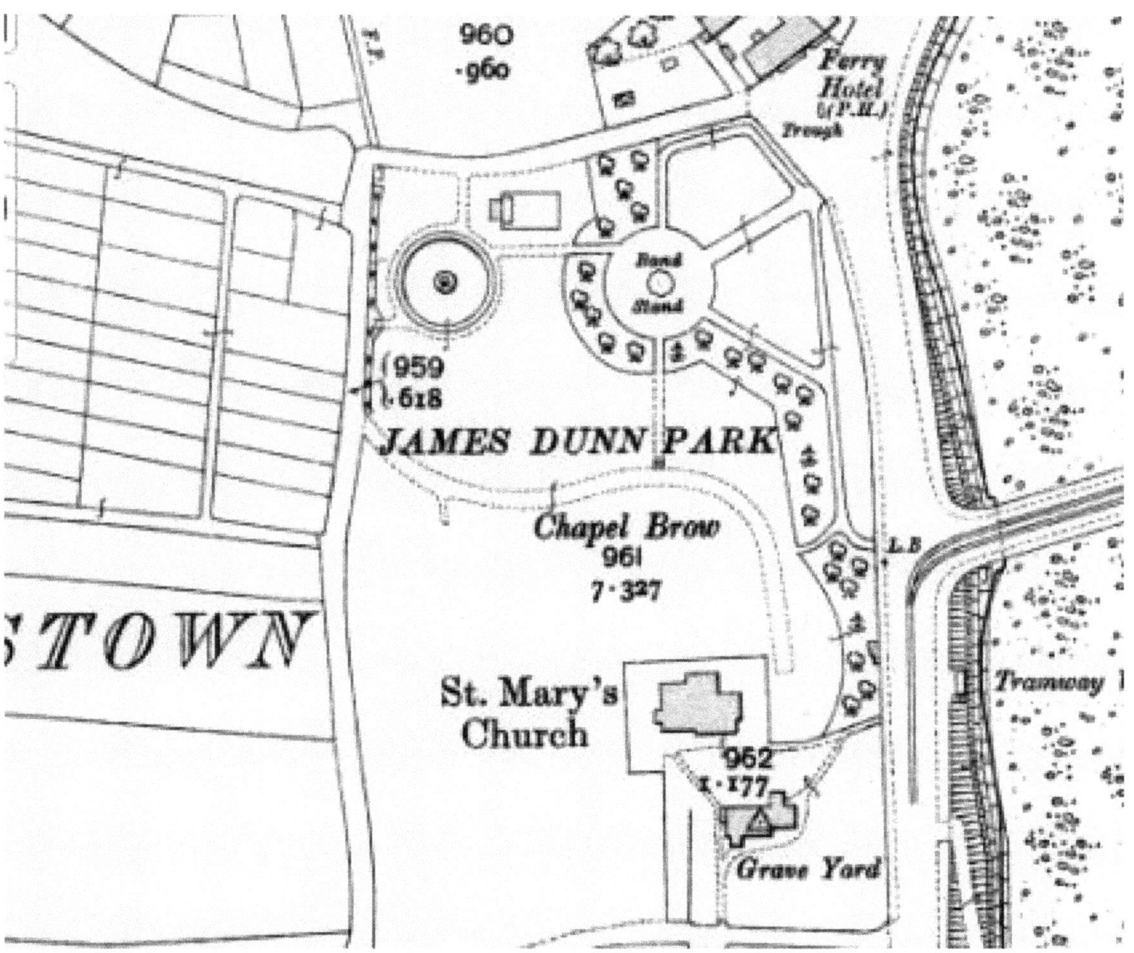

Detail OS map 1914, showing the park stretching from the Ferry Hotel to St Mary's Church.

++++

The only way to get onto Walney for hundreds of years was by using the fords, or by boat. That there had been fords is evident from many documentary sources. The fords and crossings were used not only for carts, but also for the Abbot's workmen. In a deposition to the Attorney General of the Duchy of Lancaster in 1582, one Richard Bancks of Walney had stated that:

> "The Abbot of Furness Abbey, after many breaches of the bancks (sic) and walls of Wawney (sic), by reason of the storms or rage of the sea, did send his own carriage laden with timber and pyles (sic), and likewise did send workemen (sic) to repair and amend the same upon his own costs and charges.'[132]

The fords remained the same for hundreds of years and may have remained so if it hadn't been for the rise of Barrow. The 1848 OS map shows at least eight crossing Walney channel and until the passing of the Barrow Harbour Acts in 1848 and 1855 the fords remained untouched.
From north to south the first ford crossed from Ormsgill Nook, approximately where the Cocken tunnel is now and went north-west, over Walney meetings,[G] to the North End Farm and the

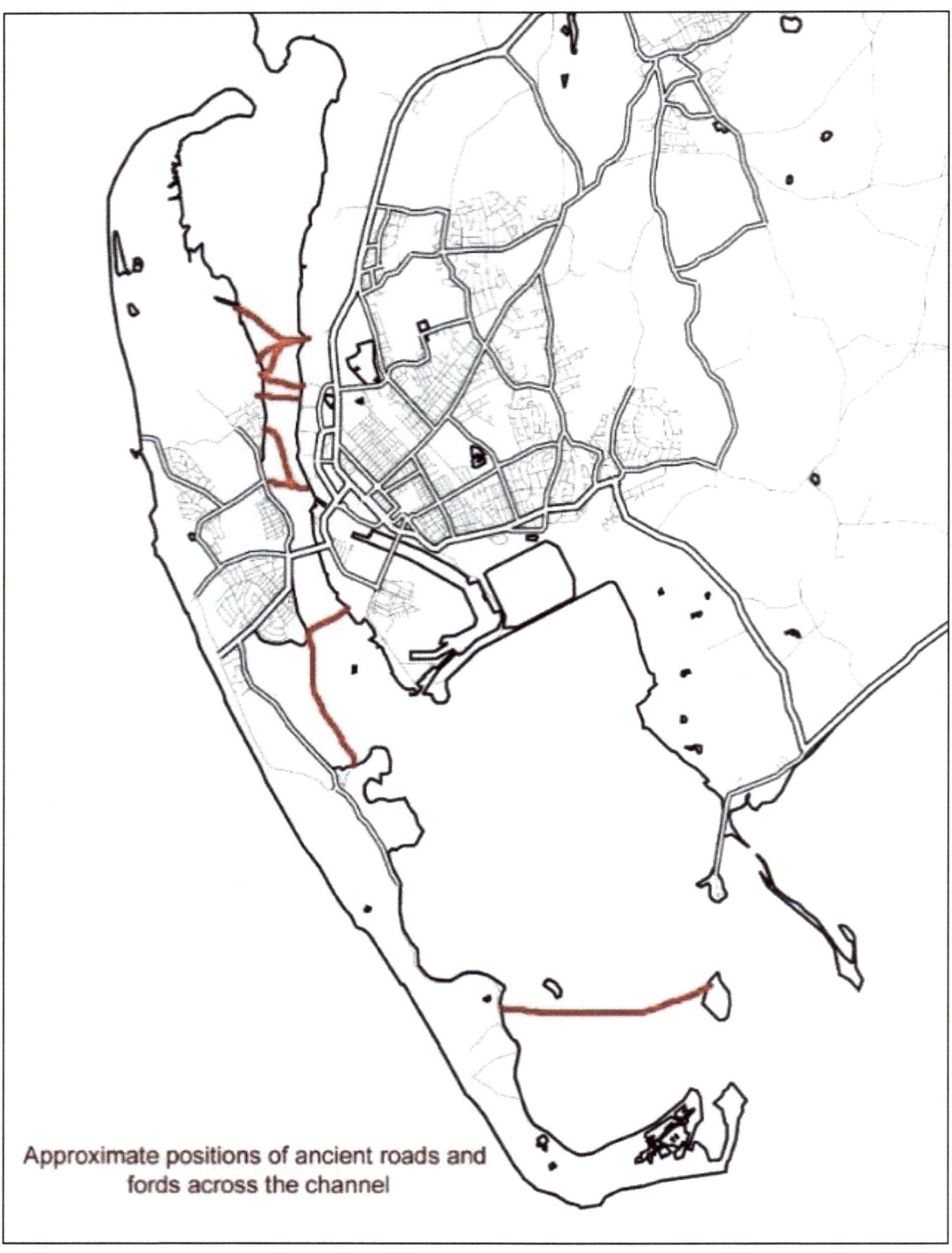

[G] Walney meetings is the place in the channel where the north and south currents meet windmill. Another crossed from the same mainland point, known as 'Cocken Cross', but it went in a south-westerly direction to Lenny Hill, with a branch off to Croft Brow.[134] Next, the fourth went near Middle steps to Croft Brow. The fifth crossing used stepping stones and this one was eventually converted to the footbridge which is still there today (although in need of repair). This became a regular route to the Iron and Steel works, tide permitting.

The sixth, came from a point just above where the graving dock was situated (now the Dock Museum), and went to the smithy in North Scale. The seventh, Ashburner Wife ford, was opposite the end of Mill Lane.

Dova Haw ford went from Biggar, across the marsh to Watergarth Nook and then across Christy Pool to Barrow Island. There was also a road across the sands to Piel. When the fords were under water a number of rowing ferries plied their trade across the channel.

A crossing which still exists and is used by locals at low tide, albeit with a short jump necessary in the middle due to broken sections. Taken from the Barrow side looking towards North Scale in 2019.

The Mail reported on 12 February 2023 that repairs were due to start *'later this year'*. I was on the causeway not long ago and it's still in need of repair. Improvements to the full length were also expected to be completed. (A similar report appeared almost exactly a year earlier on 21 February 2022 – so don't hold your breath.

Lo and behold – literally the day I go to publish and the repairs on the footbridge have started. So no more wet feet.)

Walney Ferry.

When The Furness Railway Company constructed the dock system,[135] they obtained powers to dredge the channel, thus destroying some of the fords. The company published the required notices in the *London Gazette* and in some Lancashire papers (which were not read on Walney) and they omitted to insert notices in the two Ulverston newspapers published at that time. [136] The two principal fords from Walney to Barrow Island, Dova Haw and Ashburner Wife Ford, were destroyed. In February 1876, a council meeting discussed a proposal for a bridge across the channel. Councillor Whittam saw no need and claimed it is *'a foolish project which had no use at all.'* He went on to say that the Furness Railway Company should be compelled to make good the approaches they had taken away.[137]

The footbridge to North Scale had been erected in 1860 by John Storey, surveyor for the Hawcoat Division of the Parish of Dalton, Walney was still part of Dalton parish at that time. The footbridge had been widened and lengthened in 1868 and raised and lengthened again in 1872.[138] In February 1876 the council discussed the needs of the people of Walney with regards to the loss of easy ford access to the mainland. One thing which came from this was a decision to repair the footbridge.

Approaches to Walney.—Tenders as advertised for the woodwork of the footbridge at North Scale were laid before the committee. Resolved, to instruct the surveyor to prepare plan and estimate for a bridge wide enough to admit of carts crossing. Subsequently.—Memorandum.—The surveyor submitted estimate and drawing for the construction of cart bridge at North Scale, which were approved. Resolved, that the construction of a cart bridge be proceeded with, and that the surveyor procure tenders and submit them to the committee at the expiration of one month from this date, unless, in the meantime, the committee receive a representation to the contrary from the inhabitants of Walney. Resolved, to instruct the surveyor to advertise for tenders for the construction of 120 yards of wood fencing at the highway, near Walney School, leading from the shore to New Lane.[139]

Barrow Herald 9 February 1876. Tenders for the repair of the footbridge.

An early photo of the footbridge at North Scale. Photographer unknown. (Cumbria Archives Z/3384)

On 4 November 1875, the inhabitants of Walney gave notice to the Furness Railway Company, that if the company did not forthwith make arrangements to restore the ancient communications, they would take legal action to enforce their rights. The notice was signed by 83 owners and occupiers, 35 from North Scale township, 19 from Biggar township, 3 from South end, 3 from Ulverston, 2 from Barrow and 1 from Dalton.

In August 1876, the council decided the following;

> Highway to Walney.—Resolved, to instruct the Town Clerk to call the attention of the Secretary of the Furness Railway Company to the damage being done to the highway to Walney by Ormsgill through the dredging of the channel. [140]

The result of the islander's representations was that on 6th April 1877, an agreement was entered into by the owners and lessees of lands at Biggar and South End and the Furness Railway Company, with the company agreeing to construct a steam ferry between Barrow Island and Walney, and to complete the same within nine months. An Act of Parliament of 1879 authorised the company to continue and maintain a ferry. [141]

FERRY ON WALNEY CHANNEL.—We have high authority to state that Sir James Ramsden has made an agreement with the inhabitants of North-scale and neighbourhood, under which a steam ferryboat will be put on the station within twelve months after signature of the agreement. The fares are to be low—we believe not to exceed 1d. per passenger, and for other service equally cheap. [142]

Barrow Herald. 21 April 1877

Part of the Ferry agreement between Furness Railway and the islanders.   (BDBUC/43/4/8. Cumbria Archives)

It was reported in September 1877 that the keel of the ferry had been laid.[143] It was launched on 27 May 1878 by the Barrow Shipbuilding Company and began operation on 30 June 1878. This was Steam Ferry No1.[144] It was a chain ferry and had a waiting room on the Barrow side of the channel. The ferry ran from 5.30am until midnight.

On its first day out, after only completing a few crossings, it was involved in an incident:

'An accident happened just before noon, which might have proved very disastrous. Five lads were in a boat as the steamer was crossing the channel, and they were either desirous of crossing the bows of the steamer or were led too near by the spirit of boldness, when their boat was caught by the chains and was soon smashed to pieces by the steamer. '

[All were rescued safely] **Barrow Herald, 6 July 1878**

Steam Ferry No1 c1900. Photographer unknown. The chains can be clearly seen either side.

Walney Ferry No1 was replaced with a larger ferry, Steam Ferry No 2, on 26 March 1902. It was 72 feet long, 38 feet wide and as well as passengers in the deckhouses either side it could hold ten horses and carts in the centre section. The seats inside were made of teak and it could carry up to 1,200 people. Like Ferry No1, it was a chain ferry.

Steam Ferry No2. Post 1902. Sankey Family Photography Collection No. 230. © Cumbria Archives.

Walney Ferry tickets.   (Cumbria Archives   Z/1912)

On the Walney side of the channel a ferry terminal building was built in 1881.[145]

A cropped image from Sankey Family Photo No 7854, of the ferry landing on Walney. © Cumbria Archives

The first Ferry master was a Captain Latham[146], but I can find no mention of him in the 1881 census for Walney. In the 1891 and 1901 censuses, a Peter Bartholemew was Ferry Master living in the Ferry House (landing) on the Promenade.[147] Peter Bartholomew was still there as Ferry Master in 1901.[148]

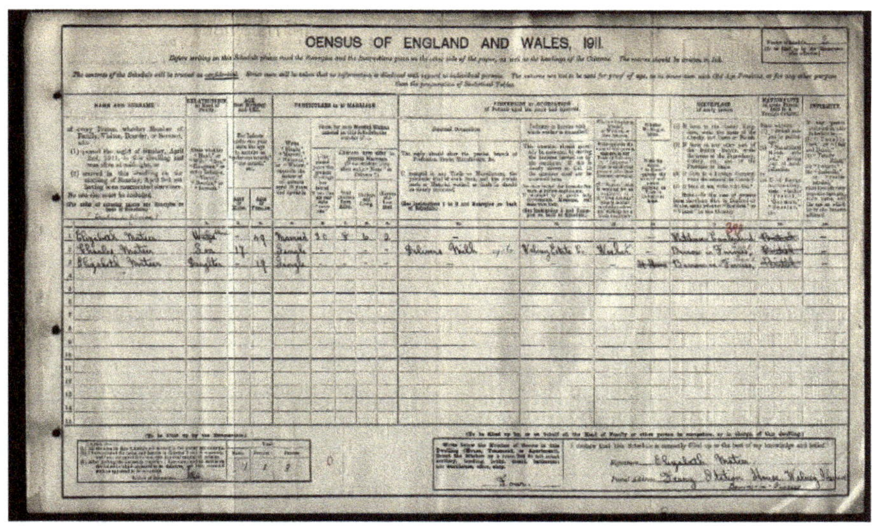

Taken from the 1911 census (above), we can see that after the ferry stopped running on 1 August 1908, the terminal building, or Ferry House, on Walney was occupied – by Elizabeth Mateer with her son, Charles, and daughter Elizabeth.[149]

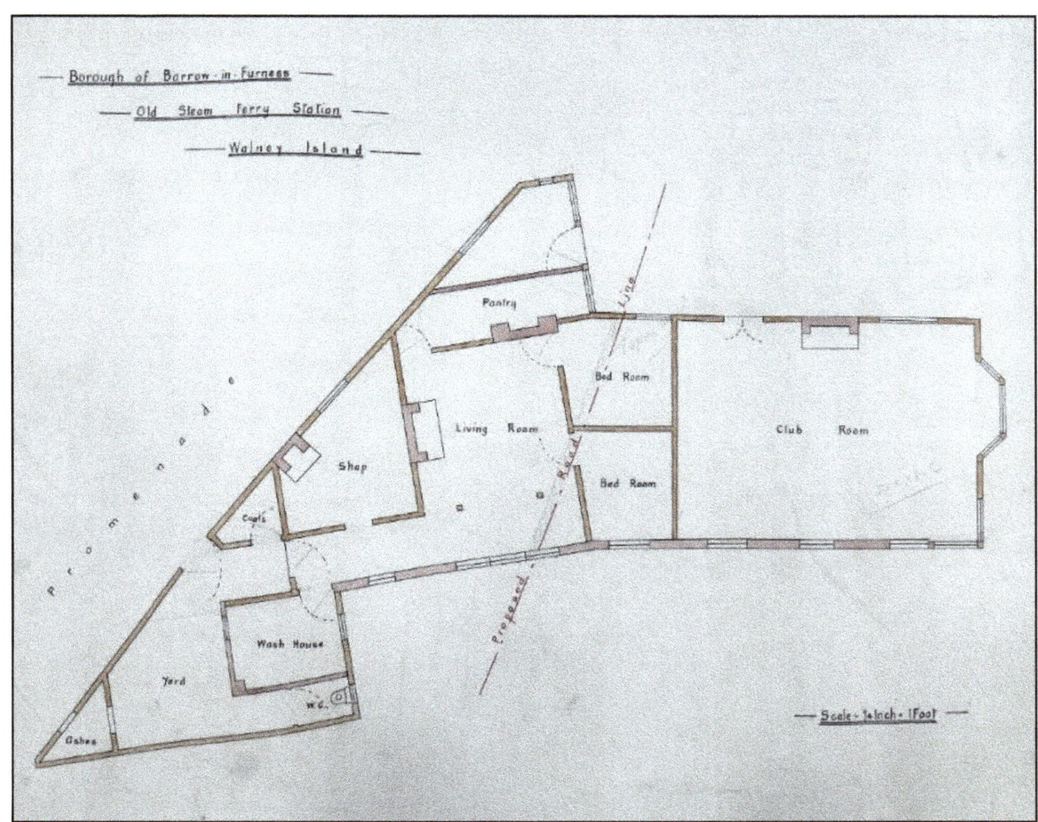

The Ferry House on Walney was demolished around 1930 when Walney Promenade was altered. As the plan, left, shows, the new road was to go straight through the building.

The section to the left of the red line was needed for the widened Promenade.

The Ferry House.   Improvement, Walney Promenade Oct 1930. Cumbria Archives. BA/S/BC/D7/75

The Promenade was altered many times at various places along its length over the years. For example, electric lighting had been provided on the Promenade in January 1903 between Latona Street and Empress Drive.[150] The road from the Ferry Hotel up towards Ocean Road, which had previously been described as *'steep'*, was *'very considerably lowered'* in 1903.[151]

Other operators continued to run their ferries across Walney Channel as they had for many years. One Ephraim Pickthall is listed in the 1891 and 1901 census as Ferryman.[152] John Jackson is a Ferryman in 1901.[153] Another well-known for his rowing skills was a man named Strong. He competed in the many regattas held on the channel. In 1878 he began running a steam launch, the 'M.A. Strong' on the channel. Hour excursions were 6d each.

The steam ferry fares were reduced in January 1891 to one half-penny and so the independent ferrymen had to follow suit thus halving their fares.[154]

A rowing boat service was put on from Vickers slipways in November 1902. It could hold 60 men and ran to the opposite bank on Walney so that the workers from South Vickerstown could get home and back for lunch.[155] It was replaced by an electric ferry in March 1903 which could accommodate 240 people.[156]It was nicknamed 'The Mudlark'.

<table>
<tr><td>

NORTH SCALE FERRY.

Dear Sir,—Is it not time that something ought to be done towards making this, the oldest ferry to the Island, approachable from either side of the channel? It is simply disgraceful that on a fine day after using this ferry you have to appear with boots covered with mud. If some of our "Council" were compelled to use this ferry, no doubt the state of things would soon be changed. In the face of splendid approaches to the steam ferry yet another landing is made, and the wants of a whole village ignored.—Yours, &c.,

UNSELFISH.

</td><td>

One disgruntled user of the North Scale Ferry complained in the local press, in September 1883.[157]

</td></tr>
</table>

Ferry boat 'Swift'.   Sankey Family Photography Collection No. 1017.   © Cumbria Archives

The Swift, used as a ferry, was built by Mr D McGruer of Barrow about 1905. It could hold 60 passengers and was powered by a 2-cylinder petrol engine of 12 brake-horsepower.[159]It was run by the Walney Express Ferry Company. The Furness Railway Company, who owned the foreshore either side of Walney Channel near the existing steam ferry, disputed the legality of the Swift running at this point and sought an injunction against the company.[160] In any event the Swift continued to run.

FERRY BOAT CAPSIZED

An exciting incident took place on Walney Channel on Sunday, a ferryboat, with twenty-five passengers, composed of men, women, and children, capsizing. A strong flood-tide was running at the time. The boatman, John Bradley, in trying to clear a small boat, fouled a moored yacht, and the ferryboat was at once overturned. The accident was witnessed from the shore, and the screams of the people struggling in the water raised great excitement. Many small boats at once put off to the rescue, and it is believed that all were got out. Many were in an unconscious condition, but they all recovered. Four of the passengers succeeded in jumping into the yacht.

Herts & Cambs. Reporter & Royston Crow. 28 August 1903

There were complaints due to the fact that the ferry didn't run between midnight and 5.30am.[161]One complainant having missed the last ferry by two minutes then had to wait until 5.30am Sunday morning.[162] The Ferry would sometimes run aground, as it did between 6.00am and 10.00am on 1st February 1903, leaving Walney residents reliant on the smaller ferries for over 4,000 people.[163] It grounded again on 19th June 1904.

WALNEY FERRY AGROUND.

A HARVEST FOR SMALL BOATS.

On Sunday morning visitors to and from Walney were surprised to find the steam ferry high and dry on the Barrow side. It appears that by some means she grounded at 5.30 a.m. and could not be floated again till the next tide. She was safely got off at 2 p.m. Naturally, with the great number of people going to Walney on Sunday morning, the small ferry boats reaped a rich harvest, and it is to the credit of the ferrymen that they coped with the extra traffic thus thrust upon them. Supporters of the Walney Bridge scheme—the Corporation Bill, being, as is well known, now heard before a committee of the House of Commons—look upon this mishap as strong evidence in favour of the bridge.

Millom Gazette, 24 June 1904

The days of ferries were coming to an end with the 10-fold increase in Walney's population since the 1890s, and a more reliable means of crossing the channel was needed.

Walney Bridge.

As early as 1873, the Walney schoolmaster, Mr J R Head was publicly advocating for a bridge to Walney, but he received no encouragement.[164] By 1888 the Walneyites were demanding a bridge and Barrow Council voted to obtain powers from Parliament to construct such a bridge (without agreeing to spend the necessary funds), in November of that year.[165] Four different schemes were prepared by Mr W. H. Fox, AMICE.[166] The project was then abandoned. In 1897, a public meeting was held to consider the commemoration of Queen Victoria's Jubilee, when erection of a bridge was suggested.[167] In 1901, Sir Benjamin Baker was called in to advise on the subject, and submitted a report and estimates for four alternative schemes.[168] In December 1903, Sir Benjamin Baker's amended scheme was approved by the council and they decided to promote a Bill. Once Vickerstown had been built, (between 1900 and 1904), there had been a huge rise in the population of Walney and the demand for a bridge was even greater and the need imperative.

There were different views in the town with the main protagonists being The Furness Railway Company, which was against and Vickers Sons & Maxims Ltd which was pro bridge.

The Walney Ferry, owned by the FRC, had carried 16,000 passengers on Whit Monday 1908 and in the week ending 14 June 1908 has taken £5,459 from the ferry and the bay steamers combined.

A newspaper - *The Vickerstown Chronicle,* was set up. Its main purpose being to promote the bridge. It was published between October 1902 and November 1904. Vickers eventually made a commitment to cover any costs beyond a sum obtainable by a rate of three halfpence in the pound, this prompted Barrow Corporation to seek the necessary Parliamentary authorisation to construct a bridge. The bill successfully received Royal Assent in July 1904.

The Furness Railway Company preferred a scheme with access from near Blake Street, but it was considered to be inconvenient for access to Biggar Bank and the South End.

Vickerstown Chronicle cartoon 29 January 1904.

A vote for/against the bridge was held in the town in January 1904, the result being in favour by 4,013 to 2,178.[169] There was a torchlight procession to James Dunn Park in celebration, led by the shipyard band, and with fireworks and balloons and a wooden model of the ferry was burnt.[170]

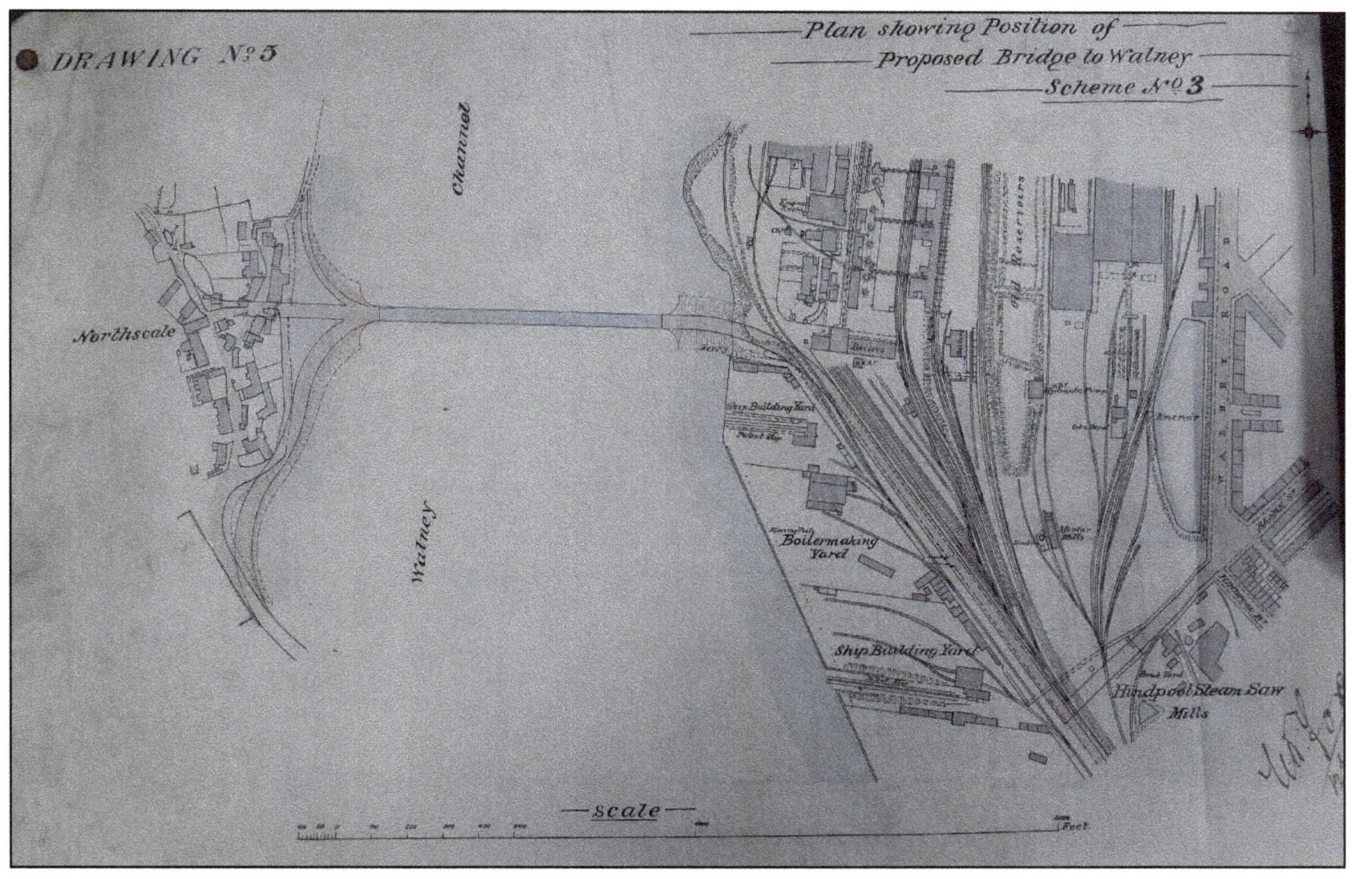

A proposal for Walney Bridge – Scheme 3. c1888.   (Cumbria Archives.   BA/S/BC/43)

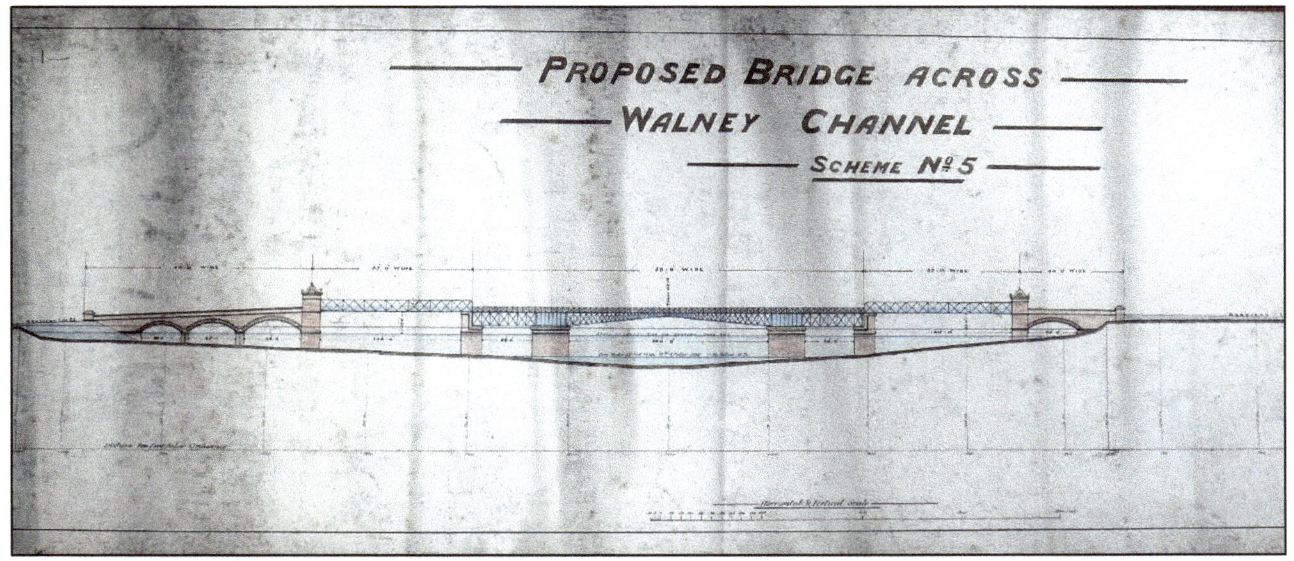

An 1896 bridge proposal – Scheme 5. (Cumbria Archives BA/S/BC/D4/20)

As can be seen from just these plans there were various proposals and designs over the years before the final design and position of a bridge was agreed.

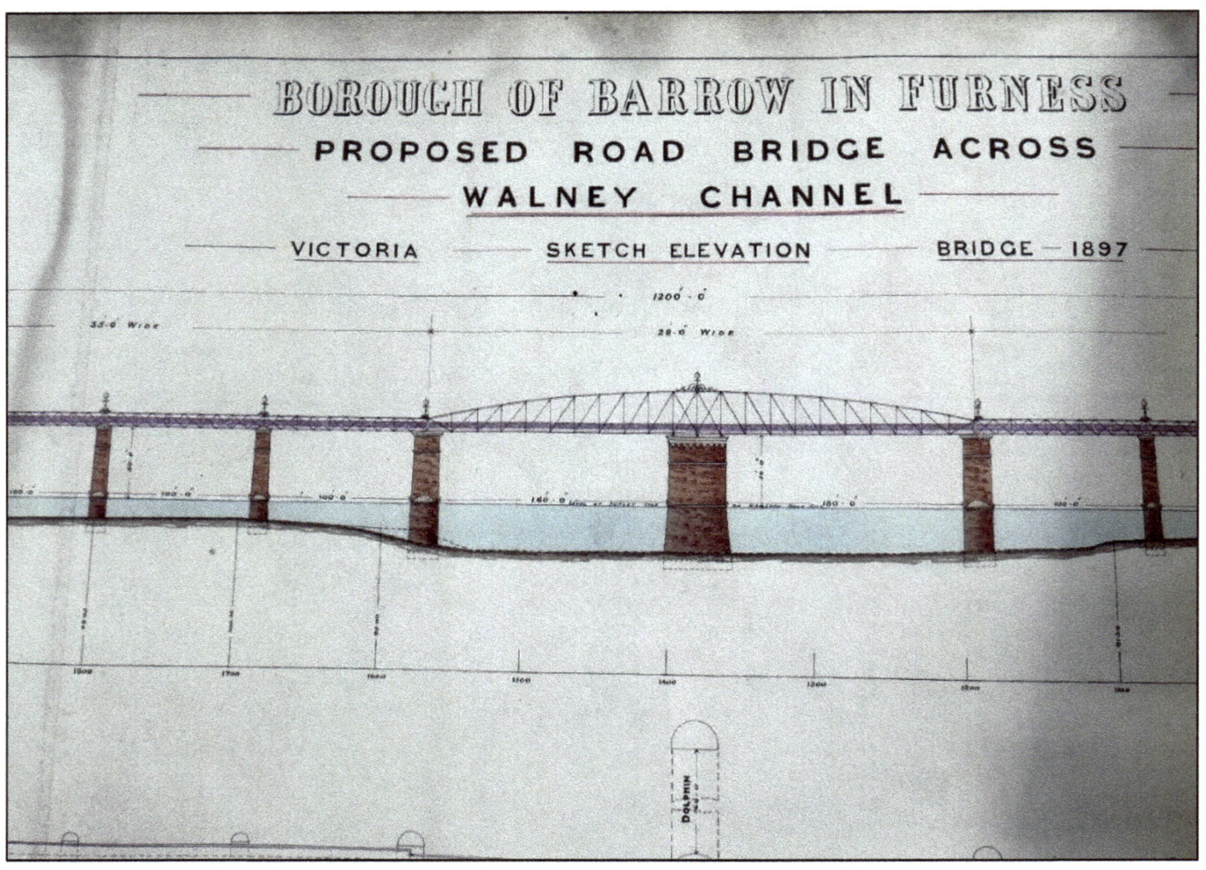

Another early proposal - 1897. (Cumbria Archives.   BA/S/BC/43)

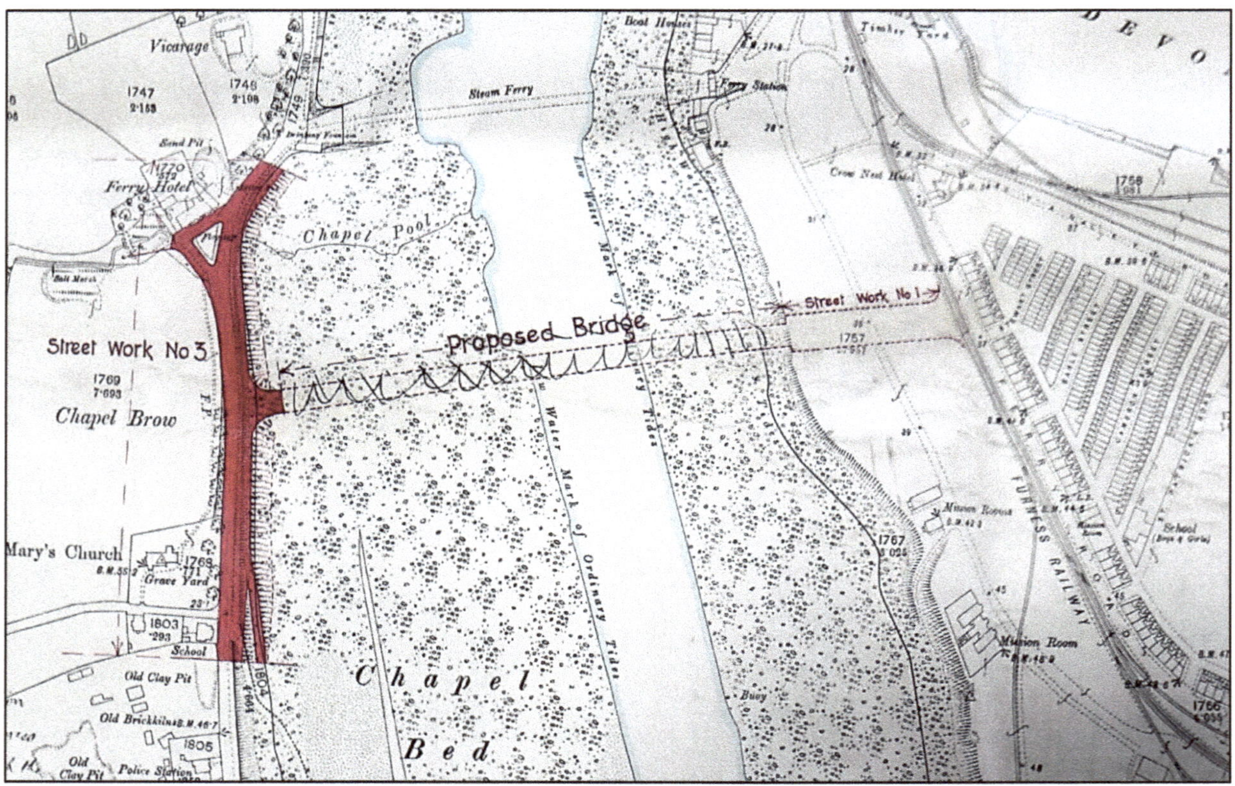

The final position for the bridge 1905.   (Cumbria Archives.   Z/2224)

In October 1905 the tender from Sir William Arrol and Company, who had built the Tay, Forth and Tower bridges, was accepted.

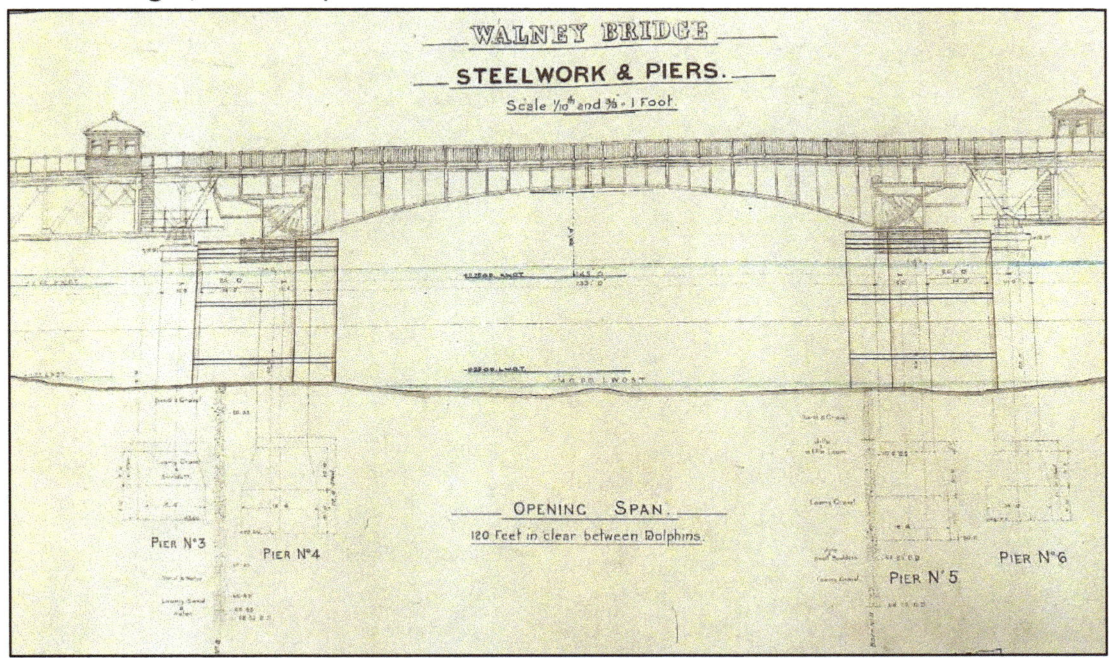

The opening span of the final design.   (Cumbria Archives.   BA/S/F/106)

Construction began in mid-1905. The bridge is 1123 ft long and 50 ft wide between the parapets. It has an opening of 120ft wide which works on the bascule principal and is powered by electric motors.

Temporary staging on the Walney Side. 11 December 1905. (Cumbria Archives BA/S)

The first three posts being pile driven Barrow side. 22 January 1906. (Cumbria Archives BA/S).

Note the steam ferry in the background.

The base of two of the cylinders in the sand on the Barrow side. 22 January 1906.

The tops of cylinders being fitted 01 July 1907. (Both images Cumbria Archives BA/S)

By July 1907 all the support cylinders were fitted and the metal framework was being added. Seen here on the Walney side. (Cumbria Archives BA/S).

You can see the temporary wooden framing between the support cylinders. The ones seen here were removed by October 1907, and the whole of the Walney side framing had been removed by December 1907.

The lifting spans were being constructed from around August 1907 – in the up position.

Almost completed. 12 May 1908. (Cumbria Archives BA/S)

The bridge ready for opening. July 1908. (Cumbria Archives from a glass plate. BA/S)

Originally it was hoped that the King and Queen could open the bridge but later that was cancelled and the bridge was opened by the Mayoress, Mrs T.F. Taylor, on 30th July 1908.[171]

The opening ceremony. Sankey Family Photography Collection No 301. © Cumbria Archives.

The bridge was fully completed in the Autumn of the same year. It was a toll bridge with the toll set at ½d. per person.

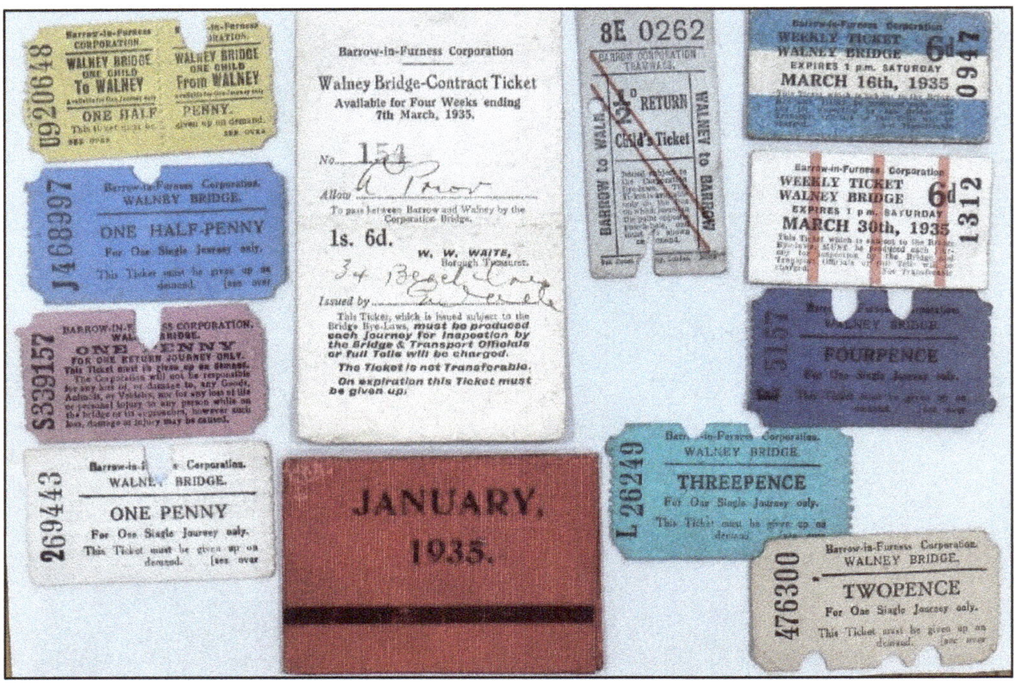

Bridge tickets.   (Cumbria Archives. BDX 882/1/17)

In the first week of operation 80,556 people crossed the bridge and these figures were reported weekly in the local press.[172] The toll receipts were also reported in the local press.

The bridge was estimated to cost £90,000, but the corporation also agreed to buy the Walney Ferry and the rights of the Furness Railway company for £30,000. The total cost including alterations to the Promenade and approaches on the Barrow side, would amount to at least £175,000.[173]

Furness Railway Company reported receiving £25,000 for the Walney Ferry *and* £12,538 for the ferry land.[174]

Plaque on Jubilee bridge. © Peter Laird

To digress from our story for a moment -The fact that it was a toll bridge was not universally popular, and during the depression of the 1920s this became a focal point for the disgruntled workers. In February 1922 a union demonstration crossed without paying, and on returning, finding the gates locked, forced their way across.[176] Then on 8th May 1922, a crowd of 2,000 crossed the bridge without paying the toll.[177]

++++

In July 1918 the workforce at Vickers had been 23,195, but by January 1923 that had fallen drastically to 3,769.[178]

In May 1922 the *Barrow Guardian* reported 11,000 out of work and another 5 -6,000 in dispute in Barrow. There were pickets and demonstrations in town and outside Vickers.

On 13th May 1922 there was a huge demonstration. The participants assembled near the Coliseum, on Abbey Road, and, headed by a band, paraded the streets of the town. The parade was followed by a meeting in the Barrow Public Park.[179]

NO EVICTION

Word went round at Vickerstown Barrow, on Monday, that a plater's helper who is out of work, was going to be evicted from his house. Unemployed men to the number of 500 went to the house and mounted a guard of 12. These, with scouts to run to headquarters, were relieved by others in shifts until Tuesday in order to prevent the man being deprived of his home, and he remained in possession.

Hull Daily Mail, **23 November 1921**

In periods of high unemployment in the town, relief work was provided to keep at least some of the men employed.

On Walney, relief work included: -

- The construction of the Promenade in 1879,[180] where the workers received 2/6d per day.[181]
- Widening the road from the ferry to Biggar Bank in 1893 at a cost of £3,500 – this provided work for 300 men, at three days per week for 3 months.[182]
- Widening Ocean Road to Biggar Bank in 1904.[183]
- Works at Biggar Bank in 1922,[184] and that, combined with works at Sowerby Woods and the Barrow Public Park employed 300 -400 men.[185]

The 100 labourers employed in relief work on Walney Island for the Barrow Corporation have demanded redress for a grievance caused by wet weather. On Friday and Monday, they were prevented from working owing to rain, and their time was stopped. They also have to work to 5.30 at night, and they contend that walking time to the Town Hall should be allowed.

Lancashire Evening Post, **14 December 1904**

On 4 April 1935, the Duchess of York had a busy day in Barrow, launching the RMS Strathmore in the morning and in a renaming ceremony, removing the toll from the bridge.

From then onwards the bridge would be named Jubilee bridge.[187] It remains the sole access road to the island.

188

Ceremony of toll removal Jubilee Bridge, 4 April 1935. The Duchess of York prepares to cut the ribbon.   Sankey Family Photography Collection No TP71. © Cumbria Archives.

Trams

After Walney Bridge opened it wasn't until June 1909 that the tram system reached the Promenade on Walney.[189] Tram lines on the Barrow side had to be moved across from Ferry Road to Bridge Road.

Agreement between the council and The British Electric Traction Company in 1911 led to the tram system being extended from the Promenade to Biggar Bank,[190] this opened on 4 August 1911.[191] No further tram lines were laid to any other part of the island.

The Promenade tram stop and toilets on the left.

Sankey Family Photography Collection No 3527/34 © Cumbria Archives c 1915

[NOTE: This was the only tram shelter on the Promenade. The triangular building, (below), on the corner of Central Drive, was built after the trams had stopped running in Barrow which was in 1932. It was never a tram stop or a tram shelter.]

This was more than likely a bus-shelter. It was built sometime between 1943 and 1946.

It is currently, in 2024, in disrepair, but funds have been found for its repair.

Shown here in 1995.

Until the toll was removed, a passenger travelling from the Town Hall to Biggar Bank paid $1\frac{1}{2}$d of which 1d was for the tram and $\frac{1}{2}$d for the bridge toll. Children paid less, as did postmen and workers on special workmen trams.

Walney bridge construction and laying the tram lines. c1907. Sankey Family Photography Collection No 395A © Cumbria Archives

You can just make out both the old and new St Mary's churches in the background, which is how we can date this photograph. The toll house is on the left.

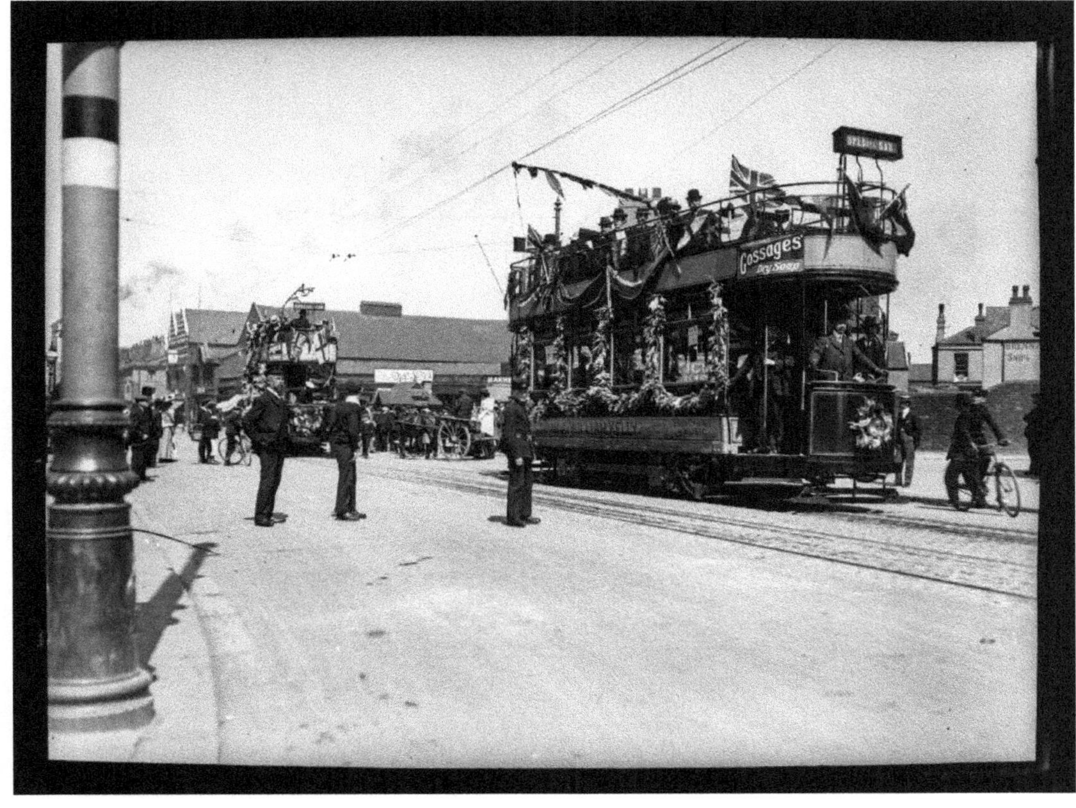

Decorated Trams Nos 3 and 6 outside the Town Hall for the inaugural run to Biggar Bank

4 August 1911

Sankey Family Photography Collection No 3346

© Cumbria Archives

The same trams at Biggar Bank.

4 August 1911

Sankey Family Photography Collection No 3349

© Cumbria Archives

Postal Services and Telecommunications

Postal Service

Travel around the country and especially around Furness was difficult until well into the 19th century. Postal arrangements were rudimentary at best. Royal Mail was carried from London to Scotland on horseback by the end of the 17th century.[192] Furness folk had to post their letters at Lancaster until a Post Office was opened in Ulverston. A letter posted to the Rev. William Hunter, at Walney, dated 13 September 1736, came via J. Collinson at Lancaster.[193] One dated 30 August 1780, to the *'Officiating Minister of Walney chapel in the parish of Dalton, near Ulverstone, (sic) Lancashire,'* had clearly come via Ulverston.[194]

By November, 1786, there was a post to Ulverston. (G.P.O.-Public Relations Department.) Prior to 1820, travel to Furness was via the 'over the sands' route. It was notoriously treacherous and many drowned in the attempt, even coaches were lost. In 1820 however, the new turnpike road from Levens to Greenodd was opened and this made travel considerably easier and therefore mail arrangements improved. By 1825 mail arrived daily at Ulverston at 8.15am and outgoing mail left by 9.00 am.[195] There was daily post to Rampside three times per week, and there were two daily posts to Dalton.[196] By 1836 there was foot-post to Dalton and Barrow leaving at 6.45am.[197] The Penny-Post was instituted in 1840.

++++

Postal rates before the introduction of the Penny Post were generally based on the number of sheets of paper used and the distance travelled. Postage was mainly paid by the person receiving the letter. The introduction of the Penny Post led to rates being based on weight and the sender paying the costs. Postage stamps were introduced at the same time.

++++

In 1841, a Thomas Shaw was employed as a foot-messenger from Ulverston and he left for Dalton and Barrow at 6.30am daily, picking up letters on his route either way – a round trip of almost 30 miles.[198] In 1863 the Barrow Post Office at The Strand, was receiving letters from Walney by 8.00am and despatching to Walney by 8.30am.[199]

In August 1851, William Housby, a shoemaker who later ran the Crown Public House, was appointed 'Letter receiver' at North Scale.[200] William was still listed as 'Letter carrier and shoemaker' in the 1861 census and he was living in the Post Office, as he was in 1871, by when he was 65, and still a shoe-maker but no longer described as a letter-carrier.[201] I can find no other letter-carrier listed on Walney in that year's census. In 1881 and 1901, Samuel Housby is listed as living in North Scale and being a 'Rural postman', yet in 1891 he is listed as a shoemaker.[202]James Fisher is in North Scale as a Postmaster in 1891.

Post office

A number of sub post offices existed on Walney until fairly recent times. The North Scale PO closed in the mid-1990s, Douglas Street PO closed in the early 2000s, Mill Lane PO closed in 2020, and Mikasa Street PO closed in the early 2000s. The only remaining PO services on the island today are as an add-on to the Co-operative store on Amphitrite Street.

Telephone exchange

A telephone exchange opened on Walney in about 1960[203], it was a Strowger electro-mechanical step-by-step system which remained in operation until it was replaced, in the same building on Church Lane, by a modern digital 'AXE10' system which opened on 21 July 1989.[204] The exchange was enabled for ADSL (broadband) in January 2004 and is currently, in 2024, able to provide fibre to the cabinet, (the little green boxes at the end of the street), and in some areas fibre to the premises and hosts four different providers, including BT. The Public Switched Telephone Network is due to be switched off for the whole country in 2027 at which time all telephony services will be via IP (Internet Protocol). In Summer 2024 a company is providing wireless broadband on Walney using fixtures on lampposts as Fixed Wireless Access points using cnWave mesh network technology. (Effectively a 60GHz Wi-Fi network).

Fort Walney

In 1879 the Admiralty had decided to erect an 8-gun battery on Walney *'at the entrance to the port'*.[205] The battery was in fact to be at the entrance to Biggar Bank.[206]

> THE BATTERY ON WALNEY ISLAND.—Mr. W. Gradwell has commenced the work of erecting the new battery for the Admiralty on Biggar Bank, near Tummerhhill. The site of the battery is at the entrance to the Bank from the Barrow-road. We think a much more favourable site could have been chosen, but the Admiralty have owned land at this place for years. We trust the presence of the battery here will not counteract the many great attractions which Biggar Bank possesses.

> THE WALNEY BATTERY.—The guns for this battery have arrived in Barrow by H.M. Screw Steamer the Lord Panmure, from the War Department of the Royal Arsenal, Woolwich. One of the guns weighs 6¼ tons with a 7in. bore, the other 3 tons 11cwt., being a 6in. bore. The guns were unshipped from the steamer in the Devonshire Dock, yesterday forenoon, and placed in the charge of Mr. Gradwell, contractor for the erection of the battery, who had everything in readiness to convey them to their destination across the channel at Northscale by low tide, which was carried out successfully. Mr. Johnson, Navy Engineer, is on the ground to direct the fixing of the guns in their proper position, and Captain Harris, who acted during the erection of the battery for the Government as Clerk of the Works, has charge of the battery. In addition to the guns the Lord Panmure brought a supply of stores and amunition for the battery. It is expected that the guns will be placed in position and the battery completed early next week.

In 1881 it was reported in the *Barrow Herald* that the guns had arrived for a battery on Walney.

Note that they had to cross the channel at North Scale, presumably because of the weight.

> THE WALNEY BATTERY.—On Tuesday afternoon the chief officer, Mr. Bailey, inspected the battery and also put the naval reserve men present through various movements, including gun practice. Eight rounds were fired at a floating target, distant 500 yards, with the 64-pounder, and 15 rounds per man with the Martini rifle, and the officer expressed himself highly pleased with their work. Dr. Sheaf, the medical officer for the northern division, was in attendance.

In September 1882 it was reported in the same newspaper that the battery was put through its paces.[207]

In 1903, The War Office announced plans to build fortifications on Walney[209] and construction began in 1909. Completed in 1911, the battery consisted of two 6-inch guns manned by two companies of The Royal Garrison Artillery.[210] There were two blockhouses, a magazine, a shelter and auxiliary buildings.

On 29th January 1915, the German submarine U21 fired upon the airship shed. (More on the airship shed later.) The battery at Walney fort returned fire and the submarine disappeared under the water.[211] The battery operated up to the second world war. After the second world war the Battery Observation Post (tower), became the Coastguard lookout tower, a use which continued until the 1990s. It is currently being converted into a house. In the immediate vicinity of the tower is an underground Royal Observer Corps post – now defunct. The other buildings had been demolished by 1973. The fortifications all sat in the centre of Furness Golf Club course.

Aerial photo of Fort Walney 1940s. Photographer unknown

Agriculture

Agriculture dominated from early times until the 19th century when several small-scale industries began to arise. These all but disappeared by the mid-20th century, with only an oyster farm operating at the present time. Today the only other businesses of note are the caravan sites at either end of the island, five public houses, and a few retail premises.

Mediaeval Period

North Scale was one of the granges of Furness Abbey and is first mentioned in documents of 1247. Of the 44 tenements of the Abbey on the island, 16 were at North Scale. The tenants shared all of the 21 fields equally, having three dales in each field to ensure no one farmer had better land than another. They paid their rental mainly in goods and services to the Abbey. [212]

The Abbey had four tenements at North End and 16 tenures at Biggar, and eight at South End. Tenants paid the whole or part of their dues to the Abbey in kind.[213]

Local Solicitor H Pearson, in a presentation on local customs to The Barrow Naturalists Field Club in 1898, tells us;

> In around 1530 *"Walney, which was then much more extensive than at present and very fertile to boot, produced grain, sheep, stricks (or yearling cattle), cheese, butter, hens and geese, for culinary purposes, in the following proportions; 30 quarters of barley at 5s. per quarter ; 20 qrs. of wheat at an average of 7s. 75d.; 124 qrs. of oats averaging 2s. 6d. per quarter ; 60 hogs or yearling sheep at 1s. each ; 30 stricks averaging about 2s. 10d. each: it seems the brethren preferred yearlings both of the flock and herd to lamb and veal; 60 stones of cheese at 8d. the stone; 26 stones of butter at 6d.; 48 hens at ld. a piece; and 24 geese at 2d. These places also paid £3. 78. 8d. in money, and the tenants were bound to carry eighty cart loads of peats to the abbey for 6d. a cart load."*[215]

Modern Agriculture

Biggar and North Scale township fields were enclosed by 1778.[216] By the beginning of the 19th century, Walney, which was very fertile, was considered to be the 'Granary of Furness' due to its production of wheat, oats and barley.[217] However, in 1834 the crop failed due to wet weather.[218] potatoes, wheat, barley and oats were the main crops grown both north and south of the island. Also, turnips and clover. A note in 1904 states that *'Walney Wheat is equal in quality to any in the three kingdoms.'*[219] In 1908, a ploughing competition was started and in 1911, 17 teams took part on Riley's farm at Biggar.[220]

Rabbit warrens were at both ends of the island too and were part of each estate and were closely protected. A £3 reward was offered for information leading to the conviction of rabbit poachers at the North End in September 1869.[221] There are numerous examples of prosecutions for rabbit poaching on the island in the press of the 19th century. Both North Scale and Biggar census returns for 1841 to 1861 show that the vast majority of households were fully employed in agricultural pursuits. It is not until 1871 that there is significant employment elsewhere.

With the building of Vickerstown around 1902, a farm was built near North Scale by the Isle of Walney Estates Company, to provide milk, cream, eggs and vegetables. It is no longer there. In 1938 North End Farm was subject to a compulsory purchase order for the construction of the airfield.[222]

Little or no crops are grown on the island in the 21st century. South End Farm in partnership with one from Biggar village run a herd of 50 pure bred Shorthorn cattle and 200-300 sheep between them. Holme Bank Farm at Urswick fattens about 300 beef cattle on Walney each year, and Harbarrow Farm at Stainton fattens about 50 cattle on Walney through the summer and 150 lambs through winter. [223]

Population

Walney's population has changed over the years as shown in the chart below.

Year	Population	Notes
1631	240	Plague year – half died
1808	239	
1841	389	
1851	323	
1861	305	
1871	338	
1881	463	
1891	433	
1901	961	Vickerstown build progress
1911	4,896	
1971	11,247	
2021	10,433	(10,519 on NOMIS)

The population of Barrow Village was about 150 in 1843 and about 8,000 by 1864. It reached 47,000 by 1872 and 67,000 by 1901 – (including Barrow Island and Walney)

It currently stands at 71,000

Walney population grew substantially once Vickerstown was built.

The current population split on Walney is almost exactly 50-50 female to male.

There are around 20% under 18 years of age, 25% between 18 and 64 and 55%, 65 years and older.

The ethnicity is over 98% white, with 98% born in the UK.

40% profess no religion and 58% Christian.

SOURCE: ONS 2021 census

Windmills

There were at least two windmills on Walney. The first stood somewhere south-west of North Scale, near the west side of the island. It was erected around 1558[224] and appears on Yates's map of Lancashire 1786. The only surviving mention of the mill is in the name Mill Lane. The fate of this old mill was rather unfortunate. It met its demise because of a pig. John Mawson, residing at the Moor House, slaughtered a pig and suspended it within the aging mill. However, the weight of the carcass proved too much for the ancient structure, resulting in a complete collapse.[225]

The second windmill, previously mentioned, stood at North End Farm, the ruins of which were demolished when the airfield was constructed in 1940 and for which photographs survive.[226]

There was a period when the Lord of the Manor tried to enforce all of his tenants to take their corn to his water mill at Roose. There were complaints, fights and the mill dam was destroyed at one time. Eventually tenants were allowed to use the Walney mills.[227]

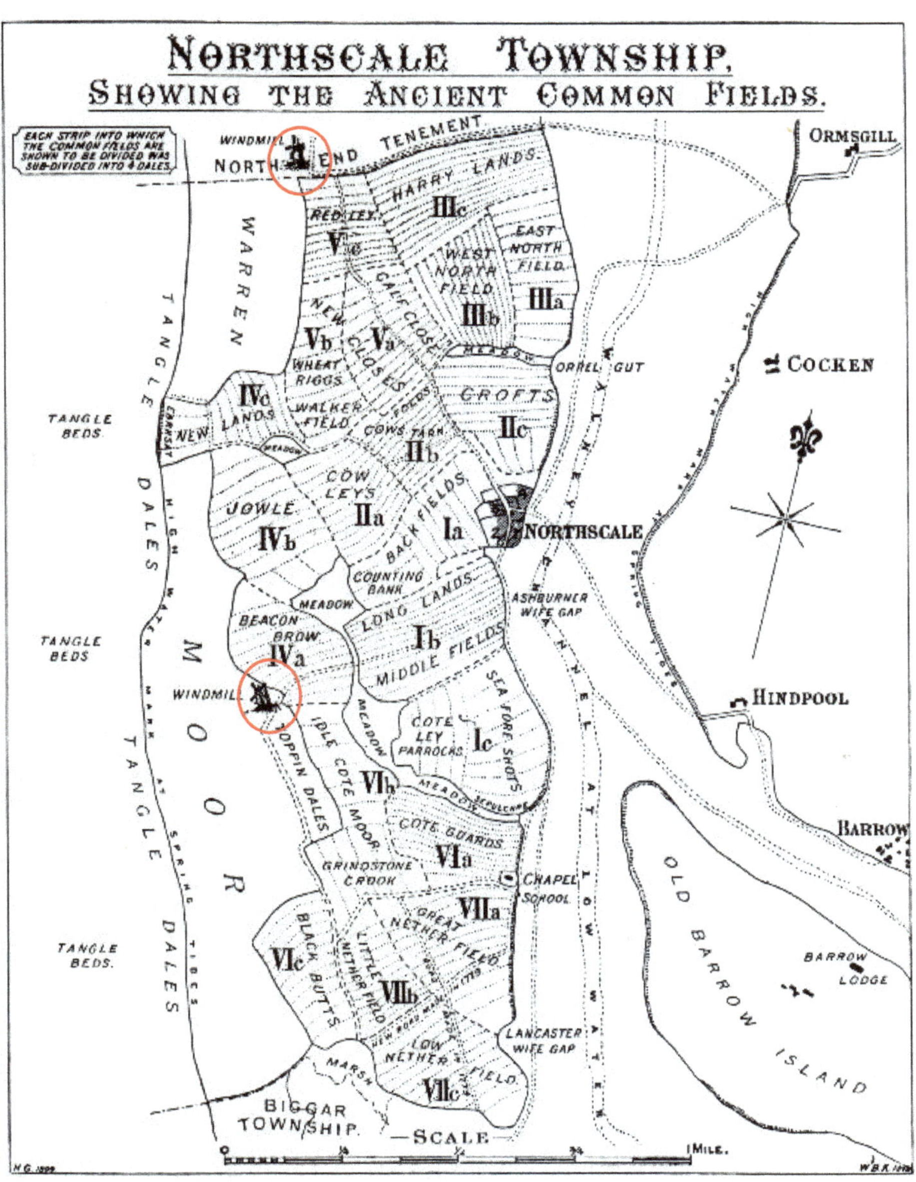

Both of these mills appear on this hand drawn map of the township of North Scale dated 1898.[228]

Retail

As previously mentioned, as part of the building of Vickerstown, a row of shops was built on Douglas Street, including a baker, a hardware store and a post office.

From 'A Vickerstown Souvenir' – a booklet printed to celebrate the building of Vickerstown. c1914

From left to right the shops were occupied by an Italian grocer, a chemist, a hairdresser and tobacconist combined, a green-grocer and post office combined, and finally a confectioner.

Other shops were built on Mikasa Street. A number of Co-operative stores also opened, on Hogue Street, Powerful Street and later, on the Promenade. The building of the estates at Rainey Park and West Shore saw the opening of another row of shops on Mill Lane. Here there was a butcher and another Post Office.

In 2024 there is one general store in the Mill Lane shops and one in Douglas Street. A Co-operative which also functions as the island's only post office is on Amphitrite Street and a small Tesco is on Ocean Road.

The shops on the Promenade were built around 1914/15 with a Co-op chemist, three shops built for Vickers and an independent shop built for J Williamson.[229] The Bank of Liverpool built a bank on the Promenade in 1915. (In 1924 it is a very small house.) There was also a bank on Chairman's Walk and another on the corner of Douglas Street.

Promenade shops. Sankey Family Photography Collection No 7856. c1916 © Cumbria Archives

In 1932, an unusual shop was approved as a temporary building at North Scale. It sat south of the garden of The Crown Hotel and consisted of an ex-railway carriage.[230]

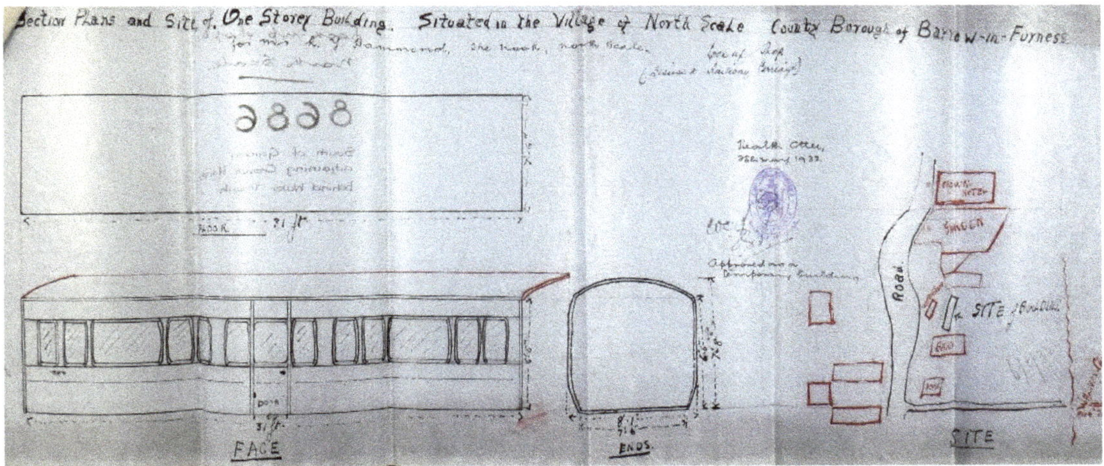

The old railway carriage shop 1932. (Cumbria Archives BA/S/BC Building Plans 8686.)

Lady Luck

The old Women's Auxiliary Air Force canteen building just south of North Scale, became first a 'Remploy' factory by around 1950; then Lansil Ltd of Lancaster took it over around 1960; J & P Jacobs of Liverpool followed in 1965, making items for M & S. Later it became the Lady Luck factory, known to locals as the 'knicker factory'.[231] It eventually closed and was used by Manpower Services as a training centre for a short time.

Airship shed

An attempt to build an airship by Vickers, Sons & Maxims Limited in 1911 had resulted in a catastrophic failure when His Majesty's Airship No 1, (called Mayfly by the locals because it may fly or it may not), snapped in half whilst being brought out of its shed on 24 September 1911.[232] This was not the end of the airship story though as *The Barrow Herald* was reporting on 7 June 1913 that an Airship Shed was to be built on Walney.[233] By August the same year it is reported that an order for five airships had been received from the Admiralty and construction of the shed was proceeding quickly.[234]

THE WALNEY AIRSHIP FACTORY.

HOW IT WILL INTERFERE WITH THE GOLF CLUB.

Messrs. Vickers' scheme of erecting an aircraft factory at the north-west of Walney Island is slowly forging ahead. A rude sort of road has been constructed from Cobler's-lane approaching the site, but as yet the only men employed on the work is a number of navvies, who are busy excavating for draining purposes. The land which the firm's project will necessitate is going to considerably interfere with the Furness Golf Club, whose links, it is well-known, are situated along the west shore of the island. For sometime now they have had notice to quit that part of their course, which comprises holes numbered 4, 5, 6, 7, and 8. The area involved is of substantial proportions, and will deprive the club of about one-third of their present pitch. The officials have been seriously considering the position, with a view to making arrangements which will make up for the encroachment on the north end of the green. A scheme is on foot to secure an additional piece of land at the Biggar Bank end of the links, and at present it is thought that this remedy will be effected with very little difficulty.

The shed was built on land occupied by Furness Golf Club who had been given notice to quit their holes 4 to 8.[235] A gasbag factory with 100 employees was built next to the shed. Work began on HMA No 9 at the Barrow Airship shed at Cavendish Dock at the beginning of 1914. R9 was designed by HB Pratt and Barnes Wallis, (of bouncing bomb fame).

Walney Airship Shed, c1920   Sankey Family Photography Collection. No 7752.   © Cumbria Archives

Experimental work was started on the building of hull girders, but great difficulties were found in the manufacturing of sections of the thin and light Duralumin, an alloy of aluminium and copper. It was only after a long time and great expense, that these difficulties were overcome and the manufacture of the girders could proceed. In March 1915, the Admiralty instructed Vickers to suspend work.

After the effective work done by the German Zeppelin airships at Jutland and elsewhere was seen by the Admiralty, they decided to complete HMA No 9 and to develop further airships.[237] HMA No 9 flew on 27th November 1916[238] and left Barrow on April 4th 1917.

After the capture of a wrecked Zeppelin in the autumn of 1916 the Admiralty decided to put in hand a programme to build identical airships. A Vickers Airship Department book states that the amount of material needed to build a typical airship was as follows:

- 600 drawings
- 21,000 different parts amounting to 1.6 million individual parts
- 20 miles of angle and channel sections of Duralumin
- 53 miles of wire
- 30,000 square yards of fabric
- 1.25 million rivets

Also built on Walney were the R23 and R26. The R23 was completed in September 1917, and flew to Howden in Yorkshire on 15 October 1917. R26 was completed in March 1918. These were also designed by HB Pratt and Barnes Wallis.

 Two non-rigid airships, No6 and No7 were delivered. The first in June and the second in December 1917. These were 350ft long and capable of 42.5 mph.

(Rigid airships were designated R, non-rigid by a number only.)

R80 was started in November 1917 and first flew on 19 July 1920. It was damaged first time out and took until January 1921 to repair.

R80 emerging from the Walney shed. Sankey Family Photography Collection No 1912

© Cumbria Archives

The R80 was powered by four Wolseley- Maybach engines, each developing 230 brake horse-power at 1,400rpm. The drive was taken through a clutch and all controls were arranged to be operated by one man. There were 34 petrol tanks totalling 3,128 gallons, weighing around 10 tons.[239]

[It seems to me that anybody travelling in a huge machine full of explosive hydrogen gas and carrying 10 tons of fuel was taking an enormous risk. Subsequent airship disasters attest to the fact that prior to the use of Helium, airship travel was not for the faint-hearted.]

A Vickers document of 1919 states:

'Very successful results have been obtained in the use of female labour on airship work, and 65% of our total hands now engaged on airship work are females, who carry out practically all the operations of drilling and riveting and wiring, and are also now doing work of quite a skilled character in connection with the erection of the hull framework, and in assembling gondolas.'[240]

R80 with the gas bags part inflated.   *Engineer Magazine* July 1920

Production of airships was later transferred to Howden in Yorkshire and the shed closed down in 1921. It was put up for sale, with one idea being that it could be used as a film studio, but nothing materialised and it was dismantled.[241]

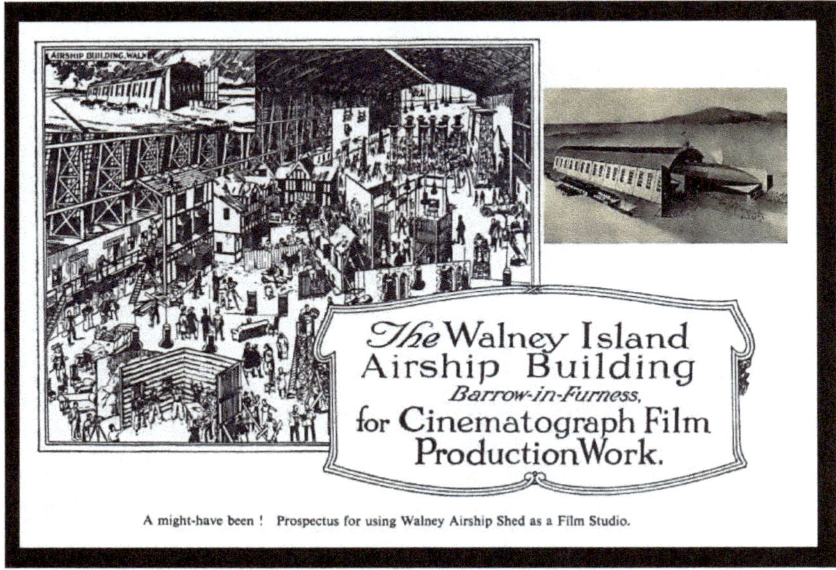

A might-have been ! Prospectus for using Walney Airship Shed as a Film Studio.

Airfield

In October 1938, Barrow Council made an order to compulsorily purchase North End farm, and 634 acres, in order to build an airfield.[243] The purchase cost was £8,030. A public enquiry was held in February 1939[244] and construction began in 1940/1. North End Farm and the remains of the windmill effectively disappeared under the runaway. The map below shows a modern map overlayed onto an older version, showing the runways. The North End windmill highlighted in red, with the farm just above.

National Library of Scotland overlay map.

In October 1941 Air Gunnery School, No. 10 was opened and remained in operation until May 1946.[245] Dozens of sites were set up for the Royal Air Force and WAAF personnel around the airfield, North Scale and Mill Lane. There were around 1,500 personnel on these sites at any one time.

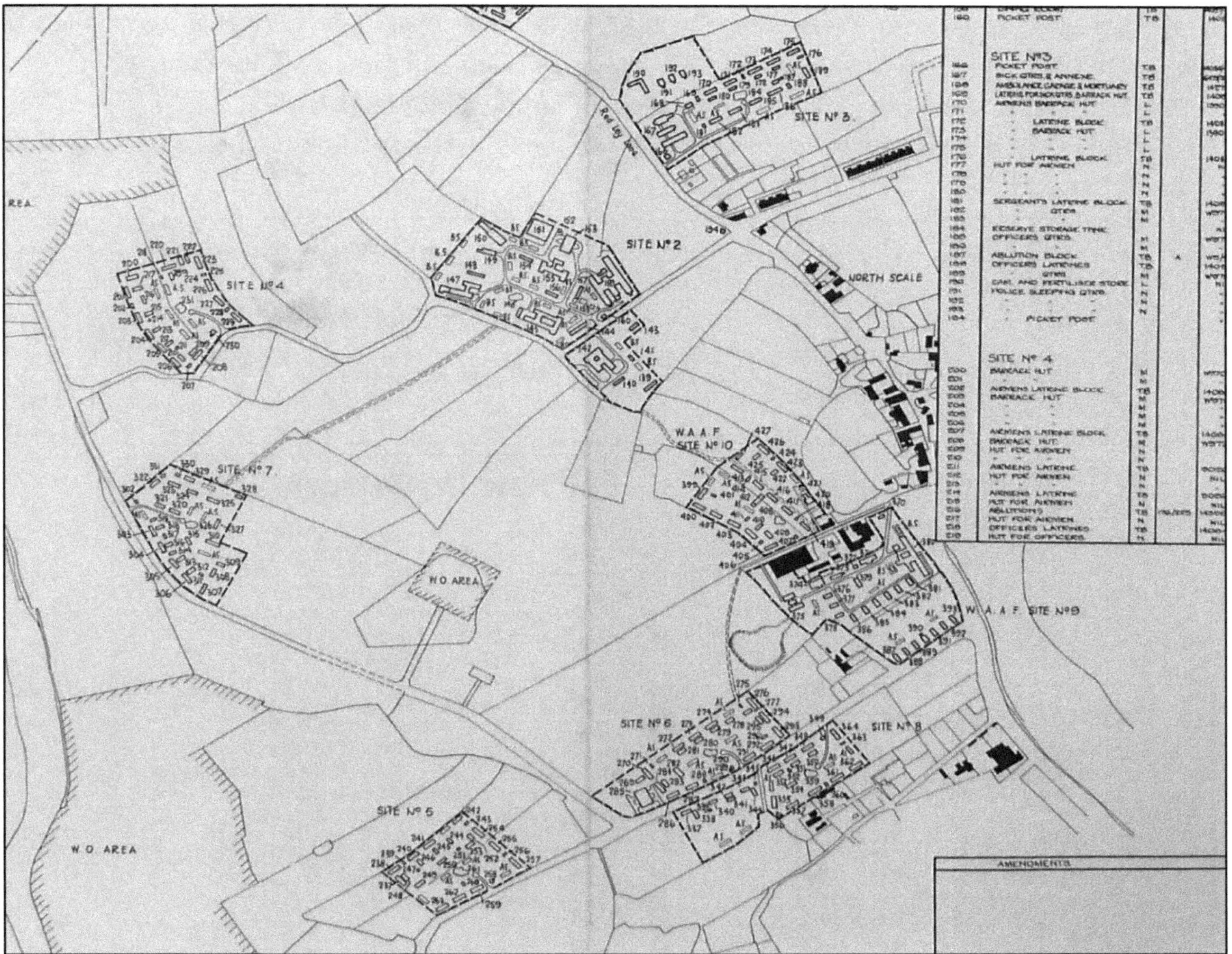

Detail from BDX/725/14/4   (Cumbria Archives)

This is detail from a map showing some of the facilities around North Walney related to the airfield. Sites 9 and 10 were the WAAF sites to the west and south of North Scale village.

The main purpose of the airfield was to teach air gunners, and to that end a number of different defence and attack skills were taught. The gun ranges on the west of the site were used to teach how to 'lead' a target using shotguns. At the north end of the site, a 'moving target' range was in operation. It consisted of a wooden dummy plane on a track, and a fixed aircraft gun turret. In the air; drones were towed over the sea to be used for target practice.

Unfortunately, flying was a hazardous business and during the operation of Air Gunnery School, No. 10, at Walney, over 40 flyers were killed whilst carrying out their duties. One incident involved an Avro Anson which crashed at Earnse Bay on 31 May 1943 resulting in the deaths of five crew members. Another involved a Wellington bomber which crashed off Roa Island on 20 June 1943 – on this occasion, luckily, there were no fatalities.

In 1945 the Mountain Rescue Unit which had been at Cark airfield moved to Walney.

Flying ceased at the base on 15 June 1946, and RAF Walney closed on 30 June 1946. The Air Gunnery School moved to RAF Valley on Anglesey, along with their mountain rescue team.[246] The sites soon had another use.

By August 1946, when many were still homeless due to their houses being bombed, quite a few of the unused RAF huts had been occupied by 'squatters' with 150 families in residence.[247] The so-called squatters intended to make arrangements for rent, water, sanitation and illumination. [248] By 1948 there were dozens of families living in the huts and registered there to vote, some were still there as late as 1952.[249]

In accordance with instructions received from the Ministry of Health, Barrow Corporation have now decided to take over the responsibility for the huts occupied by the 120 families of squatters in the town and make them as habitable as possible. A rent is to be charged which will probably vary between 8s and 10s a week for each family. This will include rates and facilities for water and lighting.
Lancashire Evening Post, 30 August 1946

Is Squatters a fair term considering their willingness to pay for their occupation?

I think not.

Barrow Squatters

Squatting continued at Barrow all day yesterday and a colony of about 150 families now exists on R.A.F. and W.A.A.F. sites at Walney Island.

Squatters have also been seen in other parts of the town and negotiations are taking-place between the Air Ministry and the Corporation.

Lancashire Evening Post

9 October 1946

Barrow Squatters

A squatter family were to-day reported to have entered into possession of a portion of the N.A.A.F.I. canteen staff quarters at Walney Island Barrow The matter has been reported to the police.

It is further reported that would-be squatters yesterday attempted to acquire a hut on the R.A.F site at Walney, which had been occupied by the mountain rescue squad who were away at the time in connection with the air ambulance disaster at Scafell. Sentries however, were able to prevent the would-be squatters from entering into occupation and the mountain rescue squad have now returned.

Lancashire Evening Post

3 September 1946

In 1947 the War Secretary brought a claim against the squatters at Walney Fort for damages amounting to £100, and also gained an injunction against them. The judge in the case sympathised with the squatters and said that the housing position was extremely difficult. He refused the claim for damages.[250]

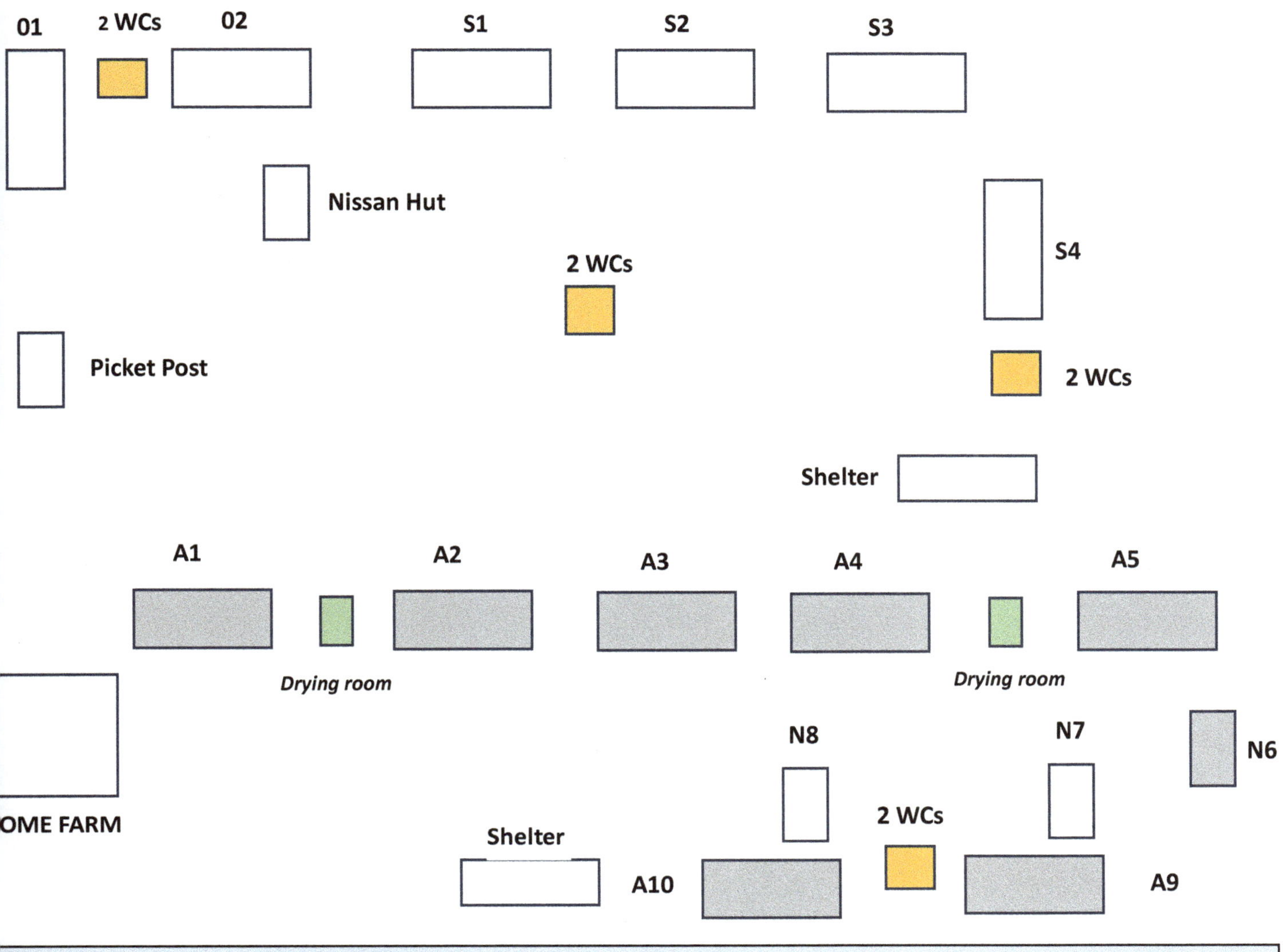

This (above), was the layout of Camp 4, (which was the easternmost part of the previous WAAF site 10,) on 15 October 1946.

The Nissan hut, the Picket post, N7 and N8 were empty. A1 to A5, N6, A9 and A10 had been filled with hay by the farmer from Home Farm, Mr T. Gilliland.

Huts 01, 02, S1 to S4 were all occupied by squatters.

01 had one adult woman and four children in five rooms.

02 had two adults and one child in five rooms.

S1 had two adults and two children in four rooms.

S2 had two adults and two children in four rooms.

S3 had two adults and two children in four rooms.

S4 had two adults and two children in four rooms.

All of these families paid rent of 10/6d per week for their timber huts. Rents depended upon the grade of the hut. Four and five -room huts were all grade A. Single room huts were grade E and paid 8/6d per week rent.

Similar huts with squatters were at all Walney sites as well as at Dane Avenue, Rakesmoor Lane, Park Drive and Rampside. Some huts initially had no electricity and were charged 6d per week less until connected.

The airfield itself was used only by glider fliers by September 1946,[257] but the *Lancaster Guardian* reported on 15 November the same year that Loxham's Flying Services Ltd was operating out of Walney, Blackpool and Middleton.

The future of the airfield was discussed with the Aviation Ministry in 1949 with a view to Barrow Corporation using the aerodrome as a civil airport. The Ministry stated that there was no prospect of scheduled services using the aerodrome.[258]

By 1952 the airfield was closed down by the council.[259] Despite being allowed to completely run down, the airfield was still in partial use in 1954 by the Furness Aero Club which had 45 members but no planes. They shared facilities with the Blackpool and Fylde Aero Club.[260]

The Lakes Gliding Club started operating from the site in 1961, but in 1968 Vickers took over the airport. They allowed the Lakes Gliding Cub to continue to operate from the site.

[261]

A number of other operators have attempted to run commercial flights from the airfield, including Air Ecosse (1982-3), who flew to Edinburgh Carlisle and Liverpool; Air Furness (1986), who flew to Manchester; and Telair (1991-2), who flew to Manchester and Blackpool. All went out of business. [262]

In 2019 BAE upgraded the airfield. They spent £7.2million pounds installing new infrastructure, avionics, and a new hangar. They also built a new control tower.[263]

In February 2023, BAE, the current airfield owners, gave Lakes Gliding Club notice to quit.[264] BAE own the site today and operates a number of planes from there, but purely for their own company use.

Saltworks

It had long been discussed in the local press that there may be coal under Furness[275] and a number of prospectors had searched fruitlessly for this 'black gold'. [276] Searches were made at Hawcoat, Stank, Rampside and Gleaston for many years and were still being reported as late as 1913.[277] It was during one such search, on Walney, that salt was discovered.[278] The quality and extent of the discovery resulted in the formation of the Barrow and Liverpool Salt Company Limited. The original lease for the salt mines was granted to Augustus Strongitharm, a Barrow civil engineer, on 19 June 1890. Over time, four different companies attempted to develop Walney's salt deposits. The Barrow Salt Company was the second of these.

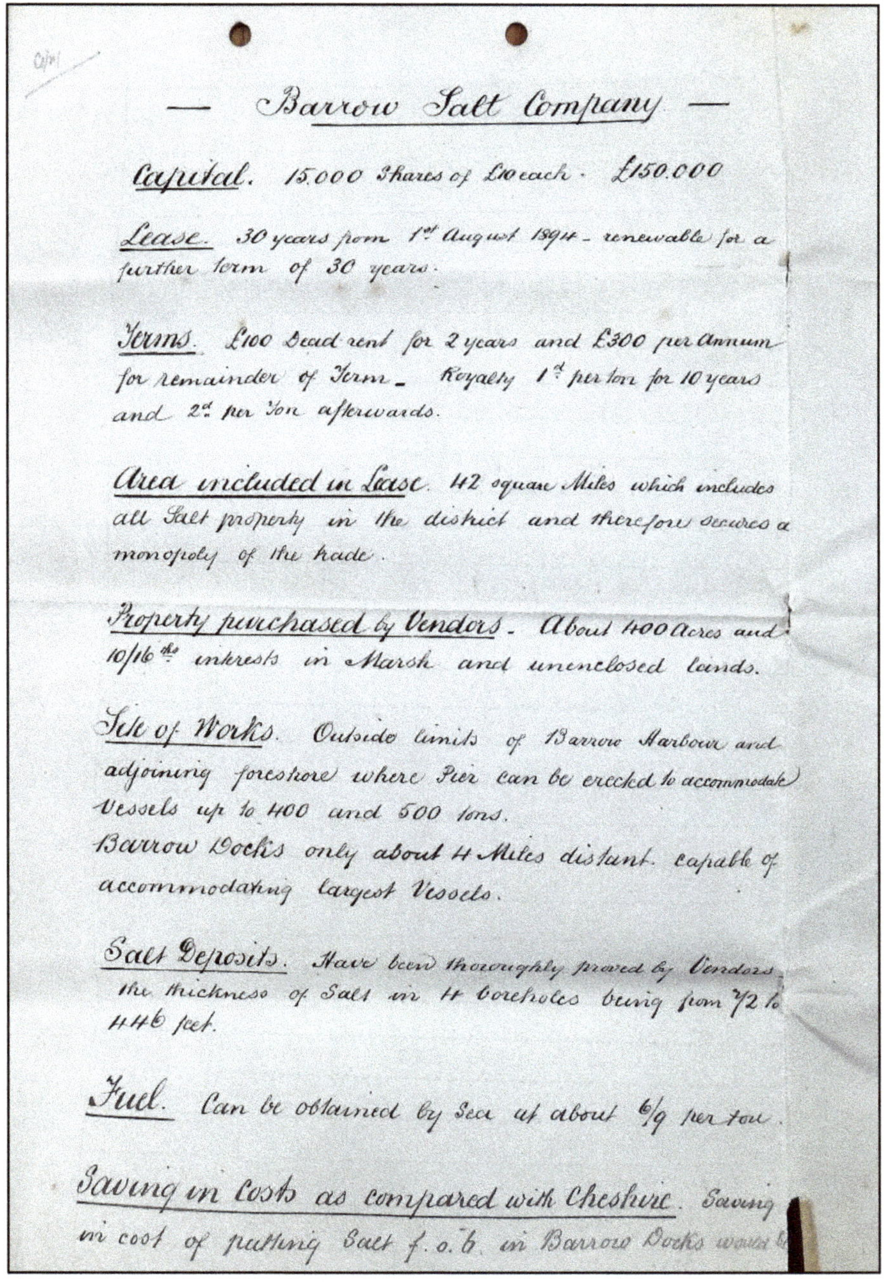

— Barrow Salt Company —

Capital. 15.000 Shares of £10 each. £150.000

Lease. 30 years from 1st August 1894 – renewable for a further term of 30 years.

Terms. £100 Dead rent for 2 years and £300 per Annum for remainder of Term – Royalty 1st per ton for 10 years and 2d. per Ton afterwards.

Area included in Lease. 42 square Miles which includes all Salt property in the district and therefore secures a monopoly of the trade.

Property purchased by Vendors – About 400 Acres and 10/16ths interests in Marsh and unenclosed lands.

Site of Works. Outside limits of Barrow Harbour and adjoining foreshore where Pier can be erected to accommodate Vessels up to 400 and 500 tons. Barrow Docks only about 4 Miles distant. capable of accommodating largest Vessels.

Salt Deposits. Have been thoroughly proved by Vendors the thickness of Salt in 4 boreholes being from 72 to 446 feet.

Fuel. Can be obtained by Sea at about 6/9 per ton.

Saving in Costs as compared with Cheshire. Saving in cost of putting Salt f.o.b. in Barrow Docks would b

A works was constructed at the south end of Walney with five large chimneys, reservoirs, filter banks and thousands of yards of cast iron pipes in use. Cottages were built for some of the workers with others using eight cottages on Piel Island nearby. Shipments were leaving the nearby wooden pier by 1898. A number of brine wells with accompanying derricks were in place and a local rail network was built on the site. However, the venture was not a success, and despite attempts to keep it going the final salt company was wound up on 29 July 1902.[279] To date this is the largest industrial venture of any sort attempted on Walney.

(Cumbria Archives BDBUC/45/9/7)

Barrow Salt Co. 1895

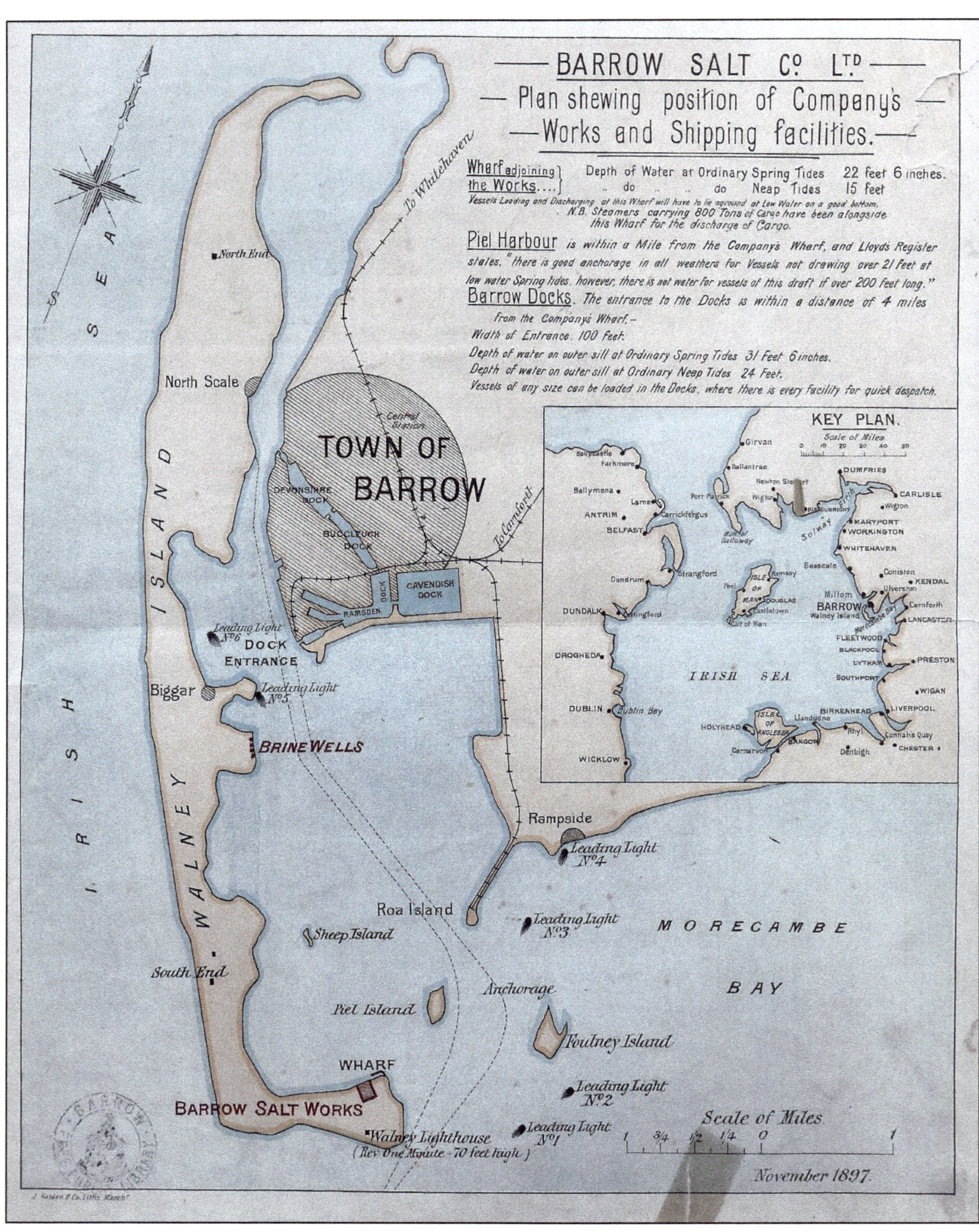

Walney Salt Works 1897   (Cumbria Archives.   BLC/PH/280/PZ/BAR)

The remains of the South End Pier in 1978. Piel Island in the background.

Sand & Gravel extraction

In the same area on the south end of Walney, sand & gravel extraction was taking place and being exported from the same wooden pier. It too utilised a railway system around the site. This 3ft gauge railway was originally built around 1880 to serve the salt works.[280] The pier stayed in use until 1962 when it closed following storm damage. The rolling stock was scrapped the same year.[281] The Piel and Walney Sand & Gravel Company became the Roose & Walney Sand & Gravel Company in 1960.

Sand and gravel were also extracted from the north end of Walney by W. Mc Lung & Sons of North Scale.[282]

From 1963, the site of the salt works and gravel extraction at south Walney has been leased from Holker estates by South Walney Nature Reserve and is a Site of Special Scientific Interest (SSSI), a Special Area of Conservation (SAC) and a Special Protection Area (SPA). It is home to a colony of grey seals as well as many species of birds.

Oyster farm

In 1978 the lagoons left over from the gravel extraction were put to good use as an oyster farm to rear seed oysters. The lagoons are fed with sea water by pumps.[283] It is still in operation today as Seasalter (Walney) Ltd.

Coastguard

For many years the Exchequer suffered financial losses due to the smugglers of tobacco, wine and brandy bringing it from the Isle of Man into England. Whitehaven 'legitimate trade' suffered. In August 1716 Thomas Crisp, High Sheriff of Lancaster, was reported as having *'executed 34 rebels at various places in the county and wants paying the expenses thereof.'* In August 1726, four vessels were stationed at Whitehaven, Liverpool, Beaumaris and Aberdovey to try to stop the Isle of Man smugglers. By 1731, these boats had been paid off and several small boats employed instead. One of these was stationed at Piel.[284]

Two plots of land were leased to HM Lords Commissioners of the Admiralty in July 1903 for coastguard cottages and a lookout hut at the south-end of Walney.[285] By 1905, three cottages and a lookout with semaphore was in place.[286] The station was in operation for many years until the press reported it was to close down in 1950.[287] In 1953 the lookout post was gutted in a fire,[288] but a temporary coastguard post was up and running within days.[289] It was closed as a full-time station by 1955.[290] However, in 1971, Walney had one full time coastguard and a two-day per week volunteer lookout watch, based in the previously mentioned, Fort Walney lookout tower, on the west side in the centre of the island on the golf course. In the 1990s this closed and the auxiliary coastguard moved to the mainland.[291]

Police

After the establishment of a Barrow Borough Police force on 1 August 1881[292] a police station was built around 1882, on the Promenade at Walney, at a cost of £427.[293] Originally it had only one constable, but following the building of Vickerstown this was increased to four officers in 1904, and by 1906 to six.

> I am glad to see that the Corporation now proposes to place two more police constables on Walney. It is well known that these are badly needed to maintain peace in an Island many miles in length, and containing 5,000 inhabitants. I have had occasion to point out several times the need for more police or detective supervision on the more lonely portions of the Promenade, notably between Latona-street schools and North Scale village. I am sorry to say that since my remarks on this subject a few weeks ago, I have had brought to my notice two more cases of women being molested at this point. These are not imaginary cases, but actual facts. But one man could not possibly look after the whole of North Vickerstown and North Scale as well.

A report from the Vickerstown Chronicle of 29 January 1904.

The police station closed after the Second World War.[294]

The old police station on the Promenade is now a private house.

The 1882 date stone is still visible above the right hand windows.

© Peter Laird

In 1891, Constable Richard Cole was living in the police house with his wife Mary Jane, along with one son and one daughter.[295] In 1901 and 1911, it was Constable Robert Postlethwaite with his family.[296]

Fire Brigade

As part of the building of Vickerstown, a fire station was built on Knox Street (in 1902) and was run by the Isle of Walney Estates Company. In 1904, the Barrow council agreed that a permanent fire station was required on Walney.[297]

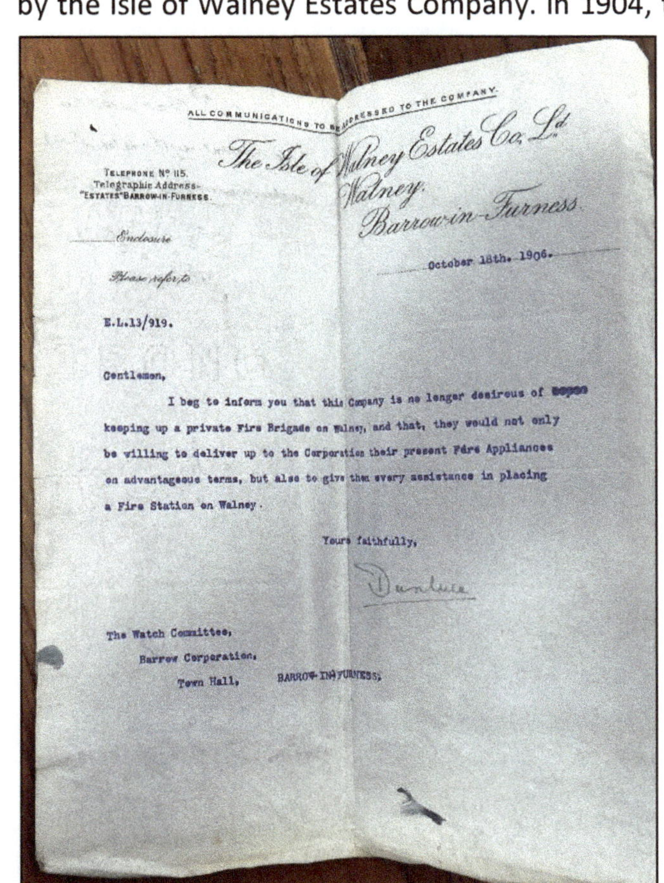

In 1906 the Estates Company informed the council that it was 'no longer desirous of running a private fire brigade on Walney'.[298]

(Cumbria Archives. BA/C/Box 4)

In 1907 the company offered to let the brigade station and land for a period of five years for 1s. per year, [299] and the offer was accepted by the council in March the same year.[300]

> *An Agreement made the _ day of_ 1907 between the Isle of Walney Estates Coy., Ltd, whose registered office is at __ in the City of London (hereinafter called the Company), of the one part and The Mayor etc of Barrow in F. (hereinafter called the Corporation), of the other part.*
>
> *Whereby it is agreed as follows; -*
>
> *The Company hereby agree to let & the Corporation agree to take All that portable wooden hut and the land on which it stands situate in (Knox) St., Vickerstown, in the said Borough for the purposes of a Fire Station at a peppercorn rent of 1/- per annum upon the following terms & conditions, viz; -*
>
> *The tenancy shall commence as from the 1st day of March 1907 & shall continue in force for a term of 5 years certain from the said 1st day of March & thereafter until determined by either party giving to the other three calendar months previous notice in writing.*

In December 1914, the Estates Company repossessed the Vickerstown Fire Station and the appliances held there were moved to Central Fire Station at Barrow.[301] A modern fire station was opened on Mill Lane, Walney, in 1974 and at that time had a day-crewed system. In 1991 it went to an on-call system.[302] The station was under threat in 2015 before it was reprieved in February 2016.[303]

Walney Fire Station 1985

Prior to the Vickerstown Fire Brigade formation, Walney had to be covered from Barrow. A case in point was when in February 1887, the Seaview Hotel, at Tummerhill near Biggar Bank, burnt down. The fire brigade had had difficulty in getting to Walney during the early hours of the morning due to the men on watch on the steam ferry not allowing the brigade to cross.[304]

A couple of days after the fire the following letter appeared in the *Barrow Herald and Furness Advertiser.* 01 March 1887

THE FIRE ON WALNEY ISLAND

Dear sir,

It is commonly reported that when the Barrow Fire Brigade arrived at the ferry on Sunday morning, on their way to the fire at the Sea View Hotel, they were met with the rejoinder by the party in charge of the ferry, that he could not take them across – although steam is always kept up to allow of it being afloat- until he had received 'an order' from a certain official who manages this department.

I presume the inhabitants of Walney pay rates, etc., like other civilised people, and are entitled to a 'deluge' on the occasion of a fire, and if ever the absurdity of the ferry being in the hands of a private company was evidenced, this occasion proves it beyond doubt. Our Town Council should now lose no time to celebrate the Jubilee by taking over this 'obstructive construction', and confer a real benefit in more ways than one; and should a fire ever occur again on the adjoining island, no such farce would be chronicled a second time. It would be refreshing to know if a man was observed drowning in the dock, would it be necessary for 'an order' to allow the use of the life-belts hung up in the various places?

Yours truly, DISGUSTED. 28th Feb 1887

The hotel had originally been called the Neptune Hotel, but the Neptune Company went into liquidation in 1876.[305] This shows one proposal for the Neptune hotel.

(Cumbria Archives BDKF/Plans 26)

The hotel as built bore little resemblance to this plan. Even after changing hands and name, the hotel was not doing well before the fire and nobody was in the premises on the night in question.[306]

WATCH COMMITTEE.

The Chief Constable and Superintendent of the Fire Brigade reported on a fire which occurred on Sunday morning, 27th February, at the Sea View Hotel, Walney, and pointed out the difficulty the Fire Brigade had experienced in crossing the channel. Resolved that the Town Clerk write to the secretary to the Furness Railway Company in reference to the matter, and state that the committee are anxious to avoid the Fire Brigade experiencing the same difficulty in crossing the channel in case of another fire breaking out during the early hours of the morning, and to ask that instructions be given to the Harbour Master to give the man on watch at the steam ferry directions to convey the Fire Brigade and their appliances across in such an event, and that they think it would also be desirable in the public interest that the boat should be available

Barrow Herald and Furness Advertiser. 12 March 1887.   The aftermath of the fire.

There was also a beer house to the left (east) of the Sea View in one of the cottages.[307]

Social History

By 1900, the days when the majority of islanders worked in agriculture were gone. With little in the way of business on the island to employ people, the vast majority spent their days off the island, making it a typical dormitory settlement. The building of Vickerstown however, in the very early years of the 20th century by the Estates Company increased the islands population substantially and brought the need for more social opportunities and communal amenities.

Theatre and Picture house

Walney Theatre and Picture House plans were approved in 1913, but that was for the plot of land fronting the Promenade and on Natal Road. That one was never built.

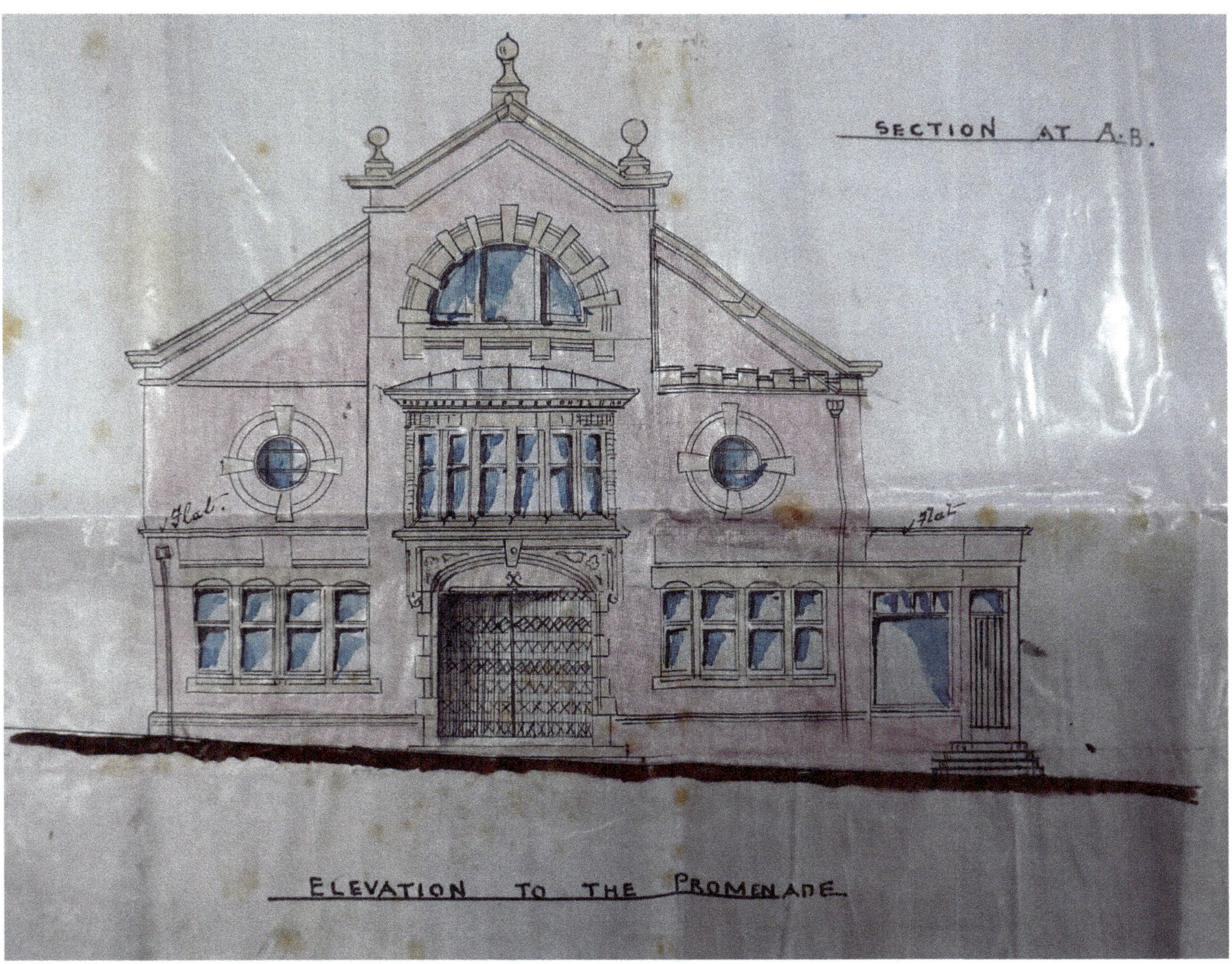

Picture Palace Promenade plans 1913. (Cumbria Archives Plans 6341)

New plans were submitted for a building higher up Natal Road in August 1915, and it opened in November 1915. [308]

The opening programme included a ventriloquist, an orchestra, a Contralto and Pierrots.

When first opened the cinema/theatre could seat 500 people, all on the same level, and it had an organ. It was altered in 1919, when the roof was raised and a balcony was added, increasing its capacity to 786.[309] Talkies, or films with sound, were introduced on 20 October 1930 [310]with the first talkie being *Sunny Side Up* with Janet Gaynor. In 1933 the Walney Parish Operatic Society performed *The Sunshine Girl* there.[311]They regularly took over the theatre for a week.

Walney cinema 1938. Sankey Family Photography Collection. No H921. © Cumbria Archives

The theatre was taken over by the Union cinemas chain in August 1936 and then by the Associated British Cinemas (ABC) in October 1937. In March 1948 it was again taken over, this time by the Essoldo chain.[312]

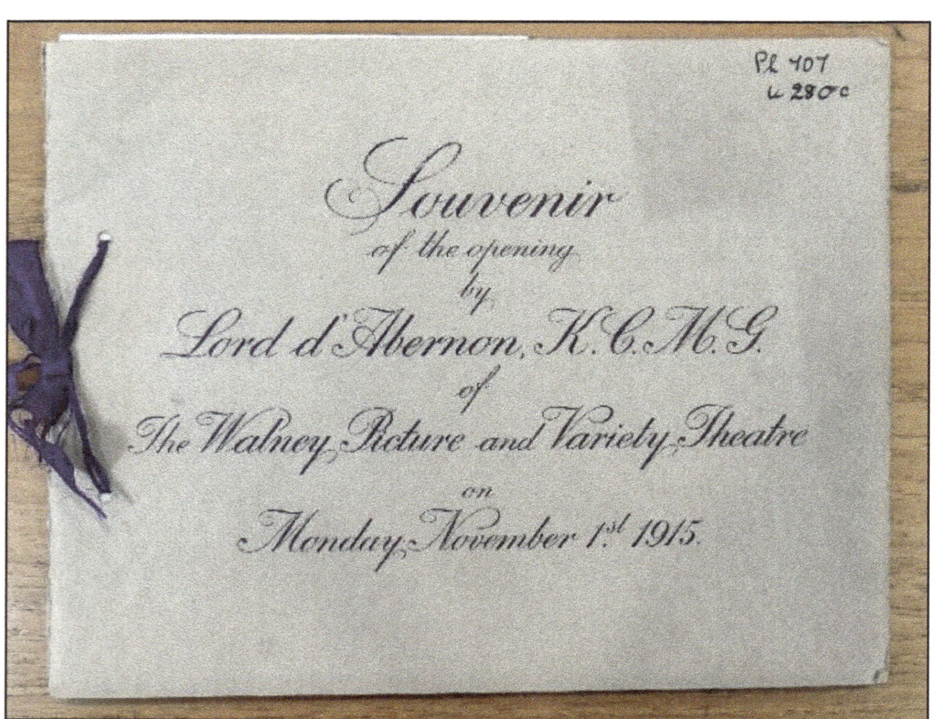

Opening souvenir 1915. (Cumbria Archives BLC/PH/280/C/OPE)

The cinema was granted permission to open on Sundays in 1955.[313]

It closed on 20 June 1959 when Richard Burton was showing in '*The Robe*.'[314] It stood empty for some years before opening as a supermarket around 1964. This venture didn't succeed and the building was demolished in 1983.[315]

Pierrots

Pierrots were a common sight on Walney in the early 20th Century. They appeared at the theatre, in James Dunn Park and at Biggar Bank.

Based on pantomime characters, they often performed in white costumes and with a whitened face. They had frilled collars and looked like clowns. They performed music, dance and comedy routines. Walney's own Pierrots were called the Walney Mascots, (left).

Sankey Family Photography Collection No 283 © Cumbria Archives

Other Inns and Alehouses

It is only in 1773 that an alehouse is first mentioned at Biggar.[320]At that time John Hool was the keeper, he was replaced first by Myles Myres in 1782, George Postlethwaite in 1787, and George White in 1795. Whether that house was the current Queen's cannot be ascertained, as traditionally most farms brewed their own beer and it may have been another, or several different places that were licensed. After 1803 there is no mention of a licensed house at Biggar for many years.

The **Queen's Arms, Biggar,** is a long low building, with a large central chimney. It has a cobbled forecourt of beach stones and is believed to be one of the oldest inns set up in the district.

Around 1838, one of the tenants of the village, a Richard Spencer, opened his house for the sale of beer and other goods.[321] The 1841 census has Richard, his wife Mary, three daughters and two sons living here.[322]

John Tyson purchased the farm around 1854, and in 1866 he obtained a licence, making his residence an Inn.[323] Originally called 'the Letters', which was a term for a house selling beer but with no definite sign outside, by 1871 the inn had become 'The Queen's Arms' and John Tyson, his wife Sarah, two daughters and two sons, a general servant, an agricultural servant and a farm servant are living there.[324] John died in December 1876 and there was court case involving a creditor, Anne Robinson.[325] The pub and associated lands were sold in August 1879 to Joseph Hunter.[326]

Isaac Robinson, as tenant, lived there with his wife Ann the innkeeper in 1881, together with a daughter, a son, a farm labourer, and a farm servant.[327]

The next tenant was Andrew Riley with his wife Sarah, three daughters, three sons and two farm servants.[328] Abraham Thompson Robinson was there in 1901 with his wife Hannah, two daughters, two farm servants and five boarders - who were all bricklayers.[329]

In 1901 Thompson, (as he was called), was still living there with another three males and three females.[330] In 1927 Mr Robinson handed over the inn to a Mr and Mrs Brookes, the latter being the tenant.[331]

The Queens, Biggar.

Early 20th century.

Sankey Family Photography Collection. No 158

© Cumbria Archives

The **New Inn, Biggar,** has a long history. The property was re-built by Richard Long in 1758, on land he had bought ten years earlier from William Shaw of Urswick. A Kendal draper, Joseph Garnett bought it in 1841 and his widow sold it to Joseph Richardson of Biggar in 1864.

According to the 1841 tithe map and schedule the inn was owned by Joseph Garnett and occupied by John Haslam. The 1841 census has John as a farmer with his wife Agnes, two children, three agricultural labourers and a female servant.

The 1851 census has John and Agnes with two daughters and three agricultural labourers. The 1861 census has John at 74 years old and Agnes 66, with two daughters and four farm servants.

The 1871 census has the house named Bear House (Beer House) and New Inn. Joseph Richardson is living there with his wife Ann and four daughters and a son.

Joseph is still there in 1881 as is Ann, three daughters, a son and an indoor servant (male). Joseph is a farmer, and Ann the innkeeper.[332]

The 1891 census has Joseph as a widower and a farmer living here with three daughters, a son, and a farm servant (male).[333]

Joseph's son, Thomas Tyson Richardson, is head of the household by the 1901 census. He is a farmer and living with three sisters and a male farm servant.[334] Thomas Tyson Richardson is mentioned in a local newspaper on 30 March 1905 as he made a discovery of a decomposed body washed up 'about half a mile below Biggar Bank.' In the article it mentions that he is from the New Inn.[335]

Richardson is still there in 1911 along with another male and three females.[336]

In 1937 a George Robinson of the New Inn, Biggar, is mentioned in the press. It states that he took over the beer-house in 1930. He was appearing at the Barrow Bankruptcy Court where it was stated that the Beer-house 'never had a large turnover.'[337] The New Inn closed in April 1973,[338] and is now a private house and a listed building.

The New Inn, Biggar Early 20th century. Sankey Family Photography Collection. No 3414

© Cumbria Archives

The New Inn. 1904 (Cumbria Archives Z 3491/1)

The New Inn farmyard. 1904 (Cumbria Archives Z 3491/5)

The pictures above, painted by the Belgian artist Abel Masson of Biggar and North Scale, shows how the inn looked in 1904, with outside steps to the loft and wooden gates which could be closed at night. The building was constructed with beach pebbles, rough cast to protect the building from the weather. Like many of the older Biggar buildings, much of the interior woodwork was from wreckage washed up from the sea.

A public house was opened in North Scale some time before 1796, as in that year John Postlethwaite and his wife Sarah sold it to William Gibson of North Scale for £80 and one peppercorn annually for 1,000 years. [339] In the Indenture, it states that the premises are connected in the west to the barn of William Boulton and to the east is the sea shore. That puts it somewhere in the region of the current No 20, North Scale. (The numbering has changed over the years.) In 1851, Ann Gibson, widow, is listed in the census as beer-house keeper,[340] but by 1861 there is no such listing in the village.

The Crown Hotel

The Crown Hotel at North Scale was in existence before 1868[341] and is still operating today.

The Crown is built on land leased for 999 years on 14 February 1839, by the Rev. John Troughton, curate of Walney, to William Housby, shoemaker, for £9, plus a yearly rent of one penny. (The same William Housby who was also the letter carrier.) William Housby had built two houses on this land before 1865 and on that date, he obtained a £200 mortgage from a North Scale farmer called Lowther.[342] The 1871 census has John Housby, son of William, as inn-keeper.[343] In 1875, in a codicil to William's will, it states that the lease of The Crown had been granted to a John Booth for a period of five years.[344]

Robert Troughton is inn-keeper in 1881 and 1891 and an Ernest Walker in 1901.[345]

SPORTS AT WALNEY. On Saturday last some good old English sport was witnessed and thoroughly enjoyed, in a field adjoining the Crown Hotel, North Scale. Mr John Pickthall and Mr Wilkins acted as umpires. The first event was wrestling, confined to Walney men…**Barrow Herald 30 May 1892**

Ferry Hotel

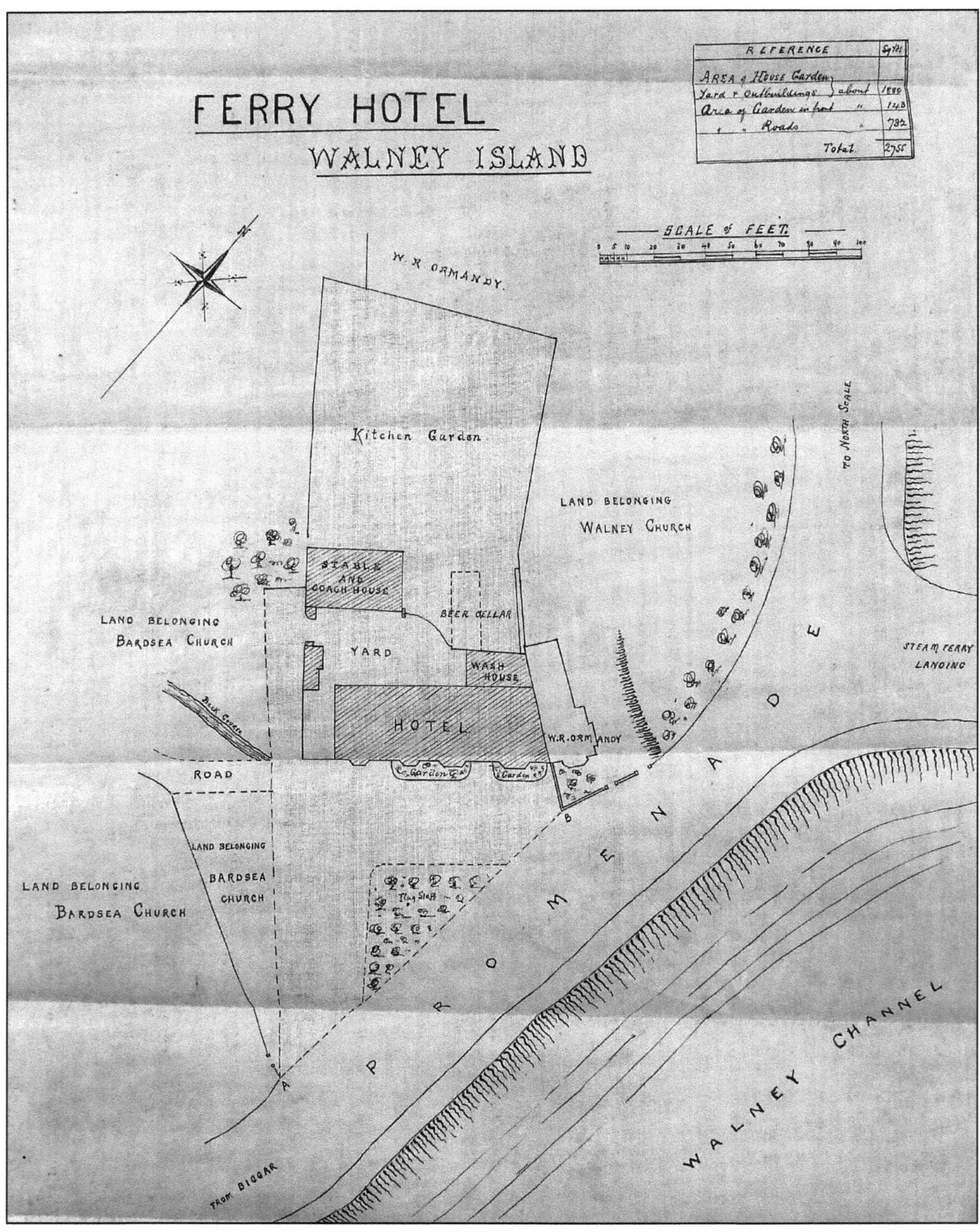

Plan of the Ferry Hotel – undated, but after 1868. (Cumbria Archives.   BDBHJ/180/13/3)

In 1868, William White built a house on Walney, at a cost of £600, which became the Ferry Hotel.[346] This was the central, lower part of the building seen below (in 1985). The addition to the left was built around 1875.[347] The building on the right, built for a Mr Ormandy[348], became the offices of both the Isle of Walney Estates Company and the Vickerstown Chronicle. To the left, out of picture, were the estate workshops.

William applied for, and obtained a licence on 2 September 1868.[349] Once the steam ferry began operating, the trade for the Hotel increased and Mr White sold it in 1879 to a Mr John Clayton for £4,370. In 1879 Mr Clayton made a claim in the High Court which in essence alleged misrepresentation. It was said that Mr White claimed 'takings' of from £16 to £30 per week but in fact Mr Clayton's average takings had been no more than £7 per week. Mr Clayton had also discovered a 'very serious defect' in one of the main walls of the hotel which should have been known to Mr White as the builder. Effectively the wall had no proper foundation and the building was in danger of falling down. Mr Clayton asked for the sale to be declared void.[350]

He must have won his case as the licence was transferred back to William in November 1879.[351] William is listed as hotel keeper of The Ferry in 1881.[352] The hotel put up for sale in 1890, was sold to Ind Coope group and in 1891, 1901 and 1911 Thomas West was the hotel keeper.[353]

The Ferry Hotel in July 1985.

As previously mentioned, the grand opening of Biggar Bank was on Good Friday 1883 and it was reported by the local press that thousands of people attended.[354] A little later a shelter and pavilion were built by the council, [355] both survived until the late 20th century before being demolished. The Roundhouse, built in the 1970s, stands on the site of the original shelter, it is now a community hub and café.

The Roundhouse in 1986. © Peter Laird

A public hotel, **The Castle House**, was built at Biggar sometime between around 1890. [It was listed as 'empty' in the 1891 census.] In 1899 George Samuel Heath applied for a licence for Castle House. Mr Heath stated that he didn't need a seven-day licence as he intended to use it as a middle-class hotel for the accommodation of visitors from a distance. Those opposed to the licence were of the opinion that a licensed house would place temptation in the way of young children. Despite backing, legal representation, and the fact that some 50,000 people came to Walney during that summer, the licence was refused.[356]

It was then used as a large boarding house and another licence application, in 1900, was refused.

During World War Two, Castle House was occupied by soldiers and was then boarded up for many years. Yet another licence application, made in 1949 was refused, but eventually, in 1950, a licence was granted to Mr John Wood who sold the hotel to Cases brewery in April 1954. It is still open today.

> **DAILY MIRROR** 18 December 1961
>
> *Customers in a crowded hotel bar yesterday helped to fight a fire with BEER. They threw pints of ale at the bar ceiling after a stove set it alight. The barrage of beer was kept up until firemen arrived and it stopped serious damage to the hotel, the Castle, Walney island.*

Castle House. Early 20th century. Sankey Family Photography Collection. No 180. © Cumbria Archives. (Note the drinking fountain to the right.)

The King Alfred has already been mentioned earlier, but a bit more detail is warranted here. The pub was named after a cruiser, not the King. It was granted a licence in April 1903 and it was opened on 15 February 1904 by Earl Grey, and was described as '*The very latest weapon for the defeat of the drink evil.*' The Vickerstown Chronicle said that the sale of temperance beverages is encouraged and the sale of spiritous liquors is not pushed. Seen below in 1982.

Other pubs on the island have included **The George**, built in 1916 on Central Drive. It wasn't granted its licence until 1919. It was another Public House Trust pub which pushed non-alcoholic beverages. Pictured here in 1985. It was demolished in 2014.

Also, there was **The Periscope**, on Mill Lane, pictured here in 1986. It was built in the 1960s and was demolished in 2012.

Other facilities

In the mid-1920s there was a putting green on the area directly in front of the Castle House, but even this was controversial with two petitions sent to the council in 1925 asking for the 'prompt removal of the obstruction'.[357] (See photo Page 127)

The latter years of the 19th century and the early years of the 20th century saw the use of bathing huts on Walney. They were mainly at Sandy Gap. The council provided at least some if not all of these.

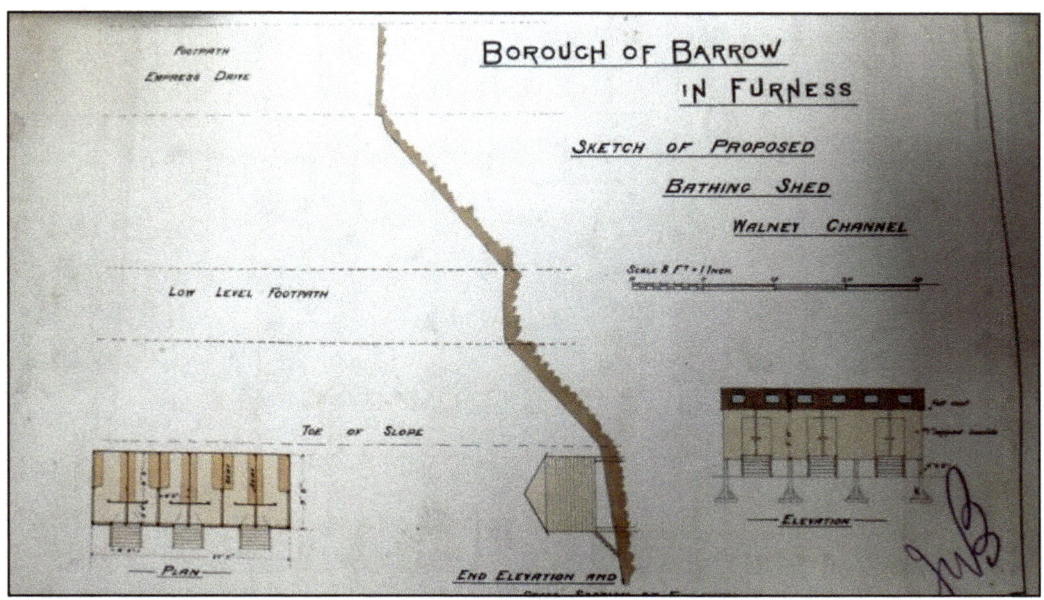

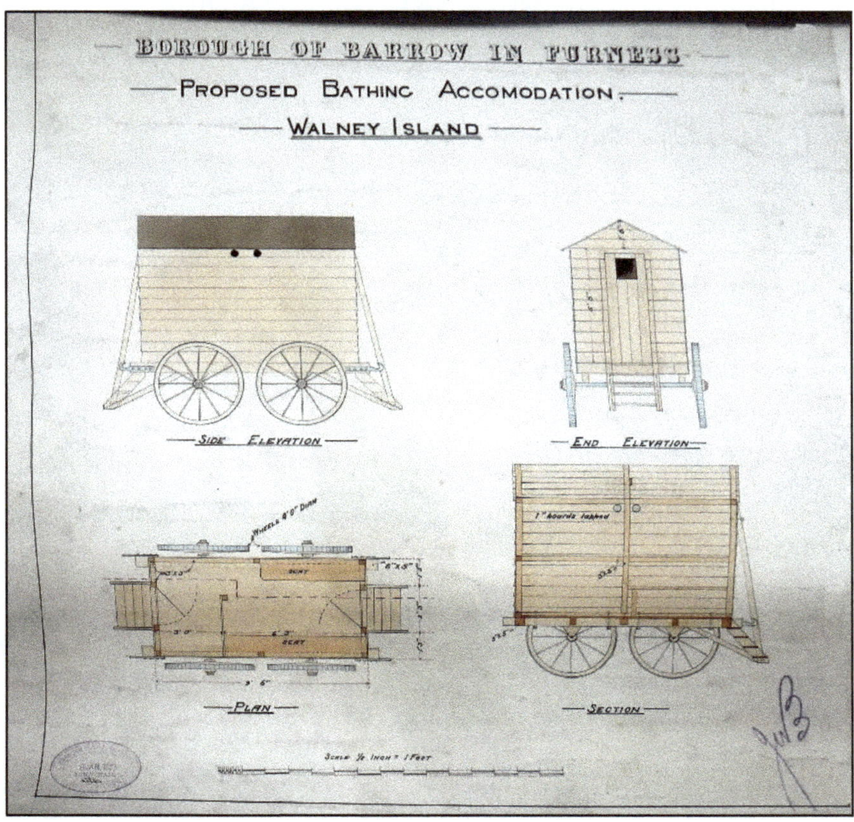

Proposed bathing huts c1903.   Cumbria Archives BA/S/BC/D8/91

Sandy Gap. c1930. Sankey Family Photography Collection No A398 © Cumbria Archives

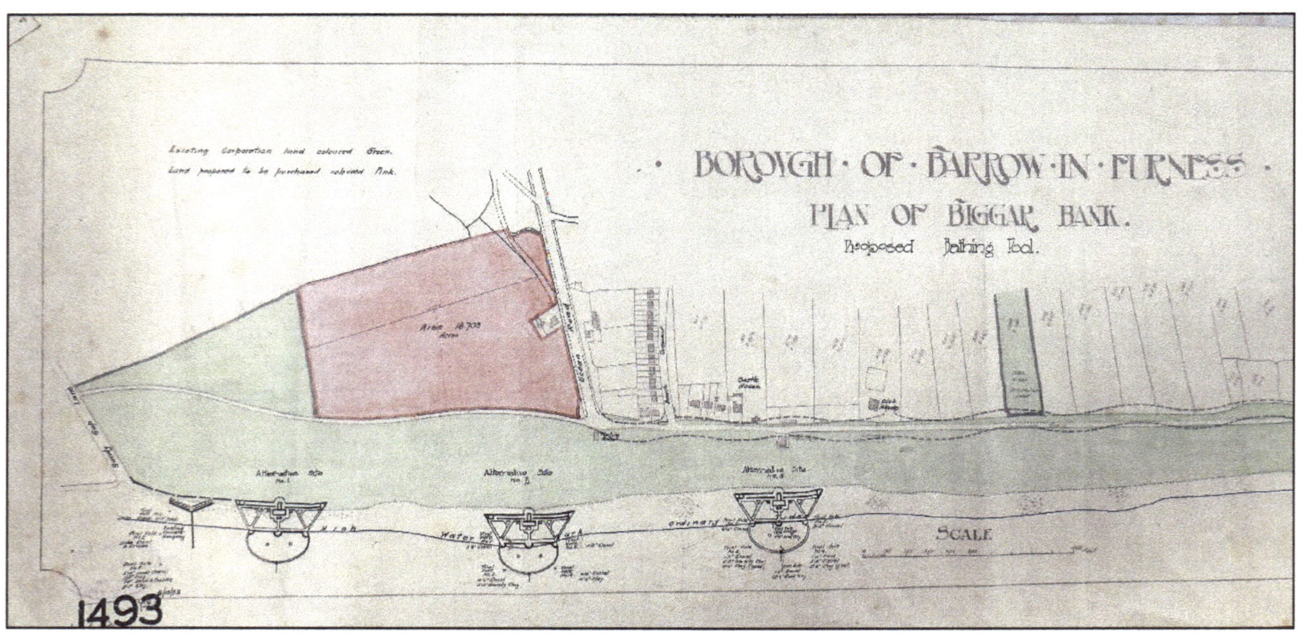

Possible sites for a bathing pool in 1922.   (Cumbria Archives BA/S/BC/D5/87)

In June 1930 it was proposed to open a bathing pool on Biggar Bank,[358] and it opened on 20 June 1931.[359] It was open each summer season - Whit to September - and swimming galas were held there. Alongside the bathing pool were a yachting pool and a children's paddling pool. The pool was popular until the mid-1960s when it closed.[360] It was demolished a couple of years later and the paddling pool filled in in 1993.[361]

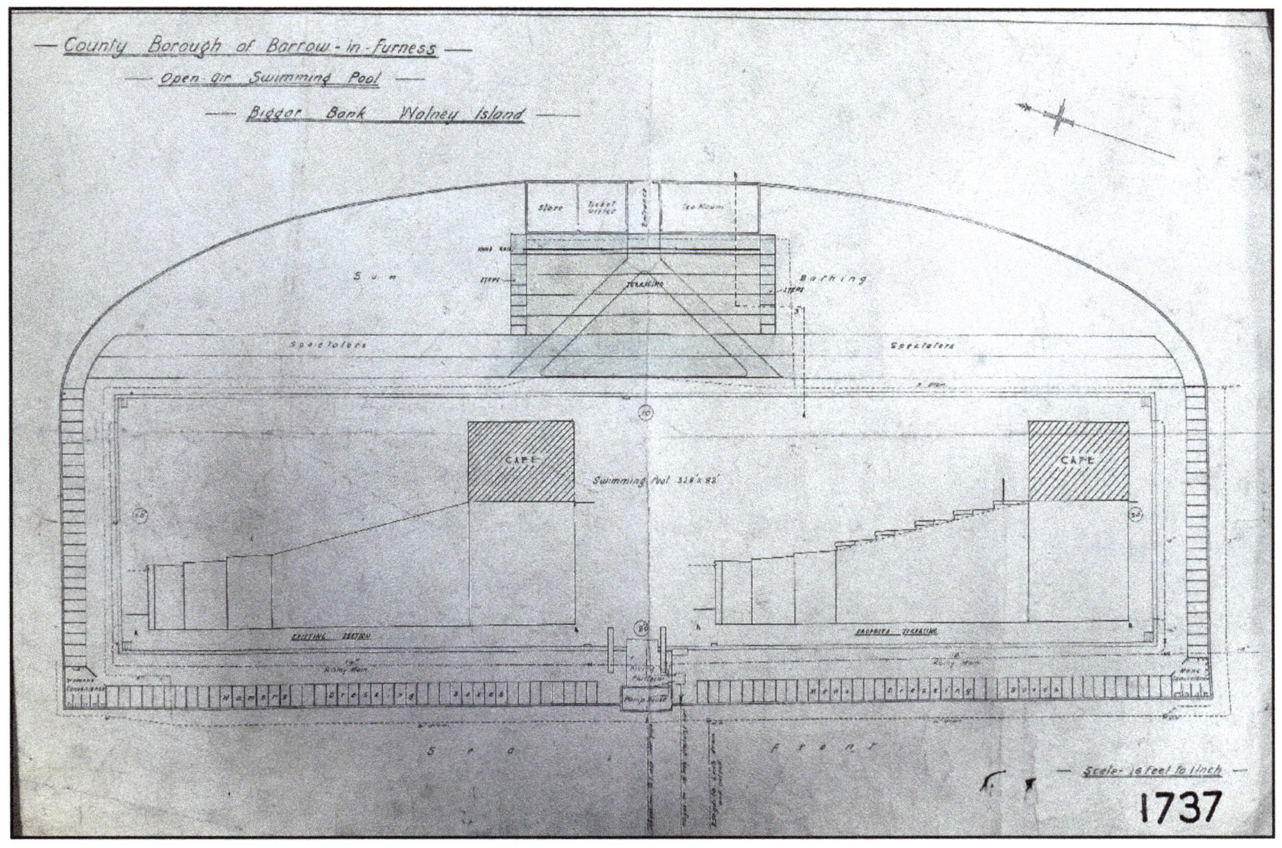

Swimming Pool plan 1940.   (Cumbria Archives. BA/S/BC/D4/175)

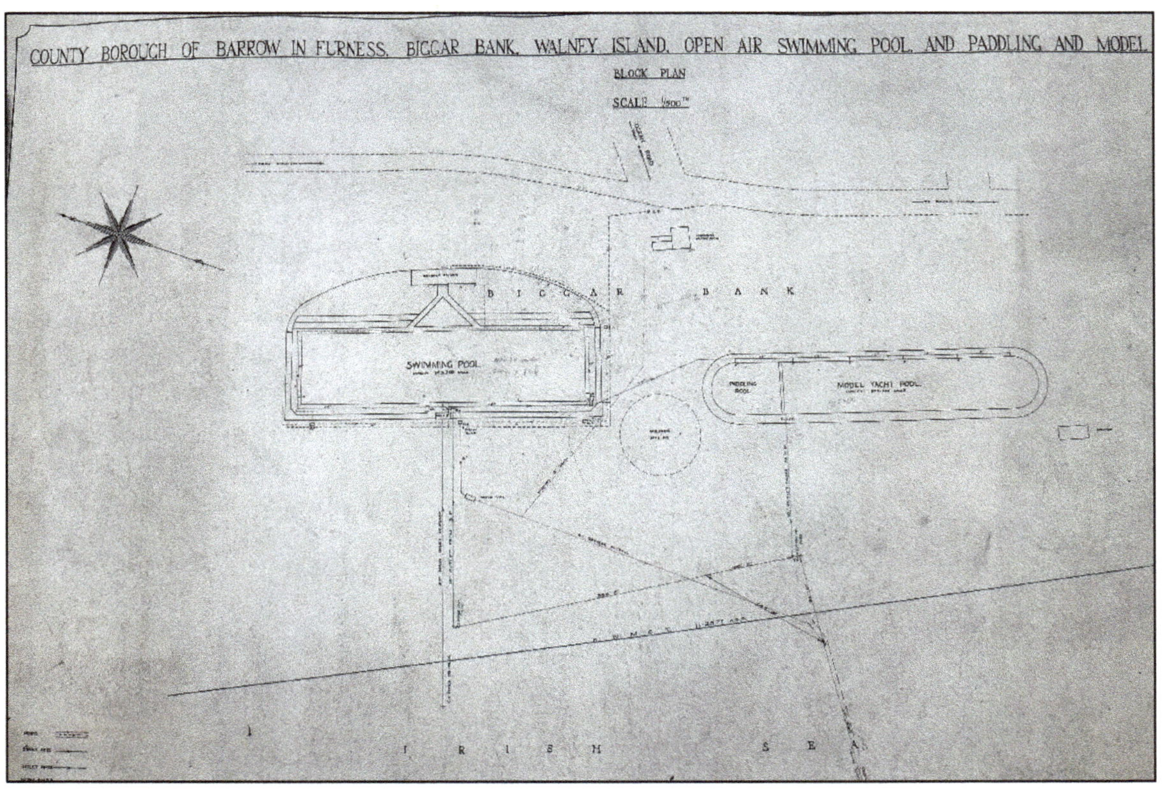

Swimming Pool and Yachting/Paddling Pool plan c1935. (Cumbria Archives BA/S/BC/D4/27)

Sankey Family Photography Collection No A556. © Cumbria Archives

In May 1939 an amusement park and play beach was opened at Biggar Bank[362] and a couple of cafes were set on land across the road from the Pavilion- one named Binder's and the other named Helling's. There was also a Brucciani's café.

I can find no mention of the Play Beach after 1946.

Was this the last straw?

> **GALE REMOVES ROOF**
>
> At the height of yesterday afternoon's gale, part of the roof of the Dodgem track at the Walney Island Play Beach Barrow, was blown off and carried through the air on to some adjoining greenhouses. An electricity pylon was also brought down and damage caused to a considerable amount of cable. Earlier in the day, Mr H.C. Gurney, general manager of the Play Beach sustained a head wound through being struck by a door blown off by the wind.
>
> **Lancashire Evening News 6 June 1946**

Schools/ Education

In 1662 the curate of St Mary's, Thomas Thompson, was licensed to teach boys at Walney. It is assumed he taught in the chapel.[363] Thomas Thompson was curate for 47 years until he died in 1709. By the early 18th century there was a 'chapel cess'[H] payment made for repairs to the church and schoolroom.[364] The curate still acted as schoolmaster into the 19th century.[365] As was mentioned in the North Scale section, there was a Dame School on one map but no further information can be found on when that was or who ran the school.

A purpose-built school was established on the Promenade in 1856 and was opened in March 1857 by Mrs Michaelson. It had been built in memory of her husband, T.Y.P. Michaelson, who had died young. The school was said to accommodate between 80 and 100 children.[366]

Michaelson School.   c1899   Cumbria Archives Z/3384

Thomas (TYP) Michaelson, was born in Michaelson Hall on Barrow Island, in 1814. The family owned the whole of Barrow Island at that time.

Educated at Shrewsbury and Trinity College, Cambridge. Thomas was a magistrate and a Captain in the Furness Troup of the Yeomanry Cavalry. He died aged 41 in 1855.

The photo above is thought to show the teacher Mr Ryden, with about 30 girls in pinafores, and about 40 boys. There were no school dinners or free transport in those days and some of the scholars had travelled long distances, especially those from the North and South ends. In winter the lunch break was shortened to enable the school to close earlier so that the children could get home before darkness.[367]

As the building of Vickerstown significantly increased the population of the island from 1900 onwards, schooling became a serious problem. A temporary wooden school was erected on Latona Street for the tenants of North Vickerstown, with access from Back Latona Street.

A permanent school, Vickerstown School, opened on Latona Street in 1902,[368] with ten classrooms and accommodation for 600 children.

In the 1980s there was a plan to close Vickerstown School due to a declining roll. A campaign was fought by the parents, teachers and local community which successfully overturned the idea.

It moved to a new site on Mill Lane in 2011.[369] Its current capacity is 210 with 176 pupils in December 2023.[370]

[H] In Walney's case, the chapel cess was a rate paid by each tenant to support the upkeep of the chapel.

Vickerstown School 1986

The building was demolished and the site is now housing.

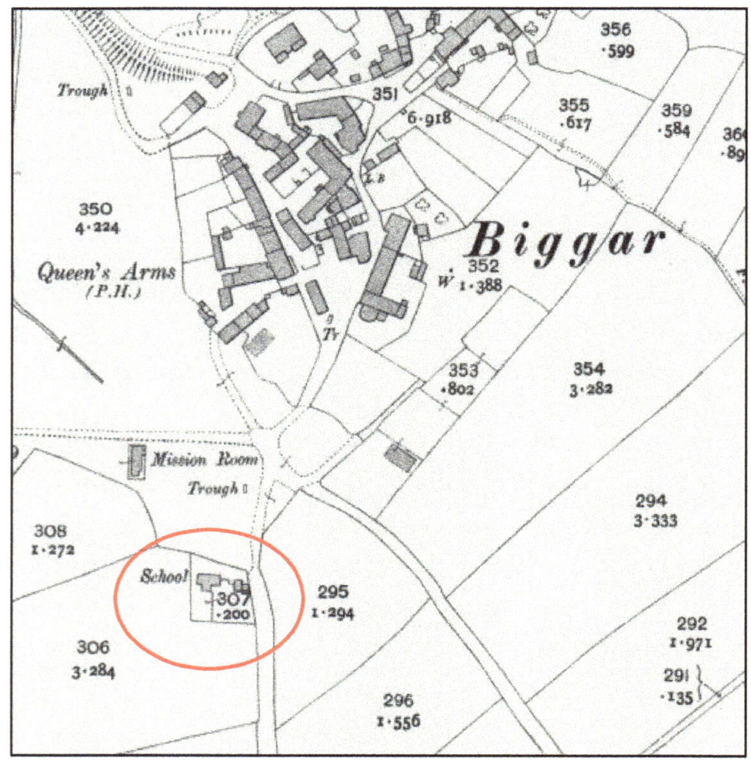

Another temporary wooden structure (circled in the map left), was erected close to Biggar Village for the children of South Vickerstown, Tummerhill, Biggar and the South End farms and the Salt Works. In 1900 the average attendance was 19 children.[371]

It had been intended for Mr Coulton Hunter of the South End to transport the children of the salt workers to the school, but owing to the condition of the road between the Salt Works and Biggar he found it impossible to do so. Alderman Cox said that there was *'as much chance of getting the road into repair as if he greased a rainbow, and tried to get a man in the moon.'*[372]

Ocean Road School opened in a temporary building in 1905, before a permanent structure opened on 28 August 1917.[373] In 1979 it merged with the Secondary Modern School at Sandy Gap (opened 1958). to become Walney Comprehensive. The original Ocean Road School building was demolished in 1993. The comprehensive currently has a capacity of 900 pupils with 479 enrolled in 2023.[374]

Ocean Road School demolition 1993. The two front doors were BOYS on the left and GIRLS right.

South Walney Primary School opened on 27 April 1954[375]and had 191 pupils on roll as of December 2023, with a capacity of 240.[376]
North Walney Primary opened, on Mill Lane, on 4th September 1956 and moved to new premises nearby in the early 1990s. It has a capacity of 161 pupils, but only 24 pupils in December 2023.[377] It was announced in March 2024 that the school was to close with effect from 31 August 2024 due to falling rolls.[378]

St Columba's Catholic School opened in 1916 with a church attached. When the new church opened in 1958, the school transferred to the old church building. New classrooms were constructed in 2020. It has a capacity of 240 pupils, with 204 pupils in December 2023.[379]

The Richard Brunskill Special School on Moor Tarn Lane opened in 1963 and closed in 1991. It was replaced by George Hastwell Special School with a capacity of 90, and had 87 pupils in December 2023.[380]

Golf Course

The first golf on the island was played by Scotsmen who came to Barrow when the Barrow Flax and Jute Works opened. That, and Barrow Shipbuilding Company's need for workers, resulted in large numbers of people from Dundee and the Clyde areas coming to Barrow.[381] They originally played on Biggar Bank.

Putting at Biggar Bank c1920s. Sankey Family Photography Collection No A120 © Cumbria Archives

A Golf Club first appeared on Biggar High Bank around 1872, although documentary records don't appear until 1875. [383]

The sixth oldest club in the country, they played a six-hole course, then nine, rising to 18 holes today.[384] The current course is laid out on the west side of the island between Walney School and Earnse Bay Caravan Park. At one time the club house, a converted deck cabin off a liner, was at the end of Sandy Gap,[385] but a new clubhouse (as per the photo below), was opened on 8 January 1916. Furness Golf Club celebrated its 150th anniversary in 2022.

Furness Golf Club House c1921 Sankey Family Photography Collection No 7400 © Cumbria Archives

As well as the main golf course there had been a miniature golf course at Sandy Gap, this was opened by the Prince of Wales (who abdicated as King in 1936), on one of his visits to Barrow in 1927.

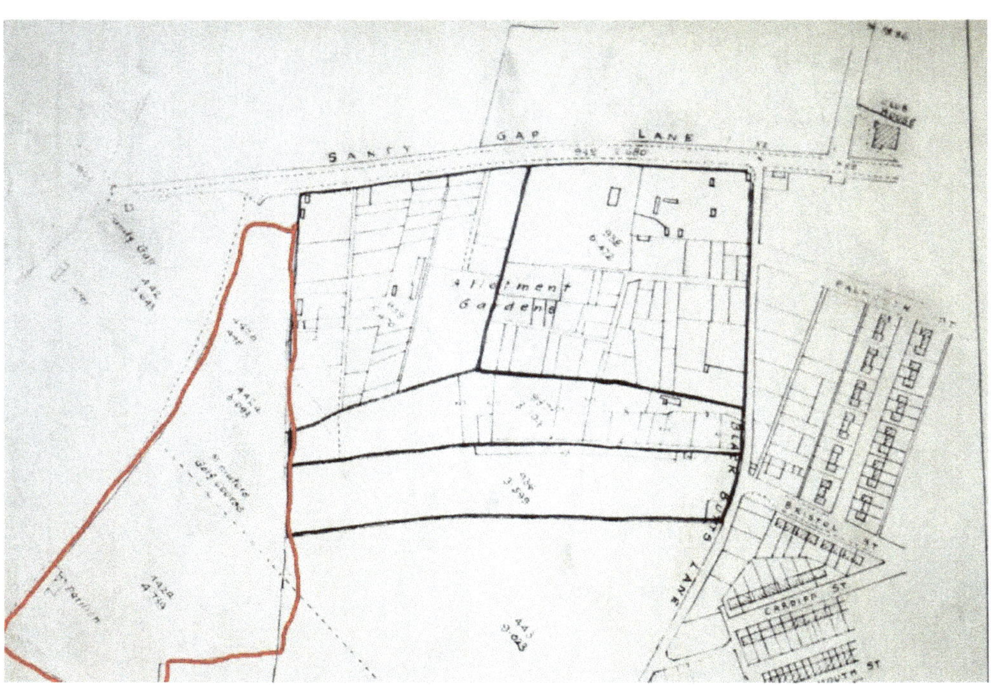

Detail showing the site of the Miniature Golf Course outlined in red. (Cumbria Archives BA/S/A/6)

The Prince of Wales opening the miniature golf on Walney on 29 June 1927.

Sankey Family Photography Collection No TP54

© Cumbria Archives

Library

A library was established by the Isle of Walney Estates Company in 1902 at Vickerstown Public Hall, Chapel Lane.[386] The library opened Mondays, Wednesdays, and Fridays 7.30pm to 9.00pm.

Librarians were Messrs. Stabler and Paitson.

Library at Vickerstown.

The Library Committee, acting in conjunction with the Isle of Walney Estates' Co., have established a branch library in Vickerstown, and we understand that through the courtesy of the Company, one of the rooms of the Vickerstown Public Hall has been fitted up to receive 500 books. Mr. W. E. Stabler and Mr. S. Paitson have, we beleive, been appointed Librarians. The library will be opened shortly and will, it is needles to say, supply a much felt want.

The proof reader missed a couple of errors here.

In 1943 a Young Men's Christian Association (YMCA), canteen was erected on the Promenade in James Dunn Park. It was converted into a community hall and library in 1948. A purpose-built library was built on Central Drive in about 1970.[387]

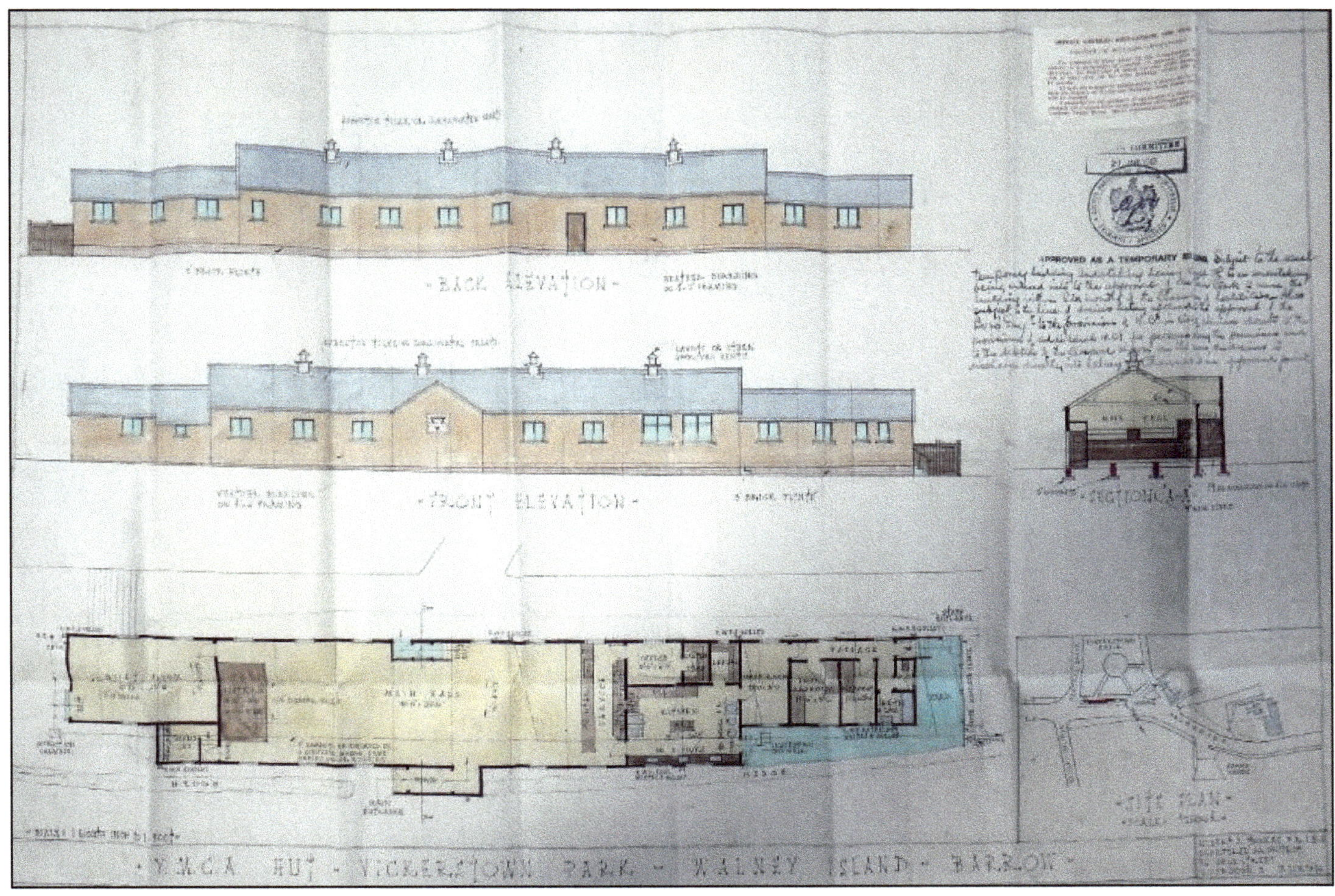

YMCA Plan January 1942. (Cumbria Archives Plan No 1943)

Religious History

Parochial organisation

From the Middle Ages, Walney was part of the ancient parish of Dalton, situated within the Archdeaconry of Richmond and under the jurisdiction of the Diocese of York. The Act of Uniformity of 1559 imposed a fine of 1s on all who should absent themselves from church on Sundays and Holydays. In 1563 a commission was established, led by the Bishop of Chester, to enforce this act across the diocese. The archdeaconry was assigned to the Diocese of Chester from 1537 until 1856, at which point it was transferred to the see of Carlisle.

A chapel-of ease on Walney is known to have existed by 1577.

++++

A 'chapel of ease' is a church building other than a main parish church. It is deliberately sited to be more accessible to certain parishioners. It made religious observance and rites such as funerals more convenient for those parishioners. For example, they no longer had to carry coffins over a great distance.

++++

It has been suggested that this chapel was one of several chapels built in the Furness area as a result of the Royal Commission of 1563.[388] The chapel, rebuilt in 1852, was subsequently referred to as a church from 1856. Its dedication to St Mary was officially recorded in 1873.[389]

Advowson,[J] Income and Endowment

The vicar of Dalton was the patron. In 1717, it was said that the inhabitants had long subscribed an annual sum of £9 14s. to pay for a curate, this amount being based on a tax of 13½d. for each tenement.[390] There was a benefaction through Queen Anne's Bounty in 1750.[391] In 1851 the endowment was recorded as £80.[392]

Religious life

A chapel of ease would have been much needed given the distance and difficulties of travelling to Dalton Parish Church. Dalton church was first mentioned in 1194 in a confirmation by Pope Celestine III.[393] Walney was served by the church there for many years.[394]

The exact lifespan of the fabric of the Elizabethan chapel before its rebuilding in 1852 is uncertain. According to the Religious Census of 1851, the existing chapel was ambiguously described as being 200-300 years old.[395] It has been said that the chapel was rebuilt and extended in the late 17th century, with a tower added about 1744.[396] The pre-1852 chapel was rectangular in plan, built of cobblestones, roughcast outside and whitewashed inside and out. There were three windows on the south side, two on the north side and one at the east end – all being square with wooden frames. A square tower which served as a porch and a belfry with a bell, projected from the west end.[397]

[J] Advowson is the religious right to recommend a member of the Anglican clergy for a vacant benefice, or to make such an appointment.

A reconstruction by local historian Harper Gaythorpe of the pre-1852 church.
Cumbria Archives   Z/2452

In 1650 there was a 'reader' at St Mary's, paid for by the inhabitants.[398] In 1652 it was noted that the minister was a Mr. Soutwerke, a Presbyterian (1649-1657). In 1652, George Fox attempted to speak with him after a service *'but he got away, and would not be seen at his house.'*[399] Thomas Thomson was appointed in 1661, he died in 1709 after having held the curacy for 47 years.[400] After that, several curates came and went, each staying for a few years.[401] This changed with the arrival of Samuel Hunter in 1741, who served as perpetual curate for the next 61 years, resigning just before his death in 1802.[402]

The earliest Registers of Baptisms and Burials for St Mary's date back to Hunter's incumbency, starting in 1744, and he recorded that there was only one Roman Catholic on the island in 1780, a man who worked as a customs officer.[403] One of Hunter's assistant curates was John Harrison, who was already schoolmaster on the island before taking holy orders.[404] Hunter's son-in-law, and one-time assistant curate, John Troughton, served as incumbent from 1805 until 1839.[405]

John Park was a non-graduate who arrived as incumbent in 1846 and remained until his death in 1875.[406] In 1851 he recorded 150 sittings, of which 120 were free. The usual attendance was 100 on Sunday morning, with 32 children at Sunday School, 40 in the congregation for the afternoon service and 32 at afternoon Sunday School.[407]

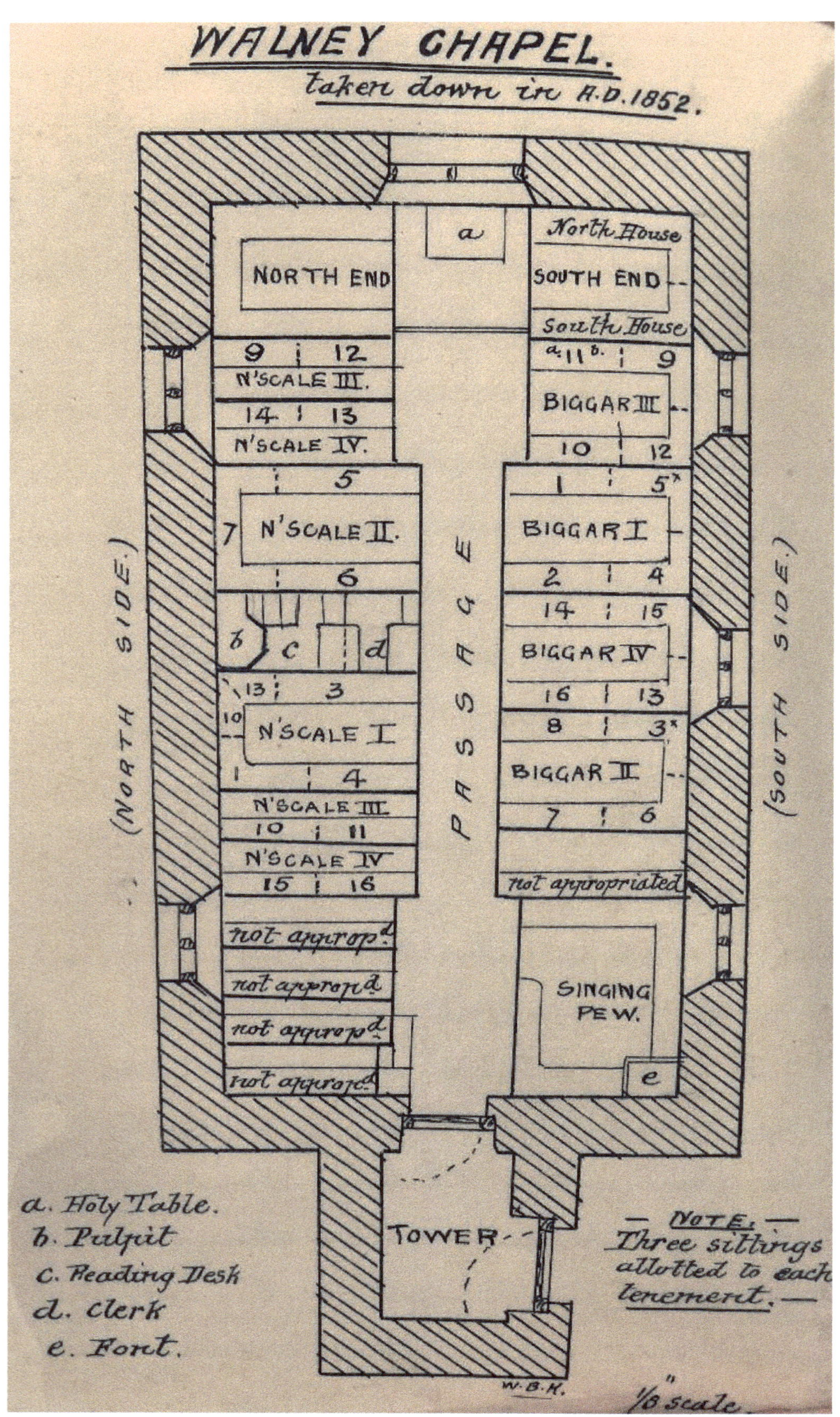

The layout of the pre-1852 chapel showing the seating arrangements.
From *North Scale and Walney Chapel Registers,* Harper Gaythorpe and W.B. Kendall, 1898.
(Cumbria Archives.   Z/K/200)

The 1853 church.   Cumbria Archives   Z/3384 This chapel remained in use for 55 years.

'The fabric of the Chapel on the Isle of Walney, a township (including Piel Island,) in the Parish of Dalton-in-Furness, having been for some time in a falling condition, and having pronounced by experienced builders to be unsafe for the congregation to assemble in for public worship, it has been deemed advisable to take down and rebuild the same. It is thought desirable, also at the same time, to enlarge the edifice according to the want of church accommodation at present existing......'

SUBSCRIPTIONS in aid of the good work will be thankfully received by the Rev. J. PARK, Isle of Walney.

Soulby Advertiser 5th December 1850

The old chapel was demolished in June 1852 and the replacement chapel was opened on 27 February 1853, [409] following the raising of the money, (£500), by public subscription and a charge of £3 10s per tenement.[410] This chapel served the purposes of its Walney congregation for the next 55 years.

The increase in the population of Walney after the building of Vickerstown made it necessary to build an even larger church. Through the efforts of the then Rev Charles Lacy Hulbert, a new church, Walney St Mary's, was built on a site adjoining the existing churchyard, the land donated by Vickers Ltd.[411] It opened in 1908 and was dedicated on 3 October in that year.[412] The chapel of 1853 was demolished sometime after, (the Chancellor of Carlisle Consistory Court gave permission for its demolition in September 1922.)[413]

The new church, constructed in 1908, was designed by Paley & Austin. Crafted from coursed, squared sandstone with ashlar embellishments, the main roof boasts red tiles, while the side aisles are roofed in slate. The nave is made up of five bays, accompanied by a single pitched south porch and aisles with square-headed, mullioned windows. The chancel, featuring an arched ceiling with a bow-string truss, spans two bays and includes a single pitched south chapel and a north vestry. [414] In 1928, the west end was completed, and further expansion occurred in 1930/31, once again under the design expertise of Paley and Austin. [415] It is a grade II listed building.

Paley & Austin of Lancaster, 1907. (Cumbria Archives. BPR/20/C/6/14)
One of the designs for the 1908 church which was unsuccessful.
There were a number of others too.

St Mary's church which opened in 1908. The west end was not completed until many years later.

You can see the 'temporary' wooden end, which lasted until 1928.

Sankey Family Photography Collection No 449   © Cumbria Archives

The two St Mary's churches side by side c1908.
Sankey Family Photography Collection No 448   © Cumbria Archives

The first non-conformist place of worship on the island was the Methodist New Connexion Chapel on Teasdale Road, North Scale. It was built on land bought from local builder William Gradwell[416]and opened in March 1881.[417] It was built in a 'Gothic style of Architecture' in a way that would allow for an extension if needed.[418] It could seat 120 worshippers.

++++

Incidentally, the name of the road was initially Teasdale Street as mentioned in a *Barrow Herald* article on the building of the chapel. It is not known when the name changed.

++++

Religious services ended at the chapel in 1907.[419] It was demolished sometime after 1979, the year the photo below was taken.[420]

One of the leaders of the Teasdale Road chapel, in a report dated 1904, stated;

> *'What our church may be in the future days is beyond my power to say, but it would be a great pity to neglect in any way the Sunday School or the Night Service. We have a work to do in North Scale. The working men on Walney – broadly speaking – are without God & consequently without hope. The Sunday for the most part is spent by the fire with some newspaper in hand. From the indifferent spirit they need to be aroused.'* [421]

Mission Hall at Biggar c1899. (Cumbria Archives. Z/3384)

In 1897 a Mission Hall was built at Biggar village. It served a dual purpose as a community centre and a church, with sliding doors at one end to close off the altar. Built of corrugated iron and wood, it was said to have been paid for by the residents of the South End.[422] In 1947, permission was given for the hall to be disposed of and after advertising in the Evening Mail it was sold to the tenants of Queen's Park Tenants' Association of Millom for £100. It served there until the early 1980s before being demolished.

Local Baptists had to make do with a sod hut built near Southend Farm on Berry's estate around 1853.[423] (See South End map earlier).

A Wesleyan Methodist church was started on the Promenade with the laying of a foundation stone on Easter Monday, 4 April 1904.[427] Opened in 1905,[428] it stood on land donated by The Isle of Walney Estates Company. [429] In 1998 the congregation moved into a nearby building on Warren Street, with the old church later being converted into six flats.   Seen here in 1986.

Plans for a Presbyterian church on Walney were drawn up by local architect William Moss Settle in 1905.[430] Built on Douglas Street in 1907, it opened in 1909 and closed in the late 1970s later becoming the Kingdom Hall of Jehovah's Witnesses. It is currently a bed and breakfast hotel.

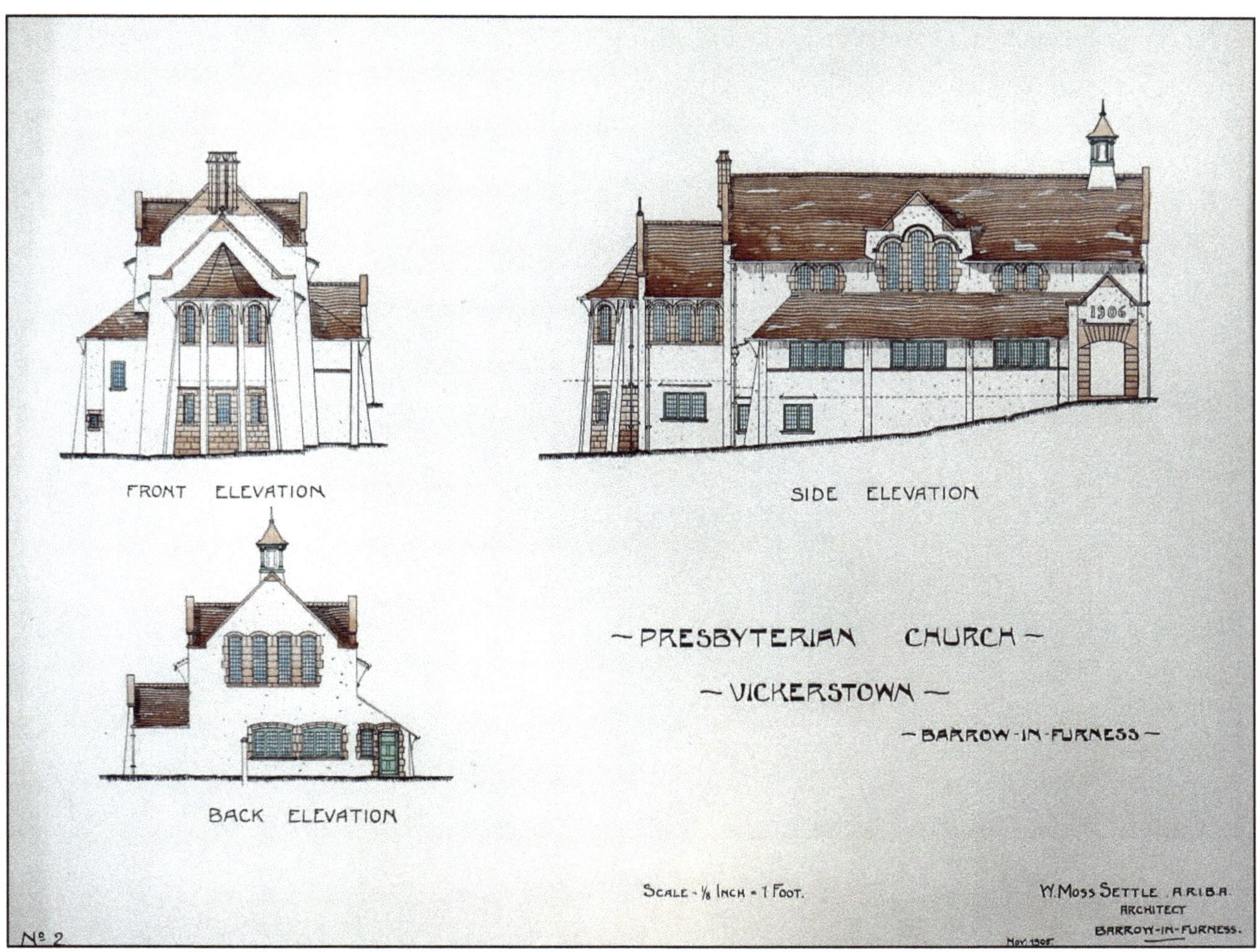

Presbyterian plans for a church 1905.   (Cumbria Archives BDFC/P/W/14)

A Congregational Mission Hall was opened in Knox Street in 1902.[432]

The Roman Catholic church of St Columba's was first built as a chapel in 1916 and was served from St Patrick's on Barrow Island.[433] The current church building had its foundation stone laid on 18 November 1957.[434] The church opened with a Christmas midnight mass in 1958.[435]

St Columba's. Seen here in 1986.

A Gospel Hall opened opposite the Co-operative on Amphitrite Street on 4 September 1966. In 2024 it is Spring Mount Church.

Over the years the religious health of the Walney community has been well served. Today, in a reflection of the times we are in, few of these establishments remain open and their influence on the lives of the people has diminished enormously. We are no longer fined for not attending Sunday services, for example.

The War Years

During both World Wars, the daily lives of all Barrovians were severely impacted.

During the First World War the number of workers employed in Vickers for example peaked at 31,000, with many of the new employees being women. Mainly employed in the New Shell Shop, which opened in 1915, they were from Barrow and elsewhere. The vast majority of Vickers workers were exempted from military service as their work was vital for the war effort.

There were shortages of potatoes, meat, sugar, beer and butter. On one occasion, the headmaster of Walney School notes that a number of pupils were absent - due to there being a delivery of margarine and meat, the children were queueing for their families.

> **January 23 1917 Ocean Road School Log Book.**
>
> The attendance, which until the last few weeks has been very good, is now being seriously affected by absence of scholars for the purpose of standing in the food queues. Last Friday morning the percentage fell to 83.4. This morning the percentage is 87.2, owing to the arrival of a consignment of margarine at one shop and meat at another. These figures contrast with a percentage of 95.6 yesterday afternoon when food queues were not formed.

School Log Book (Cumbria Archives. BDS/75/1-2)

The perennial problem of where to house the extra workers coming into the town was partly solved by the increase in the numbers of lodgers taken in by the local populace, and on Walney, in 1916, there was an agreement to build another 90 houses on Vickerstown. In 1917 the problem was just as acute and there was an agreement with the Ministry of Munitions for 500 permanent and 500 semi-permanent houses in Barrow, including 150 in Vickerstown.[436] Anzac Avenue and Verdun Avenue were built in partnership with the Ministry of Munitions, and extra houses were built on Douglas Street and Lord Roberts' Street amongst others.[437] The Bankfield Hotel at North Scale was used to house 80 men and a temporary hostel was built on Walney to house 104 women.[438] This hostel was on Church Lane and had been previously used to house women workers from the Isle of Man who came to Barrow to learn how to make airship fabric.[439]

North of Cows Tarn Lane, and West of Red Ley Lane was out of bounds to the public in 1916, probably because of the Airship Sheds, [440]and Biggar Bank was a prohibited area too.

Work had continued at the airship shed on Walney throughout the First World War – despite the submarine attack mentioned previously.

After the First World War, a number of camps, which had been occupied by soldiers at Mill Lane, Biggar Bank and at the North End were sold off as Government Surplus. A Sergeant's Mess, 70 feet by 15 feet by 10 feet, and a Regimental Institute Kitchen, 60 feet by 15 feet by 10 feet are examples of the lots for sale. Gilbert Brown and Co. of Anson Street, Barrow, was contracted to take down and load these buildings on to the railway at prices from £32 for the two buildings quoted.[441]

The Second World War brought the airfield and its 1500+ personnel who were billeted on site.

Mines were laid on the west side of Walney, the Play Beach was closed, Biggar Bank was out of bounds, as was the land south of Biggar village and mines were also laid on the 9th, 11th and 12th fairways of the golf course. Air raid shelters were built all over the island, in back streets and at schools. Fire watching posts were set up and a home guard was in operation.

Barrage balloons were tethered above Mill Lane, Moor Tarn Lane, Tummerhill and South of Biggar Village.

Bombs were dropped on Walney on the night of 29/30 August 1940 and again on the 24 September. Four High Explosive (HE) bombs hit Walney on 14 March 1941 with no casualties reported. The Barrow Blitz of May - June 1941 damaged many houses in Barrow and caused 83 civilian deaths, but luckily none on Walney. A bomb map from then shows a 'stitch' of bombs across Walney Channel and close to the Castle House, dropped on the night of 4/5 May 1941, and one HE bomb near the airfield, but no casualties were reported. The same map shows a number of bombs and two mines were dropped near Biggar village.

Many children were evacuated in early 1941, but by July, with the worst of our local blitz over, they began to come back home. The last air raid siren heard was on 25 March 1943.[442]

Victory in Europe (VE).Day was celebrated on 8 May 1945 with street parties but no official town celebration.

The RAF stopped operations at Walney Airfield on 15 June 1946. After the war, when clearing the mines from Furness Golf Course, two soldiers were unfortunately killed.

See the previous section (Page 97), on Walney Airfield, for the effects on local people of the lack of housing after the war had ended.

One of the three Second World War *fire-watchers' shelters* now on Furness Golf Course.

These were constructed from bullet-proof steel plate and would protect those inside from bomb blasts, shrapnel etc. They were used by fire watchers, ARP wardens and police. Where these three were actually sited during the war is unknown.

They have a more mundane use nowadays, being strategically placed to help male golfers who are caught short.

Miscellaneous bits and pieces

It is inevitable in a condensed history such as this that many things must be left out. For any writer it is a difficult choice to decide on what to include and what to omit. Below are a few interesting titbits.

What might have been.

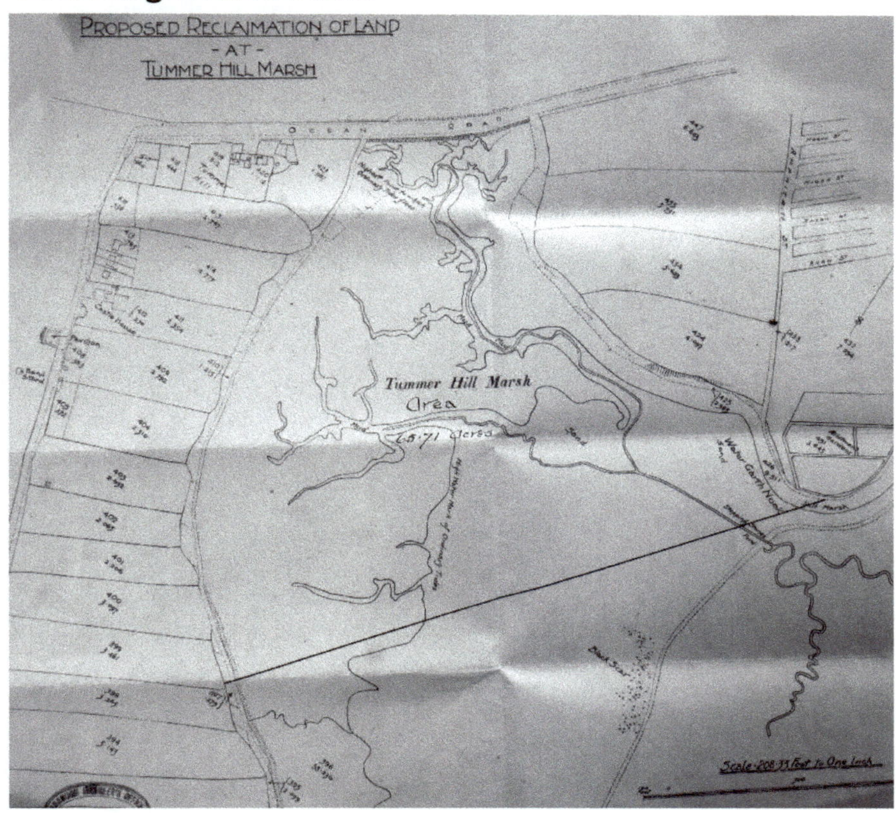

There was a proposal to reclaim the land within Tummerhill marsh in November 1920. (BDBUC/39/71 Cumbria Archives)

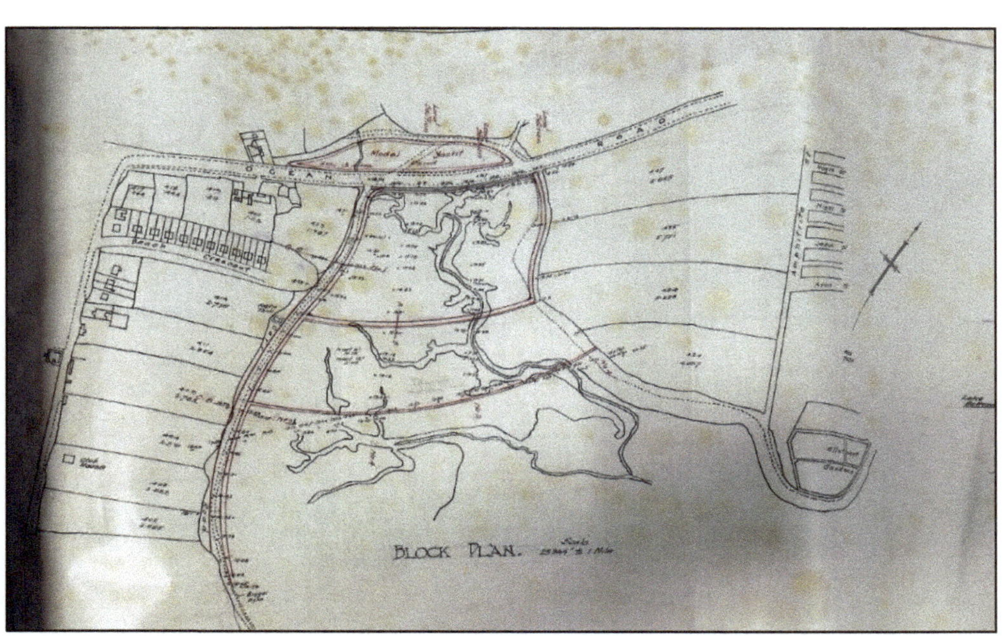

A marine Lake Proposal for Tummerhill Marsh 1930.

This never came to fruition.

(Cumbria Archives BA/S/BC/D5/89)

A proposal by Vickers to fill Tummerhill marsh with spoil from Walney channel was refused by the council in 1970.[443]

Another idea for Tummerhill, in 1893, was to put swimming baths there.

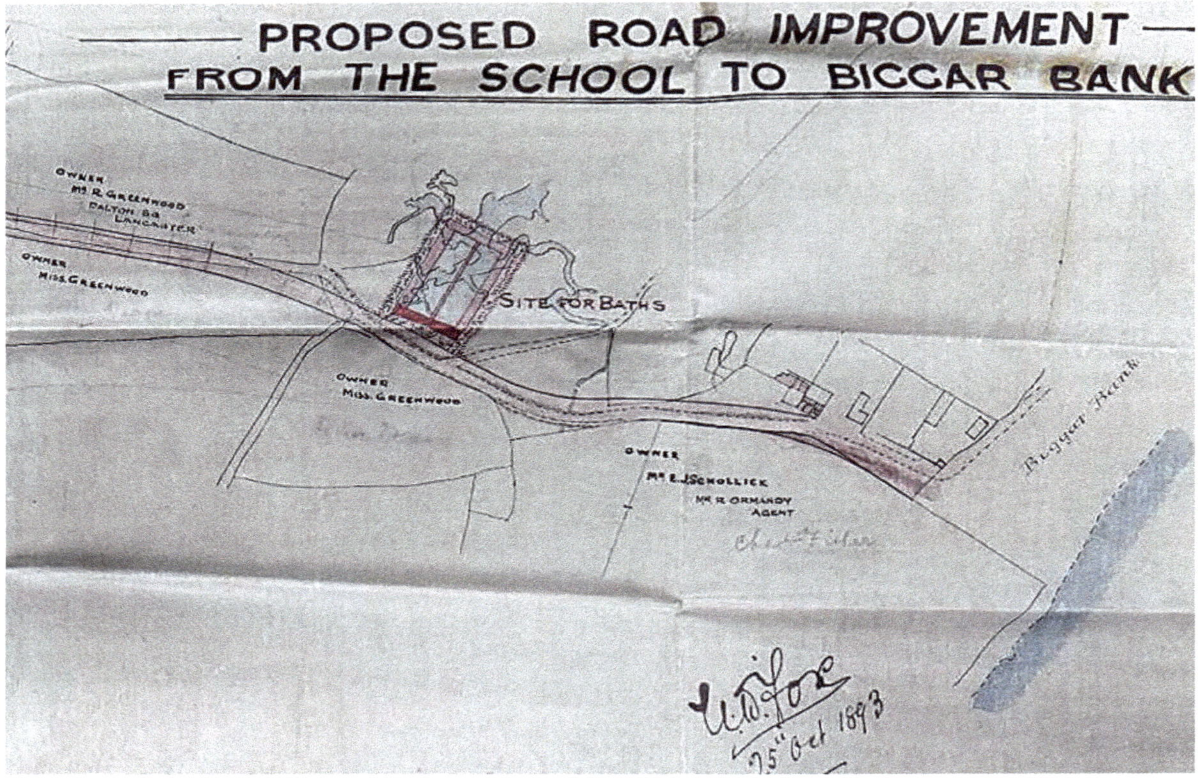

From Road improvements to Biggar 1893. (Cumbria Archives BA/C/3/4/14)

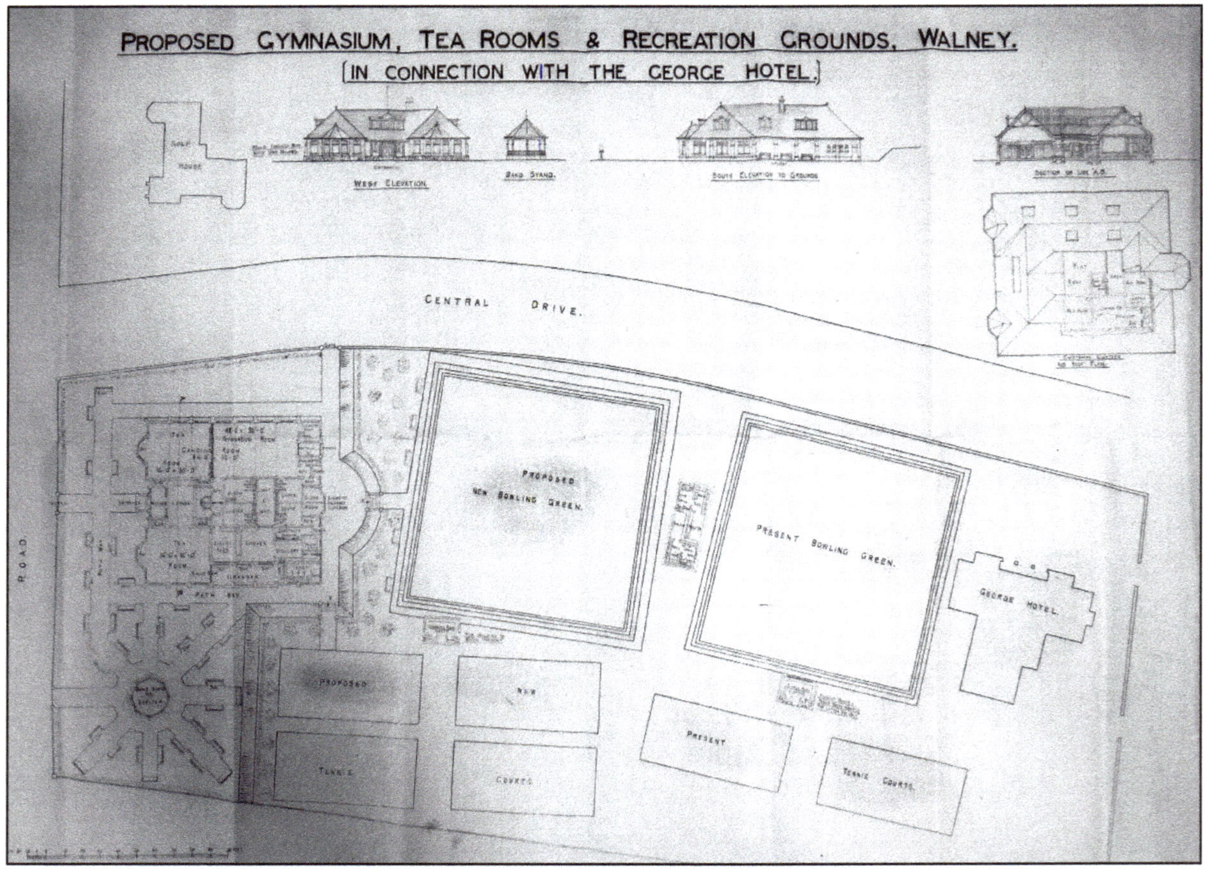

An undated proposal to considerably extend The George hotel grounds never went ahead. (Cumbria Archives Z911/1)

A grand hotel, not given a name, which never saw the light of day - proposed for Biggar Bank. c1931 (Cumbria Archives. BDX/502)

If any of the proposals, ideas, or any of the other suggestions in this section had been realised, the development of Walney would have unfolded quite differently from what actually occurred. I'm sure that any reclaimed land would have been built on for example. How would the building of more hotels on Biggar Bank have affected the peaceful enjoyment we have today? Would a pool at Tummerhill have fared any better than the one on Biggar Bank. We'll never know.

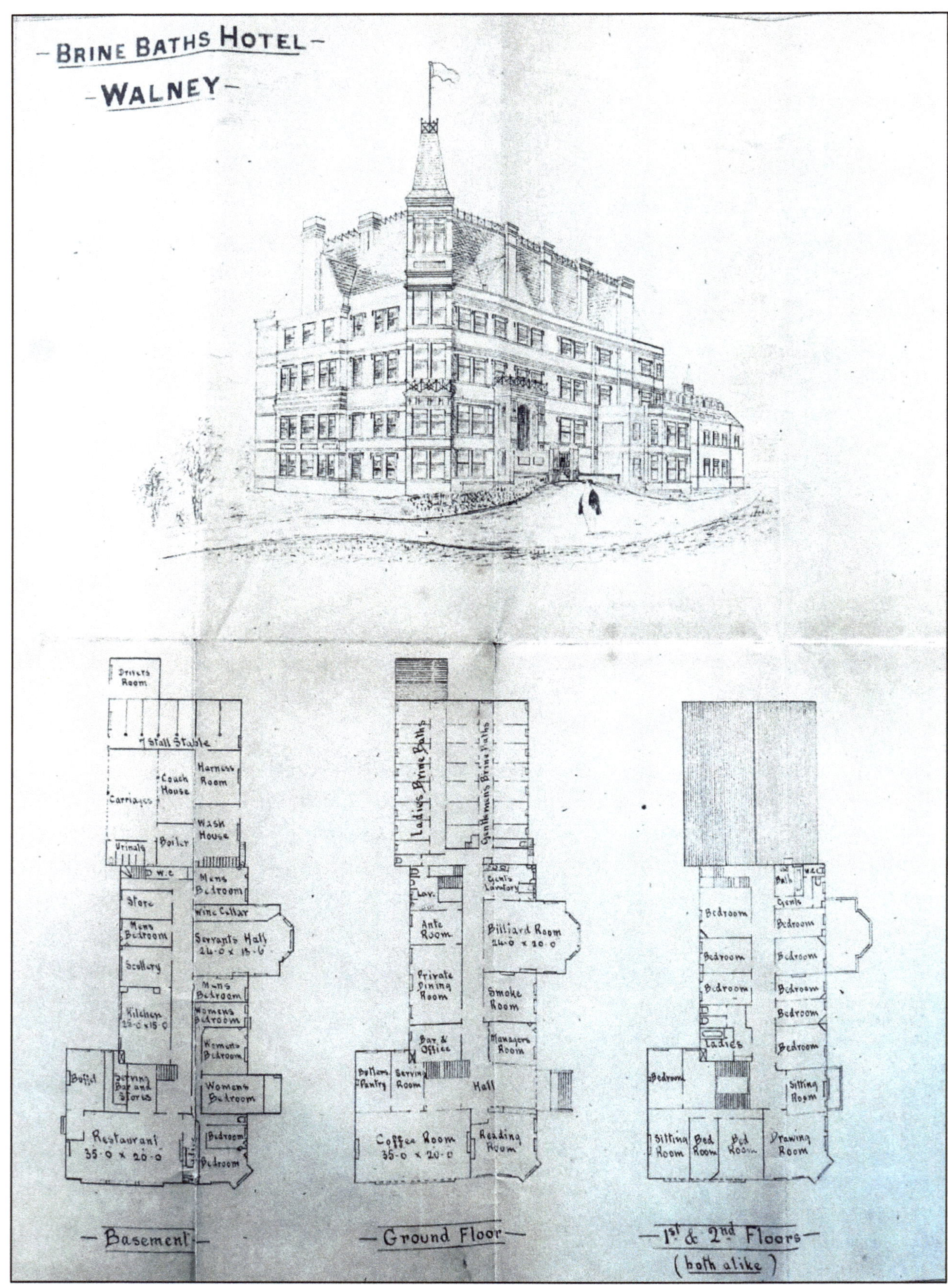

Brine Baths Hotel Biggar. (Cumbria Archives.   BDBUC/45/9/23)

An 1898 plan of an idea for a Brine Baths Hotel at Biggar Bank to take advantage of the salt from the south-end. This never happened either.

An idea for the conversion of the Bankfield Hotel on Teasdale Road into a Brine Baths Hotel (see below), in 1924 never progressed beyond the adverts.

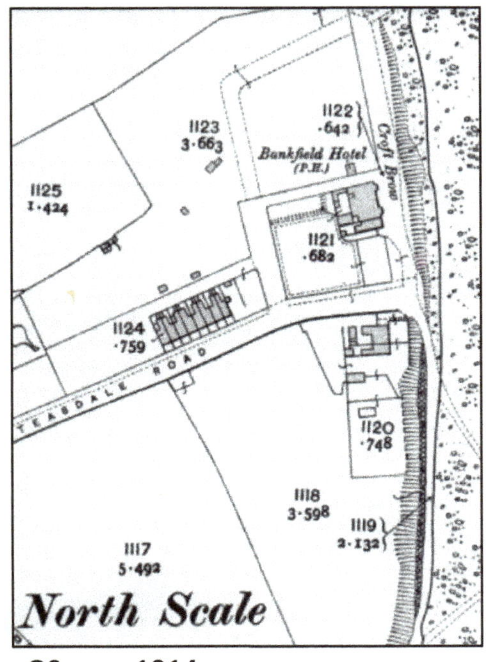

Bankfield Hotel to Brine Baths Hotel Prospectus 1924.
Cumbria Archives Z/319

The Bankfield Hotel had been built by the Neptune Company about 1895. It was taken over by the War Department during WWI.

OS map 1914

Even the enticing advert shown above didn't work. The Brine Baths idea of 1924 never materialised but The Bankfield did continue until 1937, when its licence was transferred to the Victoria Park Hotel, on Victoria Road, in Barrow.[444]

A proposed housing plan for Biggar Bank 1903/4– another idea which didn't come to fruition.

(Cumbria Archives Z/3014)

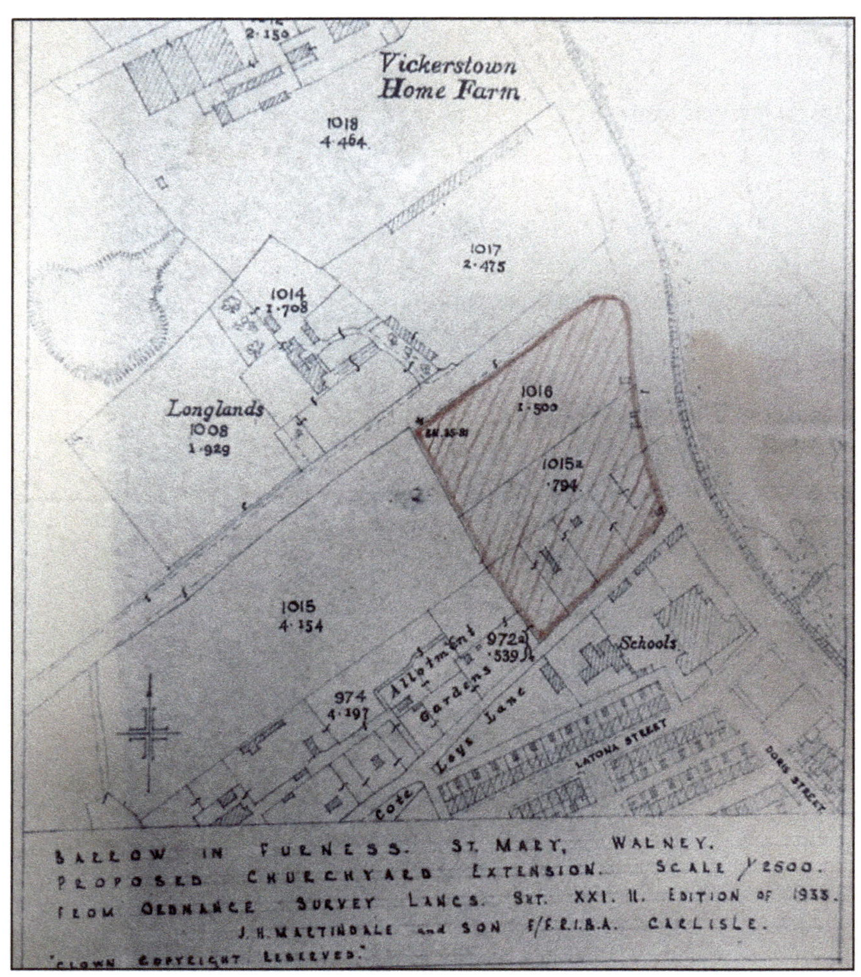

A 1930s proposal to build another church yard on the corner of the Promenade and Mill Lane, marked in red.

(Cumbria Archives. BDB/17/C/32)

Bungalows are now on this site.

The South End golf course

As has already been mentioned, golf came to Walney during the fight to free Biggar Bank for the people of the town. In 1902, a correspondent who signed themselves 'Walney' wrote an article for *Golf Illustrated*, in which it was proposed to lay out a golf course at the South End of Walney. He, (*I assume it was a man*), ventures that this is: -

> *'one of the finest stretches of golfing land that can be found anywhere. Nothing can exceed its beauty from a golfing point of view, nor its salubrity of its fine air.'*

> He goes on to say that the Duke of Buccleuch, the landowner, *'would give every facility to and generously assist any well-deserved scheme for developing the land for golfing purposes.'*

The writer invited Mr Harry Vardon, a professional golfer from Jersey who had won three British Opens and the 1900 US Open, to come and inspect the land and lay out a course, which he duly did and then played the next day. Mr Vardon stated he was impressed, and went on to describe the 18 holes he had laid out and played, saying he would *'certainly like to see this course started.'*[445] It didn't happen.

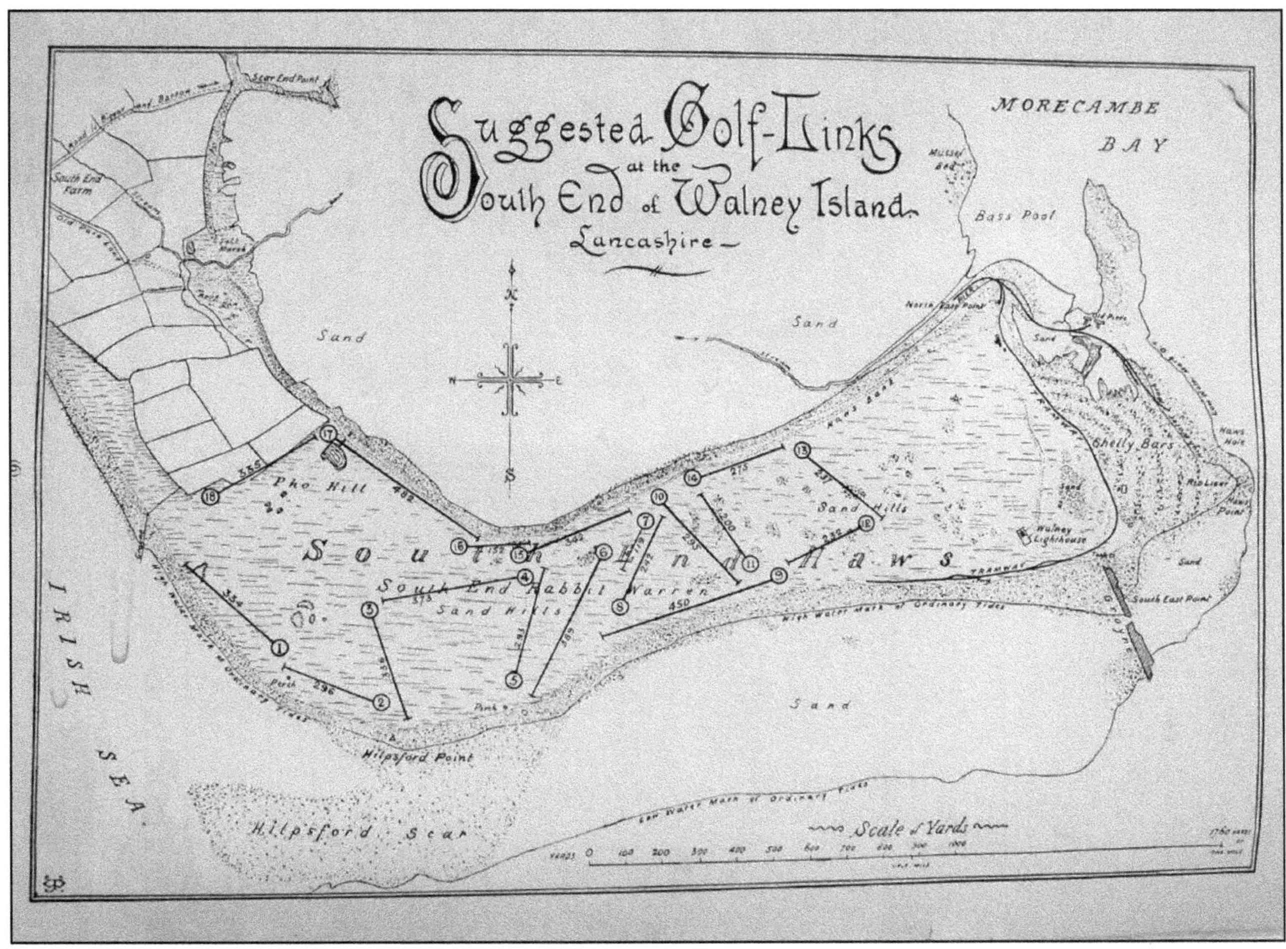

Plan from *Golf Illustrated,* January 3 1902

Racing

Biggar Bank has been used for many things over the years.

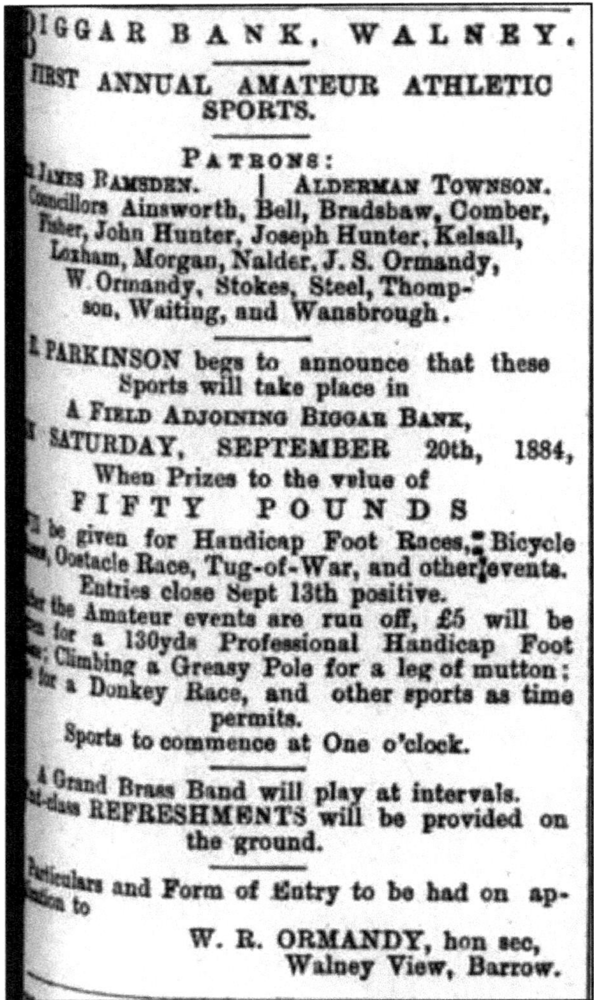

BIGGAR BANK, WALNEY.

FIRST ANNUAL AMATEUR ATHLETIC SPORTS.

PATRONS:

JAMES RAMSDEN. | ALDERMAN TOWNSON.
Councillors Ainsworth, Bell, Bradshaw, Comber, Fisher, John Hunter, Joseph Hunter, Kelsall, Lexham, Morgan, Nalder, J. S. Ormandy, W. Ormandy, Stokes, Steel, Thompson, Waiting, and Wansbrough.

R. PARKINSON begs to announce that these Sports will take place in

A FIELD ADJOINING BIGGAR BANK,

SATURDAY, SEPTEMBER 20th, 1884,

When Prizes to the value of

FIFTY POUNDS

will be given for Handicap Foot Races, Bicycle Race, Obstacle Race, Tug-of-War, and other events. Entries close Sept 13th positive.

After the Amateur events are run off, £5 will be given for a 130yds Professional Handicap Foot Race, Climbing a Greasy Pole for a leg of mutton; also for a Donkey Race, and other sports as time permits.

Sports to commence at One o'clock.

A Grand Brass Band will play at intervals. First-class REFRESHMENTS will be provided on the ground.

Particulars and Form of Entry to be had on application to

W. R. ORMANDY, hon sec,
Walney View, Barrow.

The owners of the ill-fated Sea-View Hotel held foot and bicycle races in 1884 when they advertised prizes of £50.

The same organisers ran horse races in April 1885.

WALNEY STEEPLECHASES.

On Monday a large number of people visited Biggar Bank, one of the special attractions being some pony steeplechases got up by Mr R. Parkinson, Sea View Hotel. The correct card showed four items, three of which promised to be very interesting. The prizes offered for each race were—1st, £1 and bridle; 2nd, 10s; the conditions of each race being one mile, over eight hurdles, run in heats. The results were as follows:—

Open Steeplechase for Ponies 13 hands and under, catch weight, one mile, over 8 hurdles—1st, £1 and handsome bridle; 2nd, 10s. 1st heat: Mr Riley's Polly 1, Mr Ormandy's Bendigo 0, Mr Westwood's Fanny 0; won easily. 2nd heat: Mr Parkinson's Soldier 1, Mr Hinck's Bobby 0; close race. Final: Polly beat Soldier by 100 yards.

Open Steeplechase for Ponies 12 hands and under, particulars as in above race. 1st heat: Mr Riley's Polly beat Mr Proctor's Parrafin, after a splendid race. 2nd heat: Mr Ormandy's Bendigo beat Mr Westwood's Fanny by 20 yards. Final: Polly beat Bendigo by a length.

Open Steeplechase for Ponies 14 hands and under, particulars same as first race. Soldier 1, Parrafin 2, Fanny 0; good second, poor third:

Another Pony Steeplechase for Ponies 14 hands and under brought out three competitors, Soldier winning easily.

The whole of the arrangements were carried out by Stewards Ormandy, Atkinson, Lawrence, Dickenson, and Tyson, Mr Woodburn officiating as starter, and Mr Bell as judge. The proceedings were enlivened by selections by the Volunteer Band.

The horse race course stood slightly to the south of the Pavilion but nearer to the beach.

Sankey Family Photography Collection A 148 © Cumbria Archives

Motor cycle racing at Biggar Bank in 1924.

Sankey Family Photography Collection. No A266. © Cumbria Archives.

A De-Havilland bi-plane DH6 in front of the Pavilion with a crowd of onlookers c1920.

Land Reclamation

There is one thing which didn't happen but which could have changed the course of history in the area. It would have changed the development of the town fundamentally and especially the layout of Walney.

There would have been no need for a ferry nor a bridge.[446]

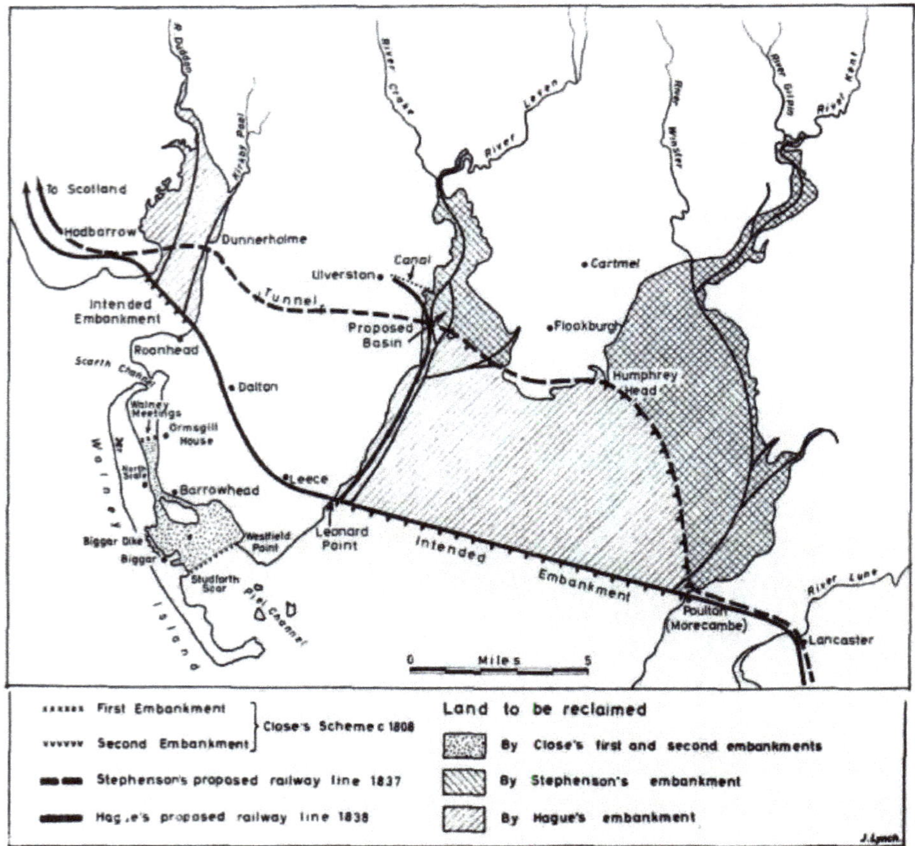

There had been a similar proposal for a railway embankment from Sandscale Haws to Haverigg in 1888 with reclaimed land behind.[447]

There had also been a plan for a railway embankment over Morecambe Bay around 1838.[448]

All three schemes seen here on a map by Bill Rollinson used to illustrate a talk in 1964.[449]

Other islands

Walney is not the only island in Walney Channel. If we start from **Piel Island**, then there is **Roa Island**, which ceased to be an island when John Abel Smith, a London banker and an MP, bought it from the trustees of Rampside Hall and then built a causeway from the mainland.

Alongside Roa Island is **Foulney**, which was connected to the causeway in 1884[450]by the Furness Railway Company, in order to protect Piel harbour. It too ceased to be an island. In 1885 there were plans to build a cholera hospital there.

Further up the channel is **Sheep Island**, a low-lying island which used to belong to the South End farms, and was used for grazing cattle. The island was fenced in by a low wall. Later, around 1890, an isolation hospital was built on the island, but it only ever had one patient – a seaman from a Spanish ship who had contracted Typhoid.[451] An isolation hospital built at Rakesmoor Lane in Barrow rendered this one obsolete and so it was taken as a residence by Captain Gracie and his wife.

Further north, on the east side of the channel is **Headin Haw** – which means Hidden Haw. Tiny, at only 270 square yards, it had a gunpowder magazine built on it at one time, used to store gunpowder from the works at Bouth and Lowwood.[452]

Dova Haw, originally called **Doufa Haw,** opposite the old slipways, is another tiny island, this time at only 120 square yards. At one time one of the fords crossed here. It later became the site of one of the navigation beacons of the channel.

Lastly was **Ramsey Island,** just below the original **Barrow Island.** It became incorporated into **Barrow Island** when the docks were extended. It sits just south of the dock gates.

All of these islands can be seen on the map on Page 34.

Finally.

While researching for this book a number of questions which I was trying to answer all came together after I was given permission to look at some of the plans in the archives. I didn't know where the hostel for women had been built (Page 142); I had been asked about a building called the Apollo; I vaguely remembered a building on Park Lane as being some sort of factory and I had seen a reference to a Central Hall but wasn't sure where it stood.

It turned out that they were all the same building.

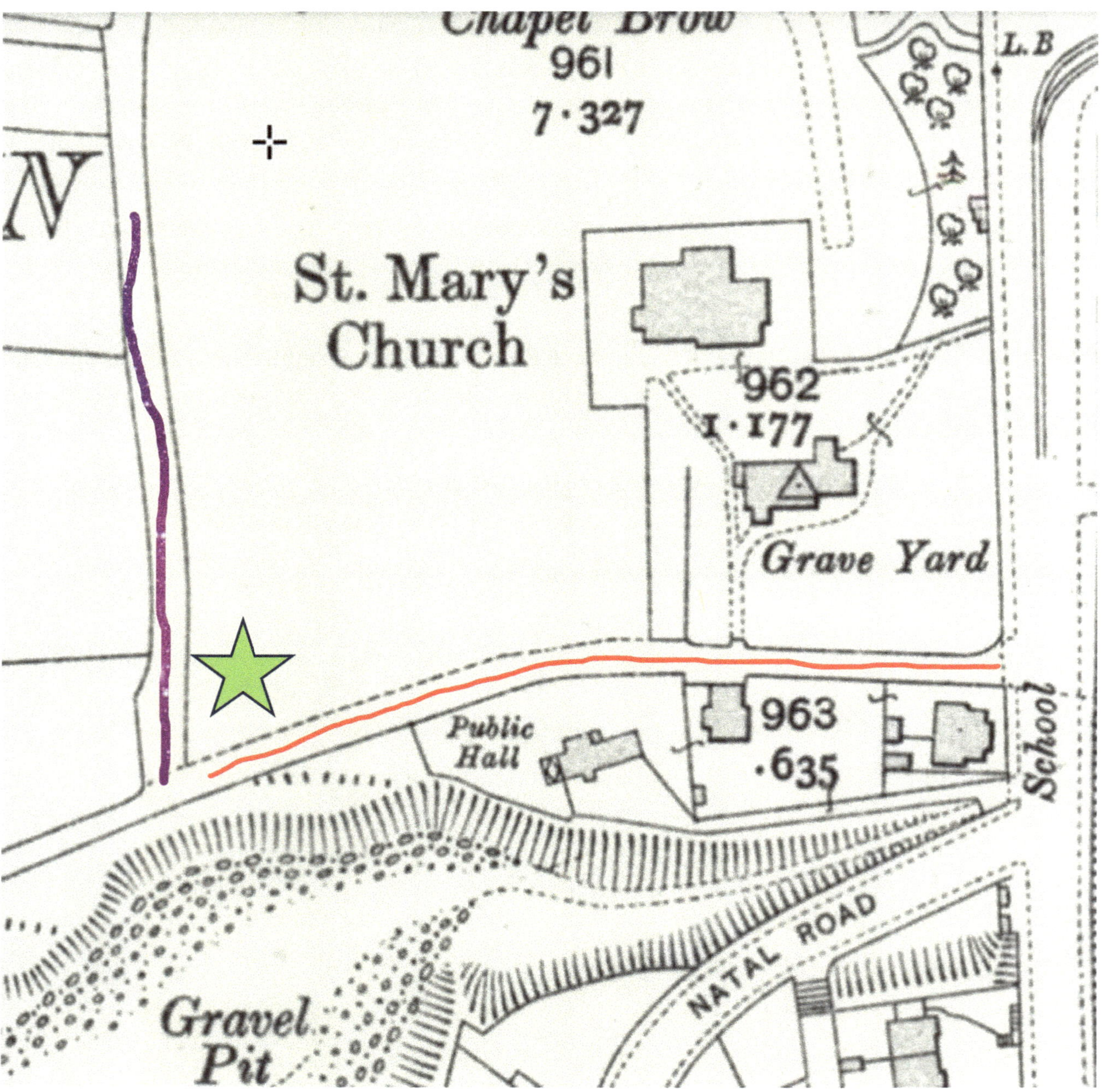

A pre-1915 map showing the area in question. The road across the middle is Chapel Lane. The road up from the corner (star) later becomes Park Lane. There is a public hall in Chapel Lane, where the telephone exchange is today, but nothing on the corner.

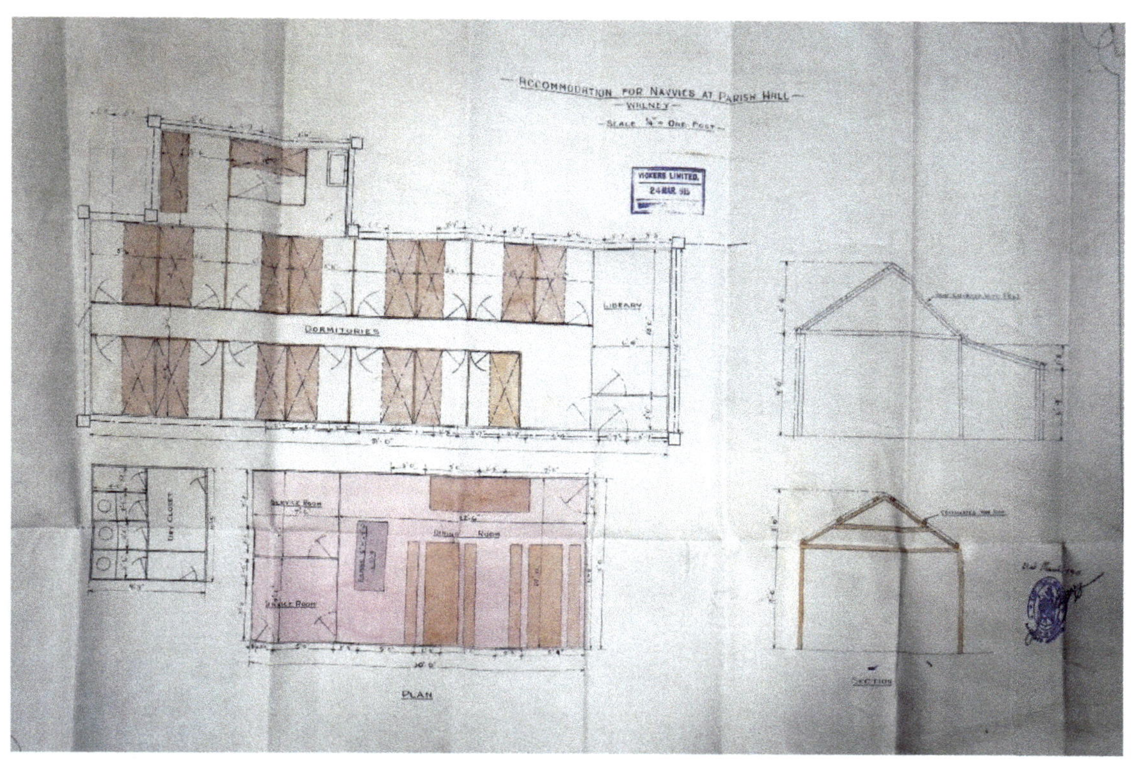

In March 1915 the Parish Hall (Public Hall) is converted to take 17 Navvies. BA/S/BC/Plan 6708

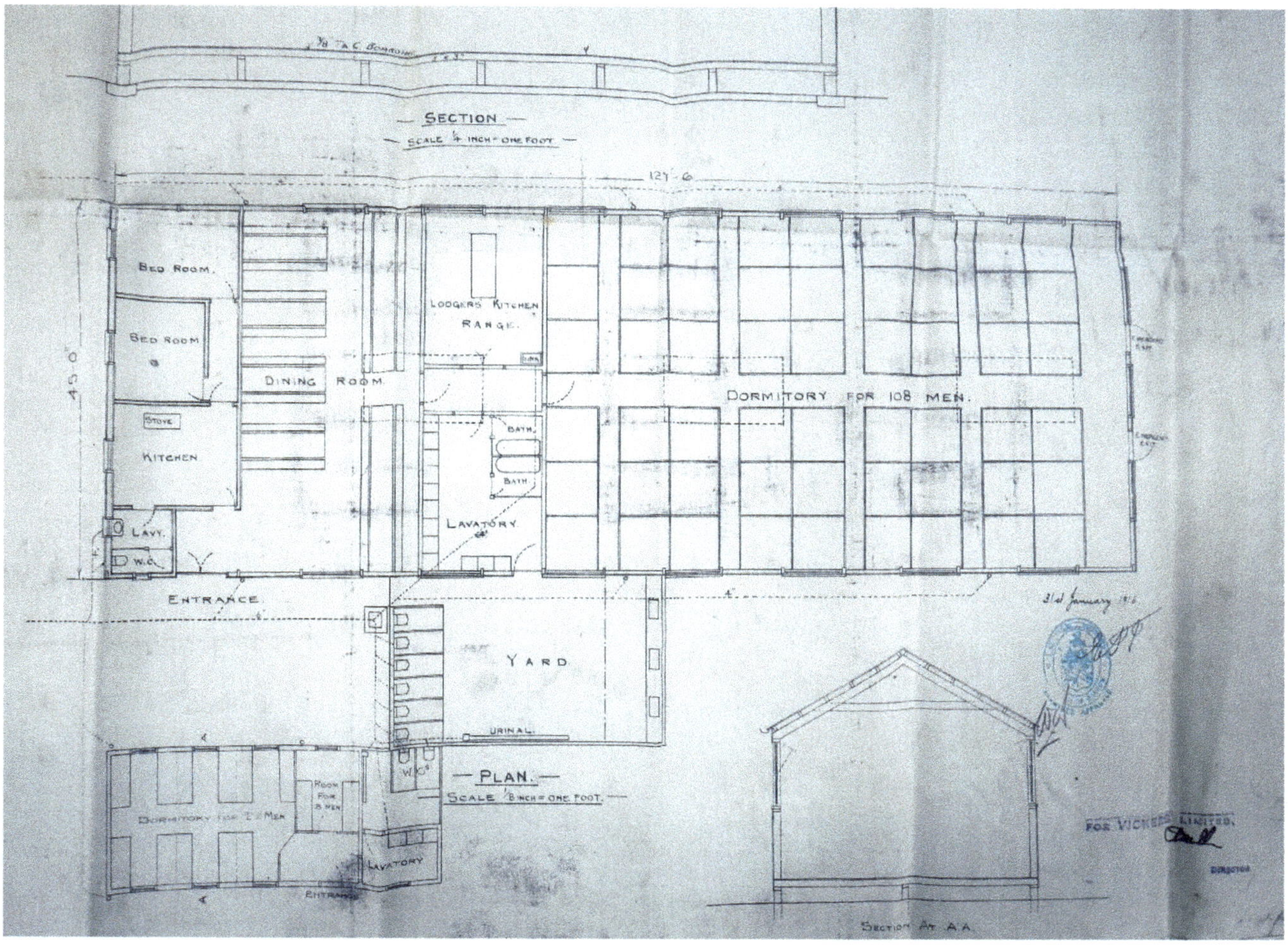

A lodging house for 108 men is built on the corner of Chapel Lane and Park Lane in 1916.
(Cumbria Archives BA/S/BC/Plan 6863)

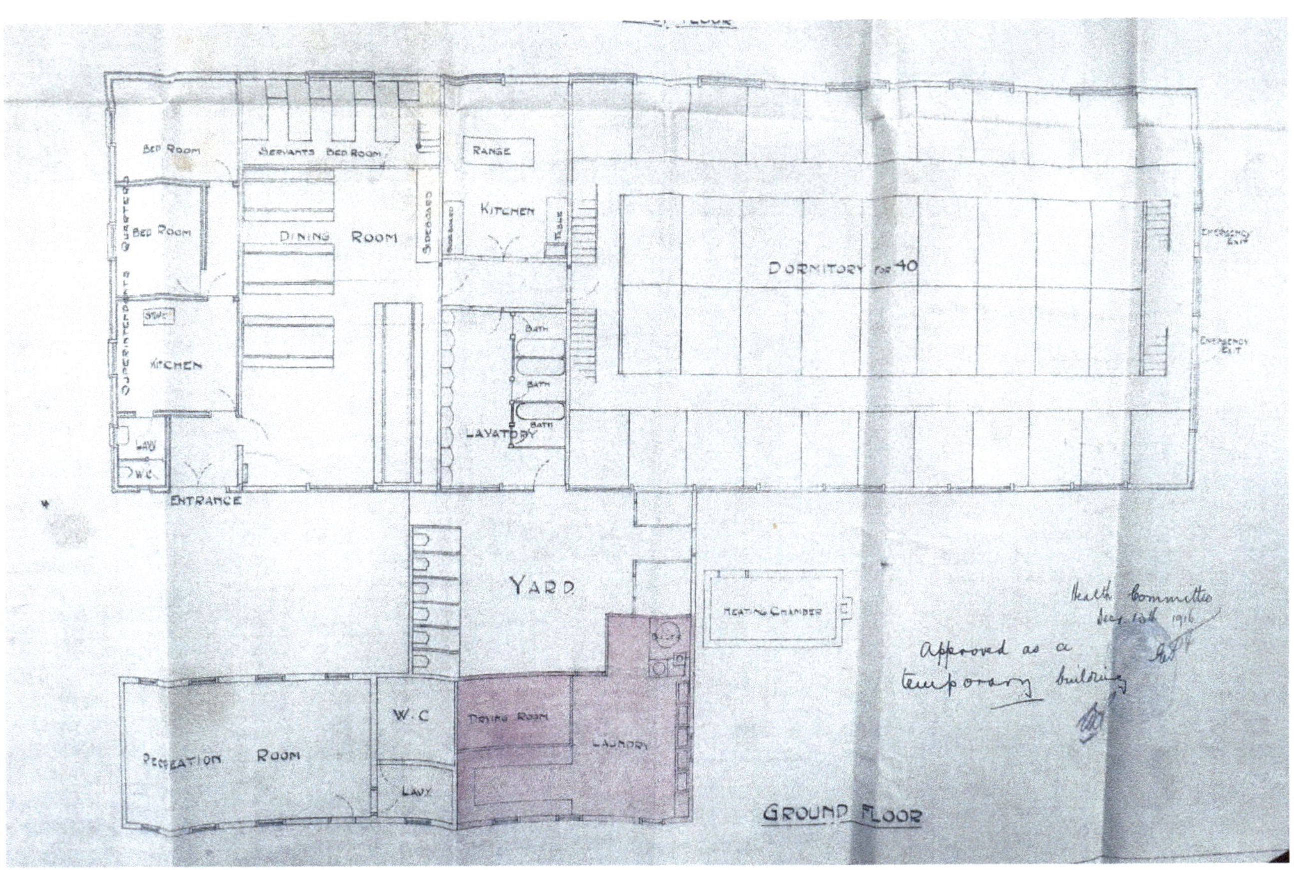

The lodging house is converted into a Hostel for 40 women in 1917. (Cumbria Archives BA/S/BC/Plan 6978)

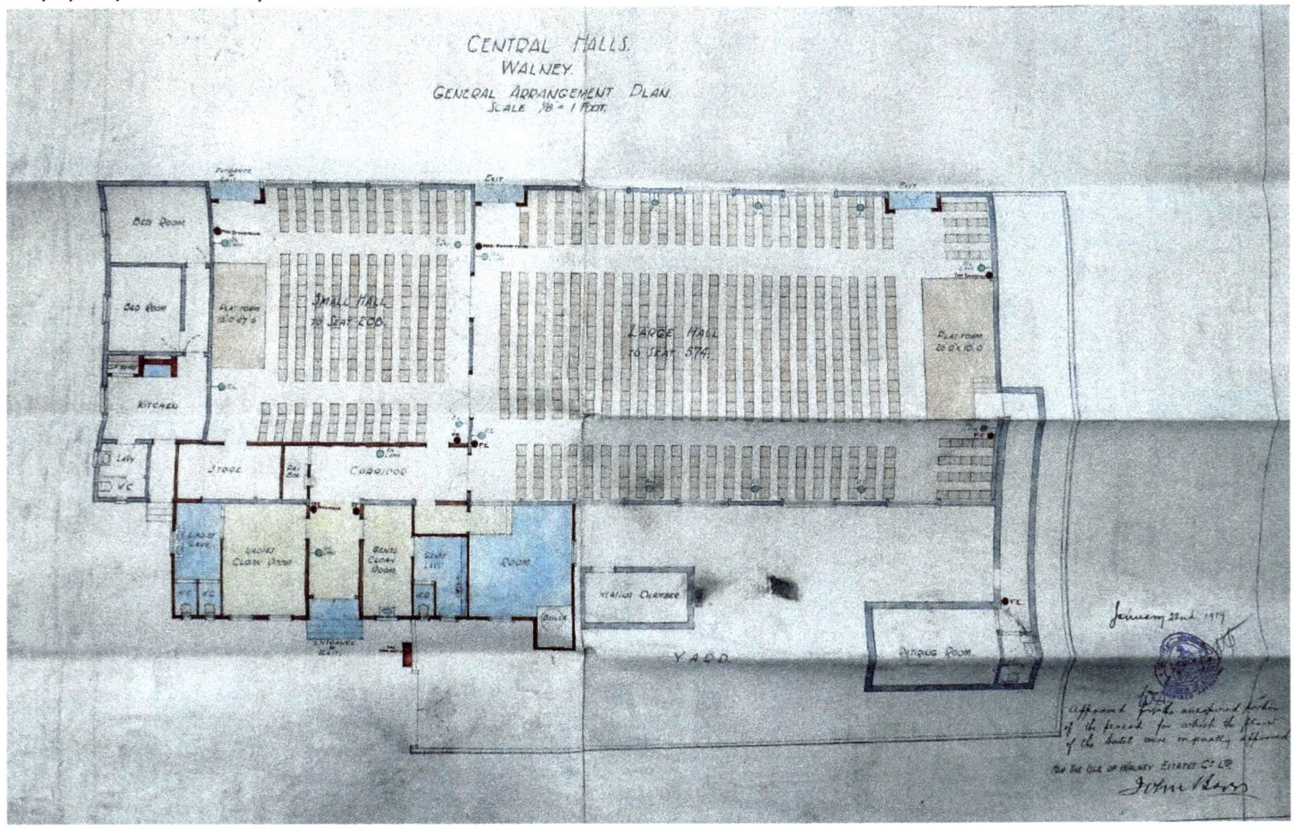

The Hostel is converted into Central Halls in 1919. (Cumbria Archives BA/S/BC/Plan 7141)

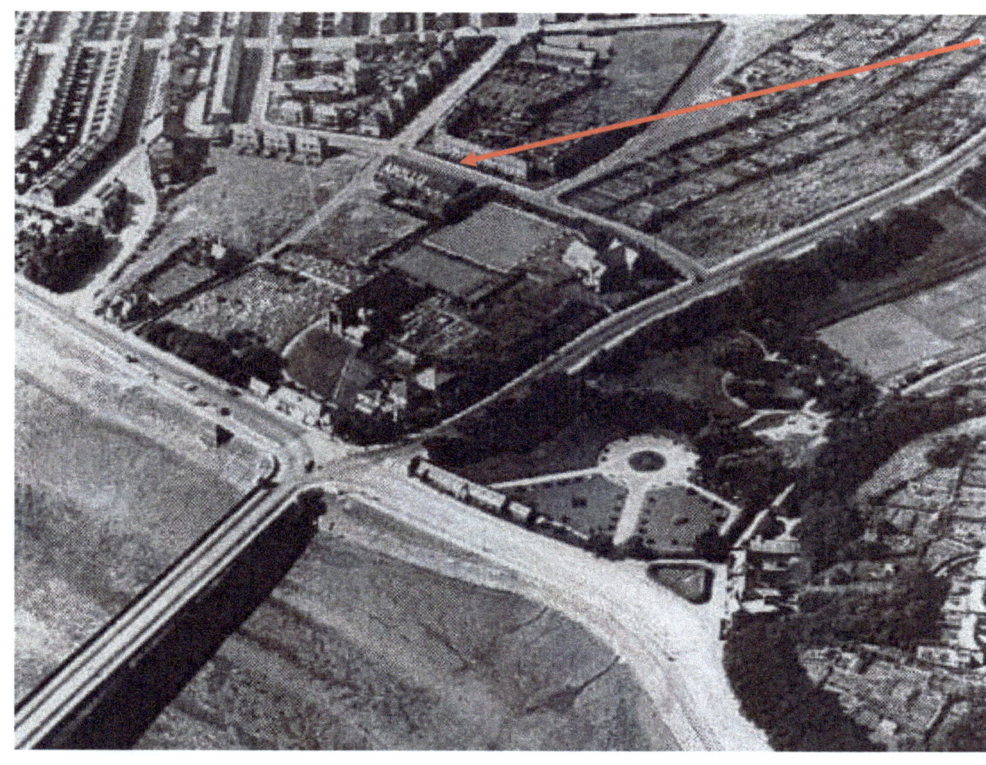

A 1947 Aerial photo clearly showing Apollo on the building roof.

I have yet to ascertain what exactly was the function of the Apollo.

This map, (below) is c1960. The Hostel/Apollo has become a factory. Chapel Lane has become Church Lane. The mystery was solved.

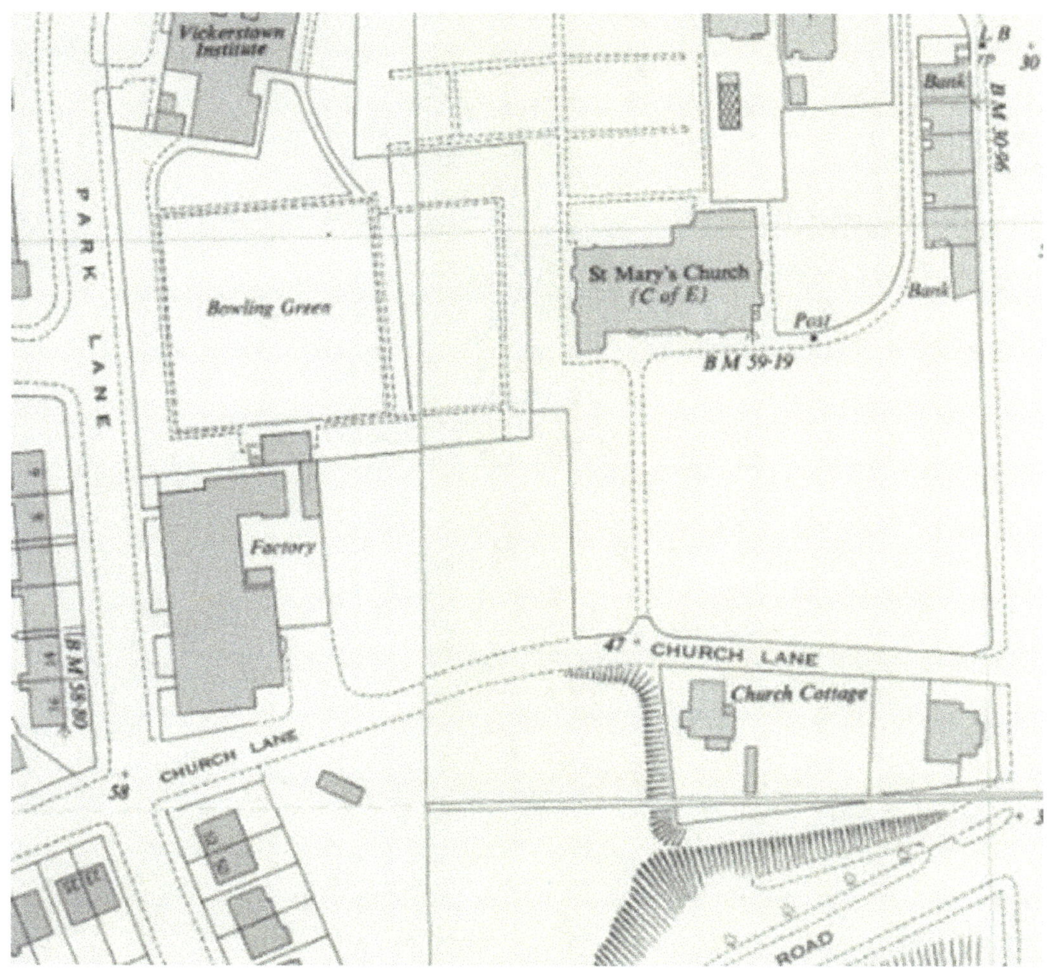

BIBLIOGRAPHY

Baines, Edward, (1824). History of the County Palatine of Lancashire;

Barnes Fred, (1968). Barrow and District;

Beck, Thomas, (1844). Annales Furnesienses; History and & Antiquities of the Abbey of Furness;

Beck, Thomas, (1844). The History and Antiquities of the Abbey of Furness.

Close, William, (1810). An Itinerary of Furness and the Environs;

Cubbon, B. D. (2015). Barrow Salt, a Historical review;

Fisher, Joseph, (1891). Popular History of Barrow in Furness;

Furness Golf Club. (1972). Furness Golf Club– A Centenary Story;

Gaythorpe, H. Collected works.

Hobbs, J. L. Collected works.

Kendall, W.B. Collected works.

Mannex directory. (1851). History, Directory and Topography of Westmorland;

Marshall, J. D. (1958). Furness and The Industrial Revolution;

Melville, James. Collected works.

Nixon, J. (2014). The Warbirds of Walney;

Richardson, J. (1880). Furness, Past & Present: Its History & Antiquities;

Rollinson, William, (1998). The Diary and Farm Accounts of William Fisher, a Low Furness Farmer, 1811–1859;

Trescatheric, Bryn, (1983). Vickerstown – A marine garden city;

Trescatheric, Bryn, (1984). Walney, A wall in the sea;

Trescatheric, Bryn, (1985). How Barrow was built;

West, Thomas, (1805). Close edition. The Antiquities of Furness 1774;

Substantial reference has been made to the British Newspaper Archive on-line: - https://www.britishnewspaperarchive.co.uk/

CWAAS – The Cumberland & Westmorland Antiquarian and Archaeological Society – On line resources: - https://cumbriapast.com/

CASCAT – Cumbria Archive Service On-line Catalogue - https://archiveweb.cumbria.gov.uk/CalmView/default.aspx

> Gaythorpe, Hobbs, Kendall and Melville are all well-known, well respected local historians.
>
> Many of their papers are in Cumbria Archives at Barrow.

> Cumbria Archives at Barrow is a fantastic resource with extremely helpful staff who go out of their way to help the budding researcher. I cannot praise them enough for their professionalism and help. The Archives are located at the rear of Barrow Library and open to the public Wednesday to Friday, (9.30am -1pm and 2pm to 5pm).

References.

[1] Barrow & District Local Board Blue Book, Oct 1887

[2] Topographical map [https://en-gb.topographic-map.com/maps/94cj/isle-of-walney]

[3] Office for National Statistics, (ONS) 2011 and 2021 censuses

[4] Whalley, Neil, *The Domesday Book of South Cumbria*. Transactions of the Cumberland and Westmorland Antiquarian and Archaeological Society. (2018). 3. 18: pp105–122

[5] Beck, Thomas, *The History and Antiquities of the Abbey of Furness*. (1844). p112

[6] Beck, p281

[7] Melville, James, *How long will Walney remain one island*. Barrow Naturalists Field Club Proceedings, 8, New Series (1956). p25-34

[8] W.B. Kendall, another local historian, wrote *Waste of coast line Furness and Walney in 1000 years*. Barrow Naturalists Field Club Annual Reports, 18, (1906). pp75-84

[9] Phillips, AW. and Rollinson, W., *Coastal changes on Walney Island North Lancashire*. Department of Geography University of Liverpool. (1971)

[10] Cumbria Coastal Strategy. (2020)

[11] Westmorland & Furness Council News. On-line. (Accessed January 2024); [https://www.westmorlandandfurness.gov.uk/news/2024/council-supporting-project-manage-coastal-flooding-and-erosion]

[12] Cross, Marjorie, *A Prehistoric Settlement on Walney Island*. Transactions of the Cumberland and Westmorland Antiquarian and Archaeological Society; (1938). pp 160-163

[13] Barnes, F and Hobbs J.L., *Newly discovered flint chipping sites in the Walney Island locality*. Transactions of the Cumberland and Westmorland Antiquarian and Archaeological Society; (1951) pp20-29

[14] *The Annals of Ulster*. Author unknown. p353.' The heathens were driven from Ireland, i.e. from the fortress of Áth Cliath, by Mael Finnia son of Flannacán with the men of Brega and by Cerball son of Muiricán, with the Laigin; and they abandoned a good number of their ships, and escaped half dead after they had been wounded and broken.'

[15] Pearson, H. G., *Biggar and its ancient customs*. (BNFC 1 ii 66)

[16] Barnes, F., *Barrow and District*. (1968). p18

[17] Tosti was expelled by the King in 1065 but returned with the Norwegian King, Harald Hardrada, and both were killed at the battle of Stamford Bridge on 25th September 1066.

[18] Image from [https://opendomesday.org/]

[19]

Sac(cum) – The power to impose fines upon tenants and vassals within the lordship.

Soc(cum) - The power and authority of administering justice.

Tol(lum) – A duty paid for felling and buying

Team (Theam) – A royalty granted for jurisdiction allowing courts to be held to judge people accused of wrongful possession of goods or cattle.

Infangenetheof – The right of the lord of a manor to try and punish a thief caught within the Liberty of Furness

[21] Barnes, F., *Barrow and District*. (1968). p30

[22] Beck, Thomas, *The History and Antiquities of the Abbey of Furness*. (1844). p14

[23] Ibid

[24] Biggar Town's Book

[25] West, Thomas, *The Antiquities of Furness*. Close edition (1805). P lvi

[26] *Barrow Herald and Furness Advertiser*. 16 May 1868

[27] Stock sale North End farm; Cumbria Archives. BDB/17/SP/209

[28] Census returns 1841 to 1911

[29] North End farm report. Cumbria Archives. BDHJ/303/11

[30] It is derived from the verb 'skala', which means 'to divide, separate, or shelter'. This word is also the origin of the word 'shall' in English. The word 'skali' is the first element in many place-names in Scandinavia and England, such as Skalholt, Skalby, and Scawby.

[31] A burgage is a term for a type of land held in tenure in return for service or rent

[32] Kendall, WB., *North Scale: The history of a Furness village*. Z/2447 Cumbria Archives (CA)

[33] A cote is a shelter, or small shed

[34] Kendall, WB., *North Scale: The history of a Furness village*. Z/2447 Cumbria Archives (CA)

[35] Northscale tenant's agreement. Cumbria Archives; BDHJ/272/1

[36] The Grave Book for North Scale covering 1820 – 1922 is in Cumbria Archives; BDBUC/50/5/1

[37] Office for National Statistics. (ONS) 1841 census
[38] https://historicengland.org/listing/the-list

[39] ONS. 1841 census
[39] CAS(Barrow); 1841 tithe schedule BDBUC/45/10.
[40] ONS. 1851 census
[41] ONS. 1861 census
[42] ONS. 1871 census
[43] ONS. 1911 census
[44] Gaythorp, H., *Biggar Dyke*. ZK/198, Cumbria Archives
[45] A copy of the Biggar Grave Book is held at Cumbria Archives covering the period from 1830 to 1895: Z/503
[46] ONS. Censuses 1841 to 1911
[47] Melville, James, *Biggar and its Inns*. Cumbria Archives. BAMH/1/52
[48] Biggar Village. Cumbria Archives. BDMH/1/17
[49] Ashton, John., *Chap-books of the eighteenth century*, (1882)
[50] *Barrow Times*. 11 January 1871
[51] Notes on wrecked ships off Walney. Cumbria Archives. BDY/124
[52] Ibid
[53] *Barrow Herald and Furness Advertiser*. 25 Mar 1876
[54] Ibid. 12 Jul 1876
[55] Ibid. 19 Aug 1876
[56] *Lancaster Guardian*. 9 Jun 1877
[57] *Soulby Advertiser*. 2 Aug 1877
[58] *Barrow Herald and Furness Advertiser*. 8 Dec 1877
[59] Ibid. 3 Aug 1878
[60] Ibid. 7 Sep 1878
[61] Ibid. 16 Nov 1878
[62] *Preston Herald*. 16 May 1883
[63] *Barrow Herald and Furness Advertiser*. 15 May 1883
[64] Ibid. 29 Sep 1883
[65] *The Mail*. 11 Jul 2018
[66] There are at least four different datestones built into the current building -1641, 1691, 1757 and 1764
[67] Melville, James, Evening Mail article on *North End and South End*. 19 Jan 1969
[68] Tithe map South Walney. BPR1/I/3/1/2. Cumbria Archives
[69] ONS. 1841 census
[70] ONS. 1851-1911 censuses
[71] Ibid; 1841-1891 censuses
[72] Extract from the Walney lighthouse visitors book No1 transcribed. Cumbria Archives. Z/274/1

[73] [https://lancasterport.org/history/] (Accessed 30th Dec 2023)
[74] Walney lighthouse notes. JL Hobbs. Cumbria Archives. BAMH/1/14
[75] Lancaster museum
[76] *Lancaster Gazette*. 24 Dec 1803
[77] ONS. 1841 census
[78] Ibid. 1851 census
[79] Ibid. 1861 census
[80] Lighthouse management: *The report of the Royal Commissioners on lights, buoys and beacons, (1861)*, Vol 2. p324
[81] *Barrow Herald and Furness Advertiser*. 18 Feb 1871
[82] ONS. 1871 census
[83] Furness Stories Behind the Stones [https://furnessstoriesbehindthestones.co.uk/stories/the-geldarts-of-walney-lighthouse/] (Accessed 10th March 2023)
[84] Biggar Town Book. Cumbria Archives. Z274/1
[85] ONS. 1881 census
[86] Ibid. 1891 census
[87] Furness Stories Behind the Stones [https://furnessstoriesbehindthestones.co.uk/stories/the-geldarts-of-walney-lighthouse/.] (Accessed 10th March 2023)
[88] Harper Gaythorpe's lighthouse notes. Cumbria Archives. Z/275
[89] ONS. 1901 census

90 *North Western Evening Mail.* 10th October 1953

91 ONS. 1911 census

92 Interview with the only female principal lighthouse keeper, Peggy Braithwaite,1993; [https://www.youtube.com/watch?v=m9PoVNh8t5A] [Accessed 3rd April 2023]

93 *Evening Mail.* 9th Dec 1949

94 Ibid. 10th Oct 1953

95 *Walney lighthouse and its keepers.* Various. Cumbria Archives. BDX 650:

96 The Medical Officer of Health in 1884 reported that 344 huts had been demolished.

97 *Soulby's Ulverston Advertiser and General Intelligencer.* 06 July 1899

98 *The Barrow Herald.* 14 Jan 1899

99 *Soulby Advertiser.* 4 May 1899

100 *Glossop-dale Chronicle and North Derbyshire Reporter.* 10th May 1899

101 *Liverpool Mercury.* 3 Oct 1899

102 Tracing of projected scheme on Walney, 1899. Cumbria Archives. Z/312

103 *Liverpool Mercury.* 15 May 1899

104 Town Planning report. *The Herald.* 22 July 1911

105 *Sheffield Evening Telegraph.* 5 Jan 1901

106 *Lancashire Evening Post.* 2 Nov 1900

107 *Vickerstown – A marine garden city.* Bryn Trescatheric. 1983; Hougenai Press

108 *Lancashire Evening Post.* 1st June 1903

109 *The Advertiser.* 11 June 1903

110 Trescatheric, Bryn, *Vickerstown – A marine garden city.* (1983). Hougenai Press

111 Building plan 6989, Cumbria Archives BA/S

112 Vickerstown Story for Lord Dunluce. Cumbria Archives. Aug 1909; Z/286

113 *Vickerstown Chronicle;.*12 Feb 1904

114 Ibid. 30 Jan 1903

115 Building register No 3, Cumbria Archives

116 Trescatheric, Bryn, *Vickerstown – A marine garden city.* (1983). Hougenai Press

117 *Lancashire Evening Post.* 28 Jul 1934

118 Ibid. 30 Mar 1935

119 Ibid. 15 Feb 1935

121 Ibid.

122 Trescatheric, Bryn, *How Barrow was built.* (1985). Hougenai Press

123 Trescatheric, Bryn, *Walney, A wall in the sea.* (1984). Hougenai Press

124 *Council Health sub-committee;* Plan 20971; 9 January 1957, Cumbria Archives, BA/S/2/8/7

125 *Morecambe Visitor.* 13 February 1963

126 First registered at Companies House in Oct 1986. [https://find-and-update.company-information.service.gov.uk/company/01137109/filing-history?page=4]

127 *Soulby Advertiser.* 19 Apr 1849

128 OS maps 1847 to 1873 sheet XXI

129 *Road Improvements Walney. Cumbria Archives.* BA/C Box 4.

130 Trescatheric, Bryn, *Vickerstown, A Marine Garden city.* Hougenai Press, (1983). p31

131 Plan of Proposed New Road. Cumbria Archives. BA/S/BC/D7/7

132 *Walney Fords.* BNFC; 1903, p118

134 Croft Brow would now be the eastern end of Teasdale Road.

135 They had taken over the Barrow Harbour by Act of Parliament in 1863

136 *Evening Mail.* Walney Fords. James Melville. 2 Feb 1968

137 *Barrow Herald.* 12 Feb 1876

138 Gaythorpe, Harper, *Walney fords.* Cumbria Archives. Z/2452

139 *Barrow Herald.* 09 Feb 1876

140 Ibid. 12 Aug 1876

141 Furness Railway Act 1879. [https://www.legislation.gov.uk/ukla/Vict/42-43/146/contents/enacted] [Accessed 4th April 2023]

142 *Barrow Herald.* 21 Apr 1877

143 Ibid. 1 Sep 1877

144 Gaythorpe, Harper, *Walney Ferry Notes.* Cumbria Archives. Z/286

145 Building plan 1562, Cumbria Archives BA/S

[146] *Barrow Herald*. 6[t] July 1878

[147] ONS. 1891 and 1901 census

[148] Ibid. 1901 census

[149] Ibid. 1911 census

[150] *Vickerstown Chronicle*. 30 Jan. 1903

[151] Ibid. 09 Jan. 1903

[152] ONS. 1891 and 1901 censuses

[153] Ibid. 1901 census

[154] *Barrow Herald*. 16 May 1891

[155] *Vickerstown Chronicle*. 21 Nov. 1902

[156] Ibid. 8 Mar. 1903

[157] *Barrow Herald,* 22 Sep 1883

[159] *Engineering Magazine*. 9 Feb. 1906

[160] Unreferenced document, Cumbria Archives.

[161] *Vickerstown Chronicle*. 2 January 1903

[162] Ibid. 8 April 1903

[163] Ibid. 13 February 1903

[164] *Barrow Herald,* 15 Mar 1873

[165] Ibid. 27 November 1888

[166] *Soulby's Ulverston Advertiser and General Intelligencer*. 30 July 1908

[167] Ibid.

[168] Ibid.

[169] *Liverpool Daily Post*. 25 January 1904

[170] *Soulby's Ulverston Advertiser and General Intelligencer*. 28 January 1904

[171] *Barrow Herald and Furness Advertiser*. 30 July 1908

[172] *Soulby's Ulverston Advertiser and General Intelligencer*. 13 August 1908

[173] Opening of Walney Bridge pamphlet. Cumbria Archives. Z/2466

[174] *Soulby's Ulverston Advertiser and General Intelligencer*. 18 August 1908

[176] Unemployment correspondence, Cumbria Archives, BA/C5/1/44/Box 48

[177] *North Western Daily Mail,* 9 May 1922

[178] Trescatheric, Bryn, *Vickerstown, A Marine Garden city*. Hougenai Press, (1983). p33

[179] *Barrow Guardian,* 13 May 1922

[180] *Barrow Herald and Furness Advertiser,* 19 July 1879

[181] Ibid, 8 Feb 1879

[182] *Lancaster Gazette,* 2 Dec 1893

[183] *Soulby Advertiser,* 27 Oct 1904

[184] *Lancashire Evening post,* 8 Jun 1922

[185] *Penrith Observer,* 3 Oct 1922

[187] Ibid. 4 April 1935

[188] *Lancashire Daily Post*. 3 Apr 1935

[189] [https://localtransporthistory.co.uk/fleetlists/tramways/barrow5/] [Accessed 24 May 2023]

[190] British Electric Traction Company Agreement with Barrow Council 1911. Cumbria Archives. BA/C Box 9

[191] Dated Photograph. Cumbria Archives. BLC/P/281/GT/TRA1

[192] *Furness Travelling and Postal Arrangements in 18th and 19th Centuries*. CWAAS. Melville and Hobbs. 1946; PP77-107

[193] Ibid.

[194] Ibid.

[195] Ibid.

[196] Baines, Edward, *History of the County Palatine of Lancashire*. Vol II.(1824)

[197] Melville, J, and Hobbs J., *Furness Travelling and Postal Arrangements in 18th and 19th Centuries*. CWAAS. (1946). pp77-107

[198] Fisher, Joseph, *Popular History of Barrow in Furness*. (1891). P21

[199] Barrow Herald; 24th October 1863

[200] Kendall, WB., *North Scale: The history of a Furness village*. Cumbria Archives. Z/2447

[201] ONS. 1861 census

[202] Ibid. 1881, 1891 and 1901 censuses

203 It is not on the 1959 OS map, which was surveyed in 1957 but is on a 1964 aerial photograph. (LC280_CX_WAL3 at Cumbria Archives)
204 The author was the Clerk of Works for the exchange on Walney responsible for overseeing the building, then commissioning, testing and opening of the new BT exchange equipment.
205 *Dundee Advertiser*. 8 April 1879
206 *Barrow Herald and Furness Advertiser*. 4 Sept 1880
207 Ibid. 12 Sept 1882
209 *Manchester Courier*. 2[1] September 1909
210 *The Herald*. July 29 1911
211 *Illustrated Police News*. 16 January 1919
212 Kendall, WB., *North Scale: The history of a Furness village*. Cumbria Archives. Z/2447
213 Beck, Thomas, *Annales Furnesienses; History and & Antiquities of the Abbey of Furness*. (1844). p13
215 Ibid. 1844. P335
216 Rollinson, w.,. *The Rural Landscape of Low Furness*, unpublished M.A. thesis, Manchester, (1961)
217 Close, William, *An Itinerary of Furness and the Environs* (1810).
218 Rollinson, William, *The Diary and Farm Accounts of William Fisher, a Low Furness Farmer*, 1811–1859, (1998)
219 *Soulby Advertiser*. 30 Jun. 1904.
220 *Barrow Herald*. 31 Jan. 1911.
221 Ibid. 23 Sept. 1869.
222 *Lancashire Evening Post*. 5 Oct. 1938.
223 Information from Mike Mulgrew at South End Farm, December 2023.
224 Melville, James, *Evening Mail* article: *Furnesses Windmills of Old*. 23 June 1978
225 Gaythorpe, Harper, *North Scale*. delivered as a lecture for BNFC by W.B. Kendall, 1898.
226 Photograph from Mike Garforth collection. Cumbria Archives. BDP 175/1/21
227 Biggar Village plan. 1893. Cumbria Archives. BDMH/1/17
228 Collection of photographs. Cumbria Archives Z/3405/16
229 Building register, No. 3, Cumbria Archives – all were dated September to November 1914
230 Building Plans, BA/S/BC/Plan 8686, Cumbria Archives
231 Laird, Dennis, *North Scale*. (1992)
232 *Barrow Herald and Furness Advertiser*. 30 September 1911
233 Ibid. 7 June 1913
234 Ibid. 16 August 1913
235 Ibid. 23 August 1913
237 *Vickers Airship Department*. Cumbria Archives. BLC/PH/200/PE/VIC1
238 *Airships and Aviation in Barrow*. BAE website. [https://www.baesystems.com/en-uk/heritage/airships-and-aviation-in-barrow] [Accessed 4 April 2023]. A video of the R80 in flight on Walney exists on-line [https://www.abct.org.uk/airfields/airfield-finder/barrow-in-furness-airship/] [Accessed 4 April 2023] and of the R9 maiden flight [https://player.bfi.org.uk/free/film/watch-airship-no-9-1916-online] [Accessed 4 April 2023]
239 *Engineer magazine*. July 1920
240 *Vickers Airship Department*. Cumbria Archives. BLC/PH/200/PE/VIC1
241 Barnes, F., *Barrow and District*. (1968). p101
243 *Lancashire Evening Post*. 5 October 1938
244 Ibid. 16th February 1939
245 *Industrial History of Cumbria; A history of Walney Airfield*. [https://www.cumbria-industries.org.uk/a-z-of-industries/airfields-and-early-aviation/a-history-of-walney-airfield/] [Accessed 7 April 2023]
246 Nixon, John, *The Warbirds of Walney*. Pixel tweaks publications, (2014).
247 *Lancashire Evening Post*. 16 August 1946
248 Ibid. 15 August 1946
249 Barrow in Furness. Walney Ward, North Scale. Register of Electors
250 *Dundee Telegraph*. 11 April 1947
257 'Only Glider Fliers use derelict 'Drome'. *Evening Mail*. 27 September 1946
258 'No future for Walney Aerodrome?'. *Evening Mail*; 15 November 1949
259 'Walney Airport to be closed as soon as practicable'. *Evening Mail*. 5 March 1952
260 *Evening Mail*. 29 November 1954
261 Images courtesy of Bjorn Larsson and David Zekra. [https://www.timetableimages.com/][Accessed 07 July 2024]
262 *Industrial History of Cumbria; A history of Walney Airfield*. [https://www.cumbria-industries.org.uk/a-z-of-industries/airfields-and-early-aviation/a-history-of-walney-airfield/] [Accessed 7 April 2023]

[263] *The Mail*. 3rd September 2019

[264] *The Mail*. 3 February 2023

[275] An example being *"Have we coal beneath Barrow"*. *Barrow Herald and Furness Advertiser*. 13 June 1868

[276] A search at Hawcoat quarry by the Barrow Haematite Iron and Steel and mining Company reported. *Barrow Herald and Furness Advertiser*. 23 January 1869, 6 March 1869, 21August 1869

[277] *Barrow Herald and Furness Advertiser*. 20 December 1913

[278] Ibid. 2 March 1889

[279] Cubbon, BD., *Barrow Salt a Historical review*. (2015)

[280] *Piel and Walney Gravel Co. Ltd.; Narrow Gauge Railway Magazine No 51*. July 1969.

[281] Cubbon, BD., *Barrow Salt a Historical review*. (2015)

[282] Mc Lung objected to the proposed airfield at the North End in an Air Ministry enquiry in February 1939 reported in the *Lancashire Evening Post* of 16 February 1939.

[283] *Evening Mail*. 15 June 1984

[284] *Furness Coastguard Service*. Cumbria Archives; Z/2485

[285] Plan of land plots for coastguard on Walney. 1903. Cumbria Archives. BD/BUC/43/8/20

[286] *Millom Gazette*. 27 October 1905

[287] *Evening Mail*. 31 January 1950

[288] Ibid. 1 May 1953

[289] Ibid. 9 May 1953

[290] *Fleetwood Chronicle*. 15 July 1955

[291] The author was a volunteer coastguard for a couple of years in the early 1980s based at this tower.

[292] Poster advertising a Borough Police Force. July 1881. Cumbria Archives. BDX 396/3/9

[293] *Barrow Herald and Furness Advertiser*. 1 July 1882

[294] *Evening Mail*. 17 June 1978

[295] ONS. 1891 census

[296] Ibid. 1901 and 1911 censuses

[297] Barrow Council Watch Committee minutes. Cumbria Archives. 15 July 1904

[298] Ibid. 16 November 1906

[299] Ibid. 15 February 1907

[300] Ibid. 15 March 1907

[301] Fire Superintendents' report. December 10 1914. Cumbria Archives. BDFB/49/55

[302] Cumbria Fire & Rescue service. [https://www.cumbriafire.gov.uk/about-us/fire-stations/walney-fire-station] [Accessed 30 April 2023]

[303] Fire Brigades Union web site. [https://www.fbu.org.uk/news/2016/02/04/cumbria-council-u-turn-five-fire-stations-saved-axe] [Accessed 13 April 2023]

[304] *Barrow Herald*. 5 March 1887

[305] Ibid. 25 October 1876

[306] Ibid.

[307] Building plan 1331, Cumbria Archives BA/S

[308] Ibid. 2 Aug 1913

[309] [https://cinematreasures.org/theaters/45257] . (Accessed 26 March 2024)

[310] *The Bioscope*. 5 November 1930

[311] *Lancashire Evening Post*. 12 December 1933

[312] [https://cinematreasures.org/theaters/45257] (Accessed 26 March 2024)

[313] *Kinematograph Weekly*. 13 January 1955

[314] [https://cinematreasures.org/theaters/45257] (Accessed 26 March 2024)

[315] Ibid

[320] Lancashire Alehouse Recognizances 1773 – a form of early public house licences.

[321] *Mannex directory 1851. History, Directory and Topography of Westmorland*.

[322] ONS. 1841 census

[323] Melville, James, *Biggar and its Inns*. Cumbria Archives; BAMH/1/52

[324] ONS. 1871 census

[325] Melville, James, *Biggar and its Inns*. Cumbria Archives; BAMH/1/52

[326] Sale Particulars: *Ulverston Mirror and Furness Reflector*. 19 July 1879

[327] ONS. 1881 census

[328] Ibid. 1891 census

[329] Ibid. 1901 census

330 Ibid. 1911 census

331 Melville, James, *Biggar and its Inns*. Cumbria Archives; BAMH/1/52

332 ONS. 1841 to 1881 census

333 Ibid. 1891 census

334 Ibid. 1901 census

335 *Soulby Advertiser and General Intelligencer.* March 30 !905.

336 ONS. 1911 census

337 *Lancashire Post.* Jan 16 1937.

338 *The News.* 20 April 1973.

339 Conveyance of public house. Cumbria Archives; Z/689/1

340 ONS. 1851 Census

341 *Soulby Advertiser.* 2 January 1868. (See also *The News. North Scale and the Old Crown Public House.* James Melville. 6 December 1974)

342 Abstract of title, Crown North Scale. Cumbria Archives. Z/3149

343 ONS. 1871 census

344 Ibid.

345 Ibid. 1881, 1891 and 1901 censuses

346 *Barrow Herald and Furness Advertiser.* 05 September 1868

347 Mr White applied for an extension of his licence for 'new rooms added to his premises' in May 1875.

348 Building plan 1426, Cumbria Archives BA/S

349 Ibid. 5 September 1868

350 Claim: Ferry Hotel. Cumbria Archives BDBUC/135/38

351 *Barrow Herald.* 4 November 1879

352 ONS. censuses 1881, 1891 and 1901

353 Ibid. census 1891

354 *Evening Mail* article, Biggar Bank. 6 June 1969

355 *Soulby Advertiser.* 17 May 1883

356 *The Advertiser.* 31 Aug 1899

357 *Lancashire Daily Post.* 6 Oct 1925.

358 *Lancashire Evening Post.* 3 June 1930

359 Ibid. 20 June 1931

360 *North Western Evening Mail.* 14 April 2019

361 Ibid. 19 March 1993

362 *North West Daily Mail.* 29 May 1939

363 Clergy of Church of England database. [https://theclergydatabase.org.uk/[[Accessed 14 Dec. 2023].

364 Gaythorpe, Harper, *Walney Chapel.* CW2, xx (1920), p.101.

365 Below, Religious History

366 *Soulby Advertiser*, 25 Sept. 1856.

367 Melville, James, Walney's old school. *Barrow News*, 2 June 1978

368 *Lancashire Evening Post*, 30 Aug. 1902.

369 BBC News, [https://www.bbc.co.uk/news/uk-england-cumbria-15618465[[Accessed 6 Dec. 2023].

370 [https://www.get-information-schools.service.gov.uk/Establishments/Establishment/Details/112209] (accessed 6 Dec. 2023)

371 Melville, James, Biggar village's wooden school, *Evening Mail*, 29 Sept. 1978.

372 *Lancashire Evening Post.* 23 January 1907

373 Ocean Road School Log Book. Cumbria Archives. BDS/75/1/2,

374 [https://www.get-information-schools.service.gov.uk/Establishments/Establishment/Details/141041](accessed 6 Dec. 2023).

375 Barrow Council Minutes 1954. p 197. Cumbria Archives.

376 [https://www.get-information-schools.service.gov.uk/Establishments/Establishment/Details/112212] (accessed 6 Dec. 2023).

377 [https://www.get-information-schools.service.gov.uk/Establishments/Establishment/Details/112240] (accessed 6 Dec. 2023).

378 Westmorland & Furness Council News. (Accessed 29 March 2024)

379 [https://www.get-information-schools.service.gov.uk/Establishments/Establishment/Details/112364] (accessed 6 Dec. 2023).

[380] [https://www.get-information-schools.service.gov.uk/Establishments/Establishment/Details/141993](accessed 6 Dec. 2023).

[381] Furness Golf Club, *Furness Golf Club – A Centenary Story* (1972).

[383] Ibid.

[384] *Barrow Herald and Furness Advertiser*. 1 Jul 1876

[385] Ibid.

[386] *Vickerstown Chronicle*. 1902

[387] Opening invitation Central Drive Community centre 1970. Cumbria Archives. BA/L/14/4

[388] Gaythorpe, Harper, *Walney Chapel*. CW2, xx (1920) p.99.

[389] Ibid.

[390] *The Cumbria Parishes 1714–1725 from Bishop Gastrell's Notitia, with additions by Bishop Porteous 1778–1779*, ed. L.A.S. Butler (CWAAS, Rec. Ser., Vol. XII, 1998)

[391] Gaythorpe, Harper, *Walney Chapel*. CW2, xx (1920) p.98.

[392] *Religious Census of 1851* (Surtees and CWAAS, 2019), p312.

[393] Beck, Thomas, *Annales Furnesienses; History and & Antiquities of the Abbey of Furness. (*1844) .p159 (Also [http://www.isle-of-man.com/manxnotebook/manxsoc/msvol04/v2p021.htm] [Accessed 17 June 2023]

[394] A list of the incumbents of St Mary's and a very short history appears on the web site: [http://www.walneyparishchurch.co.uk/incumbents.html] Accessed 17 June 2023

[395] Ibid.

[396] Gaythorpe, Harper, *Walney Chapel*. CW2, xx (1920) pp.99 -100.

[397] *Walney church and its registers*. Harper Gaythorpe. Cumbria Archives. Z/K/134

[398] [http://www.walneyparishchurch.co.uk/incumbents.html] (accessed 2 Feb. 2023).

[399] Gaythorpe, Harper, *Walney Chapel*. CW2, xx (1920) p.98.

[400] Ibid.

[401] [http://www.walneyparishchurch.co.uk/incumbents.html] (accessed 2 Feb. 2023).

[402] *Ibid.*

[403] Gaythorpe, Harper, *Walney Chapel*. CW2, xx (1920) p.99.

[404] [http://www.walneyparishchurch.co.uk/incumbents.html] (accessed 2 Feb. 2023).

[405] [http://www.walneyparishchurch.co.uk/incumbents.html](accessed 2 Feb. 2023).

[406] [http://www.walneyparishchurch.co.uk/incumbents.html] (accessed 2 Feb. 2023).

[407] *Religious Census of 1851*, 312.

[409] *Soulby's Ulverston Advertiser and General Intelligencer*, 17 May 1855.

[410] Ibid. 5 Dec. 1850.

[411] Gaythorpe, Harper, *Walney Chapel*. CW2, xx (1920) p.102

[412] *Yorkshire Post and Leeds Intelligencer*, 5 Oct. 1908.

[413] *Lancashire Evening Post*. 6 September 1922

[414] Walney church plans. Cumbria Archives. BPR/20/C/6/14.

[415] National Heritage List for England, no. 1291841, 'Church of St Mary' (accessed 2 Feb. 2024).

[416] Conveyance by William Gradwell. Cumbria Archives. Z/361

[417] *Barrow Herald*, 26 Mar. 1881.

[418] Ibid.

[419] *North Western Evening Mail*, 9 Mar. 1979.

[420] The author took a photograph of the chapel in 1979, it was since demolished.

[421] Teasdale Road Chapel. Cumbria Archives. BDFCBWM/2/2/8

[422] Biggar Mission Hall. *Evening Mail*. 12 December 2007

[423] [https://www.cumbriacountyhistory.org.uk/township/walney-island] (accessed 14 April 2024)

[427] *Soulby's Ulverston Advertiser and General Intelligencer*. 7 Apr. 1904.

[428] Ibid. 27 Apr. 1905.

[429] Ibid. 7 Apr. 1904.

[430] Plan St Andrew's church. Cumbria Archives. BDFC/P/W/14.

[432] Trescatheric, Bryn, *Vickerstown, A Marine Garden City*. Hougenai Press, (1983)

[433] Barnes, F., *Barrow & District*. F. Barnes, (1968).

[434] *Evening Mail*, 18 Nov. 1957.

[435] The Parish of "Our Lady of Furness." [https://ourladyoffurness.org.uk/st-columbas/] (accessed 26 Apr. 2023).

[436] *Penrith Observer*. 9[t] October 1917

[437] Trescatheric, Bryn, *How Barrow was built*. Hougenai Press, (1985)

[438] *Hutton, JE., Welfare and Housing, a practical record of war-time management.* Longmans, (1918) p41

[439] *Isle of Man Examiner.* 1 July 1916

[440] *Liverpool Echo*, 6 May 1916

[441] Sales Particulars. Cumbria Archives, BDB17/347

[442] Trescatheric, B., and Hughes, DJ., *Barrow at War.* Furness Museum, (1979)

[443] Uncatalogued letter at the time of writing. Markets and Parks committee. 19 January 1970. Cumbria Archives.

[444] *Lancashire Evening Post*, 2 April 1937

[445] *Golf Illustrated*. Jan 3 1902

[446] Dickson, R.W., *The Agriculture of Lancashire*, (1815). p523

[447] Duddon reclamation plan. Cumbria Archives, BDBUC/68/1

[448] Notes on land reclamation for the building of a railway in Morecambe Bay, Duddon estuary and Piel. Cumbria Archives, BDX 828/1/1/19

[449] Rollinson, William, *Schemes for the reclamation of land from the sea in North Lancashire during the eighteenth and nineteenth centuries, (1964)*

[450] *Barrow Herald*, 13 September 1884

[451] Melville, James, *Islands of Walney*, Cumbria Archives, BDX/828/1/2/88

[452] Ibid.